The Jews, Modern Israel and the New Supersessionism

Responses to the first edition of *The Jews, Modern Israel and the New Supercessionism*

In a day when the merit of the role of Israel is being questioned by many, including many Christians, it is refreshing to see a biblically grounded presentation of God's faithfulness to Israel that affirms the gospel for the Jewish people and the idea that God will keep his promises to Israel. How do these go together? This book takes us well down the path to a theologically sound answer.

Darrell L. Bock, Ph.D.
Research Professor of New Testament Studies
Dallas Theological Seminary
Former President of the Evangelical Theological Society

The contributors to this book exhibit the kind of scholarly balance necessary for moving the debate concerning modern Israel from the practice of firing shots from opposing trenches to a careful examination of the facts in the light of Biblical Revelation. As to the importance of their contributions, the declared ideological motivations of groups like Hamas, who vow to put an end to Israel as a sovereign state, mean that the question of modern Israel's existence must be approached in essentially theological terms.

Ronald E. Diprose, Ph.D.
Academic Dean, Istituto Biblico Evangelico Italiano, Rome
Author of Israel and the Church: The Origin and Effects of Replacement Theology *(Authentic Media, 2004)*

A book of this quality, character and courage has been needed for decades! I want to congratulate Dr Calvin Smith of King's Evangelical Divinity School for engaging in this highly charged and controversial study focusing on God's plan for the Jewish people, the nation of Israel and the Arab world. I further applaud the project for taking the very critical next step of helping to provide a matrix for understanding the relationship between the Western Church and the Christian, Messianic and Muslim communities of the East.

Mitch Glaser, Ph.D.
President, Chosen People Ministries, New York

There is a belated tide rising against almost virulent anti-Judaism. So, in *The Jews, Modern Israel and the New Supercessionism* Dr. Calvin Smith provides us with a rich resource that covers the essential issues at a substantial level. The times call for a volume like this. May it help turn Christians toward a more Judeo-centric eschatology. Supremely may it uphold the glory of the quintessential Jew, the Lord Jesus Christ, who shall return as a Jew.

Dr Barry E. Horner
Author of Future Israel: Why Christian Anti-Judaism Must Be Challenged *(Broadman and Holman, 2007)*

A large portion of the word of God in the Old Testament is being misinterpreted or deliberately avoided by those who have adopted the teaching that the Christian Church has replaced Israel and that the ancient promises made by God to Abraham, Isaac, Jacob and David are now *passé*. However, Calvin L. Smith has edited a set of chapters in a new book that makes a vital contribution towards rectifying this imbalance in interpretation. May it spark a long-overdue discussion among Evangelical interpreters of all persuasions as well as one between Jewish people of the book and believers in the Christian Church.

Walter C. Kaiser, Jr., Ph.D.
Colman Mockler Distinguished Emeritus Professor of Old Testament, President Emeritus, Gordon Conwell Theological Seminary

Any scholarly attempt to address the growth of supersessionism should be welcomed in the Evangelical community worldwide. While not perfect, modern Israel is thought by most Evangelicals to be a fulfilment of biblical prophecy, and therefore to be seen as one of the formidable signs of Christ's soon return.

Dr Calvin Smith has taken on this challenge and brought us a strong rebuttal to the position held by supersessionists, and must be thanked for giving Evangelical Christians this important compilation of writings by such a group of authors. Thanks.

Rev. Dr. Daniel Mercaldo
Senior Pastor and Founder
Church at the Gateway, Staten Island, New York

The Jews, Modern Israel and the New Supercessionism provides thorough insights, both biblical and secular, into issues related to the present, past, and future status of ethnic Israel. It is heartening that editor Calvin L. Smith along with an assortment of contributors has outlined many historic and current facets related to present-day Israel. The availability and helpfulness of the book will strike a strong note in response to growing supersessionist influences regarding God's promises to Abraham and his descendants.

Dr Robert L. Thomas
Professor of New Testament Language and Literature
The Master's Seminary, Sun Valley, California

The articles in this book, written by scholars who vary in their theological stance, are balanced and profound. They seek to answer biblically some of the oldest heresies in the Church, which sadly are advocated by many Evangelicals today, namely that all the promises to Israel have been transferred to the Church and that Israel has ceased to be within God's purpose for world redemption. I warmly commend this book and pray that it will be widely read.

Revd David W. Torrance
Retired Church of Scotland minister and author (with Howard Taylor) of Israel, God's Servant: God's Key to the Redemption of the World *(Paternoster, 2007)*

Finally, an irenic, but yet resolutely Evangelical treatment of the issues surrounding the Middle Eastern crises centred around the contemporary state of Israel! While readers will agree or not depending on their own ideological biases, all who approach this book with an open mind will come away better informed about why Bible-believing Evangelicals think the Jews remain God's people in a distinctive way and why we can be hopeful that the good news of the gospel is still applicable in the present situation for all parties involved – Israelis and Palestinians, Jews and Arabs, and Christians of every ethnicity bound up on the conflict. As valuable is the attempt of the essayists to find a middle way between the extremes of Zionism on the one side and anti-Israelism on the other. The result is registration of an important set of mediating Evangelical voices in an otherwise tumultuous discussion.

Amos Yong, PhD.
Professor of Systematic Theology
Director of the Doctor of Philosophy Program
School of Divinity, Regent University, Virginia

The Jews, Modern Israel and the New Supersessionism

edited by

Calvin L. Smith

King's Divinity Press
Broadstairs, Kent (United Kingdom)

Edited and typeset by King's Divinity Press
Printed and bound in the United Kingdom by Print on Demand
9 Culley Court, Bakewell Rd, Orton Southgate, Peterborough PE2 6XD

Contents

PART 2: SUPERSESSIONISM AND THE BIBLE

PART 3: SUPERSESSIONISM AND THE JEWISH
PEOPLE TODAY

About the Contributors

COLIN BARNES earned several degrees in Australia, including an M.Th. at Morling College, Sydney, exploring European church involvement in the Holocaust. He lived and taught in Israel for five years before moving to and serving as a missionary in Pakistan.

BRIAN BREWER completed degrees in Theology at the universities of Wales and Chester through King's Evangelical Divinity School. He is Administrator of King's Centre for Jewish-Christian Studies and is commencing doctoral research.

ANDY CHEUNG holds degrees with the Universities of Durham and Bangor and earned a Ph.D. in Linguistics and Bible translation at the University of Birmingham. He lectures in Biblical Languages and New Testament at King's Evangelical Divinity School.

RONALD E. DIPROSE (Ph.D., Evangelische Teologische Faculteit, Leuven, Belgium) lives in Italy and is Academic Dean at the Istituto Biblico Evangelico Italiano. His book *Israel and the Church: The Origins and Effects of Replacement Theology* has been translated into five languages.

RICHARD GIBSON has worked within the Messianic movement for eighteen years. He leads Leeds Messianic Fellowship, serves on the British Messianic Jewish Association executive and lived in Israel. He is currently engaged in postgraduate theological studies.

MITCH GLASER (Ph.D., Fuller Theological Seminary, California) is President of Chosen People Ministries, New York. He helped establish the Charles Feinberg Center for Messianic Jewish Studies and edited (with Darrell Bock) *To The Jew First: The Case for Jewish Evangelism in Scripture and History*.

BARRY E. HORNER (D.Min., Westminster Seminary, California) is recognised as a leading authority on John Bunyan and his writings and has published several volumes in this field. He is the author of *Future Israel: Why Christian Anti-Judaism Must Be Challenged*.

STEVE MALTZ is a popular author and broadcaster speaking widely on the Hebraic roots of Christianity. His books include *How the Church Lost the Way* and *How the Church Lost the Truth*.

TONY PEARCE leads the Bridge Lane Christian Fellowship in Golders Green, London. He speaks widely, broadcasts regularly and has written several popular books on issues relating to Jewish evangelism and Christian responses to modern Israel.

JACOB PRASCH is the founder of Moriel Ministries and teaches widely on Jewish-Christian hermeneutics. He is a fluent Hebrew speaker and has written several popular books exploring the relationship between Israel and the Church.

CALVIN L. SMITH (Ph.D., University of Birmingham) is Principal of King's Evangelical Divinity School, edits the *Evangelical Review of Society and Politics*, and speaks and publishes widely on Israel, Evangelical politics and hermeneutics.

HOWARD TAYLOR served as a missionary, minister and university lecturer, as well as teaching and lecturing widely in ethics, science and religion. He co-authored *Israel God's Servant: God's Key to the Redemption of the World* with David W. Torrance.

STEPHEN M. VANTASSEL (Ph.D., Trinity Seminary, Indiana) lectures in Biblical Studies and Systematic Theology at King's Evangelical Divinity School, is Adjunct Professor at Trinity Seminary, Indiana, and co-edits the *Evangelical Review of Society and Politics.*

PAUL RICHARD WILKINSON (Ph.D., University of Manchester, England) is the author of *For Zion's Sake: Christian Zionism and the Role of John Nelson Darby.* He is currently writing in the areas of dispensationalism, philo-Semitism and the Holocaust.

Foreword to the First Edition

You are about to embark on a theological journey to the Holy Land. The path will take you through the valleys of Scripture and the mountains of theological debate to the contemporary socio-political plains of the Middle East. Along the way, you will be introduced (or perhaps re-introduced) to a band of articulate, intelligent and biblically astute authors who will serve as your guides.

As a Messianic Jew for almost forty years, I can tell you that a book of this quality, character and courage has been needed for decades! I want to congratulate Dr. Calvin Smith of King's Evangelical Divinity School for engaging in this highly charged and controversial study focusing on God's plan for the Jewish people, the nation of Israel and the Arab world. I further applaud the project for taking the very critical next step of helping to provide a matrix for understanding the relationship between the Western Church and the Christian, Messianic and Muslim communities of the East.

It would be a sad mistake to underestimate the theological, political and even ecclesiastical challenge that Christians – both Jewish and Gentile – face in engaging the Muslim world for Christ. This book makes a profound contribution and provides information that is both biblical and relevant, thereby enabling followers of Jesus the Messiah to pray intelligently and thoughtfully consider our personal perspectives on issues relating to Israel and the Arab world. I view exploring our biblical roots and the complex, contemporary realities of the Middle East as a pilgrimage.

We cannot treat Israel as simply one nation among others. We also cannot view the Jewish people as just one people among many ethnic or religious groups, because we love the Jewish Messiah and we believe the Bible's story, which primarily takes place in Israel. Christians throughout the centuries have always recognized, rightfully, that there is something special about the land of Israel and the Jewish people. You will appreciate the chapter by Howard Taylor, who makes reference to the following quote by Mark Twain regarding the special role of Israel and the Jewish people:

> The Egyptian, the Babylon and the Persian rose, filled the planet with sound and splendor, then faded to dream stuff and passed away; the Greek and the Roman followed, and made a vast noise, and they are gone; other peoples have sprung up and held their torch high for a time, but it burned out, and they sit in twilight now, or have vanished. The Jews saw them all, beat them all, and is now what he always was exhibiting no decadence, no infirmities of age, no weakening of his parts, no slowing of his energies, no dulling of his alert and aggressive mind. All things are mortal but the Jews; all other forces pass but he remains. What is the secret of his immortality?

A Substantial Contribution
Whatever your current perspective on Israel, the Jewish people, and the Middle East conflict, it is safe to say that these topics are especially unavoidable for thoughtful, growing believers in Jesus.

It is possible that you may never board a plane destined for the Holy Land (although it is an experience not to be missed!). You may never walk where Jesus walked and experience the land of the Bible first-hand, but through this book you can journey to the homeland of our Saviour and gain a greater understanding of His "kinsmen according to the flesh." Eminent, capable, and well-informed scholars who have thought deeply about these subjects will guide you along the way.

I am grateful to Dr. Smith for the privilege of encouraging you, dear reader, to do more than simply skim this multi-author volume, but rather to read this book with a marker and an open Bible. You will want to study these chapters and talk over the issues raised with fellow believers and your pastor, as I am certain you will find the issues in this book to be critical to your faith.

I want to further commend the editor and authors for their evident passion for their subjects. They write with both mind and heart. They also strive to be fair and just in their portrayals of Jews and Arabs, Christians, Messianic Jews and Muslims. Each writer wrestles with the scriptural data as well as the books, articles and public relations information generated on these subjects.

A Balanced Approach

There's no doubt that an intelligent, biblically-based, politically astute and fair-minded volume is necessary to help Christians rebalance their views on the Middle East. I appreciate the authors' attempts to present both sides of the issues as much as possible. It is clear that this volume is attempting to rebalance the way in which Christians view the conflict in the Middle East. For many years, some evangelical Christians have been pro-Israel to the point of losing objectivity – and this certainly needs to be rebalanced. Some Christians have been driven by their eschatology to make claims and projections that have been embarrassing to many believers. As an American, I can tell you that this has been true on both sides of the pond and is not simply a concern of Christians in the United Kingdom.

But in the United Kingdom and North America as well as in Western Europe, there has been a recent pro-Palestinian swing that has pushed the church to a new stage of imbalance, as the title of the book suggests by coining the term "New Supersessionism." We cannot seek the welfare of Palestinians at the expense of Israel and the Jewish people. Unfortunately, this has been the case recently, as evidenced by the plethora of Christian books "bashing" Israel and the Jewish people.

While reading many of the books recently published about the Middle East, one gets the impression that Palestinians can do no wrong and that all the problems in the Middle East are a result of Israeli aggression. This book seeks to rebalance this perception and clarify the ways in which Islamic fundamentalists are a threat to the church, the West, and especially to Arab Christians. A number of the authors will suggest that in certain Christian circles, we have merely sanctified fundamentalist Islamic propaganda.

I have also had a deep and growing concern about the way in which the role of Jewish people in the Bible has been linked to the modern state of Israel. Of course this is true to a degree, but it is also problematic. The many popular Christian books that have promoted a pro-Palestinian Christian platform have led many in the church to lose their concern for Jewish evangelism. Great Britain has more than 400,000 Jewish people, and each one who has not already received Jesus as Saviour needs the Gospel.

I had a conversation with a Christian pro-Palestinian spokesman who has written a number of influential books that I believe have led to the imbalance that this current book attempts to correct. I asked him whether he realized that his books were actually helping to swing the Church beyond a pro-Palestinian position to one rapidly becoming anti-Israel and even anti-Jewish. I knew this was not his intention, yet it was the regrettable result of an overzealous Christian pro-Palestinian position.

Some Christians today feel that we cannot speak favourably about the need for Jewish evangelism without adding that reaching Arabs is important too! It is as if promoting Jewish evangelism is deemed unfair to Arabs, and that reaching Jewish people in London or New York City is tantamount to supporting all of Israel's political policies. There is a confusion between modern Israel and the Jewish people in general, which is hurting Jewish missions on both sides of the pond as Christians trend towards a more pro-Palestinian and anti-Israel position.

The ecclesiastical atmosphere has been profoundly charged against Israel and the Jewish people, and while many of us involved in Messianic ministry were wondering how to rebalance the viewpoint of the church, Dr. Smith and his team had already held a conference and now produced this essential volume of essays.

We now have a book that is biblical, fair, and honest, and will hopefully enrich Christians who love the Jewish people as well as the Palestinian people and who desire to see both Jews and Muslims come to Christ. This book provides the insights and theological framework for that critical and necessary balance.

Read each chapter carefully and enjoy the journey!

Mitch Glaser, Ph.D.
President, Chosen People Ministries
New York (31 March 2009)

Acknowledgements

This book represents the work of various people to whom I am indebted. Foremost among these, of course, are the contributors themselves, many of whom not only prepared essays for the book but also delivered challenging and interesting papers at the two conferences out of which much of this book has arisen.

I am grateful, too, to Dr Mitch Glaser of Chosen People Ministries, New York, for kindly providing a foreword to the first version of the book. Since then, Mitch and I have become good friends and colleagues, working together on this and related issues. His confidence in the original work was deeply encouraging at that time, as were the kind words of support from the established scholars and churchmen who also endorsed the first edition of the book.

We remain thankful to Pastor John Angliss and SORCF for hosting the very first conference. At a personal level I am also grateful to Brian Brewer and Virginia Snape, who both willingly offered their services in a research assistant capacity for one of my chapters and my on-going research into Christian-state relations in the Holy Land.

At that time Brian was one of my undergraduate students in his final year of study, but has since also completed an M.A. in Theology at King's Evangelical Divinity School (earning a distinction). It is pleasing as his longstanding tutor to see him now commencing doctoral studies in a related field. Moreover, Brian is now also a colleague, recently appointed as Administrator of King's new Centre for Jewish-Christian Studies. It is all the more satisfying, therefore, to see him contributing a chapter on the Messianic movement in this second edition. How things change over time!

Finally, my thanks to my parents who brought me up with a love based on the Scriptures for the Jewish people, together with my wife Kay and our children who, as always, patiently support my work and cheerily forgive me for working late hours and unwittingly missing family events (which seems to happen quite a lot). I have always greatly valued their patience and support.

Calvin L. Smith

A New Supersessionism?

Calvin L. Smith

Israel and the Jewish people are of considerable interest to many Christians. This is hardly surprising, given how the land of Israel is where Jesus trod and Christianity emerged. Moreover, Israel is mentioned or alluded to nearly 3000 times in the Bible, while as a biblical theology theme it appears far more than many other important themes in the Bible. Scripture refers to God as "the God of Israel" some 200 times. Jesus, the Messiah awaited by the Jewish people, was a Jew. This Jewish Messiah is described as the consolation of Israel, bringing glory to Israel (Luke 2:25, 32). The Apostles, too, were Jewish. Indeed the entire early church, headquartered in Jerusalem (the Jewish capital) was thoroughly Jewish. These first Christians – Jewish believers in Jesus – considered themselves in direct continuity with Old Testament Israel.

There is so much more, of course. Jews and Christians both draw on the Old Testament, while Mosaic (though not Rabbinic) Judaism historically and theologically underpins the New Testament. Then there are the many Scriptures highlighting the theological importance of Israel and the Jews, for example "salvation is from the Jews" (John 4:22); Zechariah records God's declaration that ten Gentiles will

1

take hold of the tunic of a Jew, saying "Let us go with you, for we have heard that God is with you" (Zech 8:23); in Romans 9 the Apostle Paul introduces his lengthy treatise on Israel by pointing out how the adoption as sons, the glory, covenants, the giving of the law and promises all belong to the Jews. Furthermore, in the Prophets Israel is referred to as God's servant (Isa 41:8-9, 44:1-3, 44:21, 49:3, Jer 30:10, 46:27), His son (Hos 11:1, Exod 4:22) and His inheritance (Isa 19:25).

These and many other passages demonstrate how Israel is inextricably woven into the very historical and theological fabric of the Bible, whether the Old or New Testaments, or passages focusing on the eschatological future, so that very many Christians hold to the view that God retains a plan and purpose for the Jewish people. In short, they maintain God has not finished with Israel. Many Christians also believe that God has restored the Jewish people to their ancestral homeland in the Middle East, in what is now the modern State of Israel.

But others take an altogether different view. Supersessionism (sometimes spelled supercessionism) is the view that the Church has displaced, superseded, or replaced Israel to become a *new, spiritual Israel* (a doctrine also known as replacement theology). This view can be traced back to the earliest church period. Indeed we even see it in the New Testament Church, where Paul writes to the Gentile Christians in Rome (11:13) and warns them not to become arrogant towards the Jewish branches of the olive tree into which they (Gentile believers) have been grafted (11:17-24). Several observers have suggested this arrogance was born out of the situation arising from Claudius' expulsion of the Jews from Rome around 49 AD. In Acts Paul meets a Jewish husband and wife, Aquila and Priscilla, who were of that Jewish population expelled from Rome (18:1-3). Eventually the Jews were allowed to return to the imperial city (Paul greets Aquila and Priscilla in his epistle to the Romans, 16:3). But during their absence the Roman Gentile Christians had apparently become arrogant through what they believed was their new status as the true Israel which had supplanted ancient Israel, as expressed towards the returning Jewish branches referred to in Paul's olive tree analogy.

Whatever the exact circumstances leading the apostle to warn in unambiguous terms against Gentile believers expressing arrogance towards the Jewish branches, the fact is it marks the emergence of a long history of supersessionism whereby the Church has sought to lay exclusive claim to God's promises to Israel. (Notice, by the way, how those holding this doctrinal position rarely accept the curses for disobedience which accompanied those blessings.) Thus in Chapter 2 Barry Horner explains in detail the transition not only from a first century Jewish New Testament Church to a fully Gentile institution over several centuries, but also a Church which rejected completely God's continued plans and purposes for the Jewish people, regarding itself as the exclusive heir of everything promised to biblical Israel.

This tension with the Jewish people – expressed through often harsh and triumphalist supersessionism, leading in some cases to disgraceful, indeed brutal instances of anti-Semitism – can be traced throughout church history, whether the Spanish Inquisition, medieval expulsions of Jews from various European countries, suspicion towards the Jews as expressed by theologians such as Martin Luther, pogroms, and so on. At its most extreme, of course, supersessionism, melded with nationalism, contributed to a mind-set that permitted one of the greatest human catastrophes of all time, the attempted genocide of a whole people resulting in the death of six million Jewish men, women and children in Nazi

Germany. As Colin Barnes demonstrates in his chapter, while Christian supersessionism does not automatically translate into anti-Semitism (and therefore when pro-Israel Christians label every expression of replacement theology as anti-Semitic they severely weaken their position), nonetheless triumphalist supersessionism is a key ingredient of the historical recipe leading to Christian anti-Semitism.

A NEW SUPERSESSIONISM

The debate surrounding the place of Israel in God's plans, then, has raged within the Church for centuries: Does God retain a plan and purpose for the Jewish people, or has the Church now replaced and become the new Israel, a *spiritual* Israel? At times the theological debate has been just that, a debate, yet for others (as has been noted above) it has spilled over into something infinitely more ugly.

Yet in the wake of the horrors of the Holocaust, leading some Christian theologians to re-examine the extent to which inherent supersessionism and negative views of the Jewish people contributed to the horrors of Nazi Germany, there emerged a more positive theological view of the Jewish people and Judaism known as post-Holocaust theology. Consider how, for example, the latter part of the twentieth century has witnessed considerable Christian-Jewish dialogue. Meanwhile within Evangelical circles supersessionism has not, until relatively recently and with some exceptions, been expressed in particularly militant (though certainly dogmatic) tones.

But many of us holding to a non-supersessionist position taking an interest in the on-going theological debate have noticed the re-emergence of a particularly militant form of supersessionism in recent years. The publication of a number of well-known books, together with growing anti-Israel activism within Evangelical circles in the past two decades or so, arguably marks the rise of a *new* expression of supersessionism (hence the title of this book), which is militant, strongly political, polemic and pejorative. Emulating a growing and somewhat simplistic anti-Israel narrative across much of wider secular society (particularly in Europe but now increasingly in the US), the new supersessionism is often deeply critical of modern Israel to the point of one-sidedness, even in some cases the demonisation of the Jewish state. Given the Church's less than illustrious treatment of the Jewish people throughout its history, this is, at best, unfortunate.

The new supersessionism is not only deeply critical of Israel, it also tends to portray any Christian who broadly believes God has not finished with the Jewish people as somehow fanatical and extreme, even heretical. The term "Christian Zionism" is thus bandied about with very little attempt at nuance reflecting the many different expressions of non-supersessionism (ignoring, for example, how some non-supersessionists can be quite critical of some Israeli policies). Rather, a straw man, a parody, is presented that feeds into a simplistic narrative within the wider world of *"Israel* [and her supporters, including Christian Zionists] *bad, Arab/Muslim world/anti-Zionism good"*.

Thus this book is not so much a reaction against, or an attempt to demonise, those who hold to non-militant theological supersessionism. While several essays and the book as a whole challenge supersessionism robustly, it is recognised that disagreement between supersessionists and non-supersessionists will always exist. Rather, the book, partly at least, is concerned more with offering a general response to the views currently being disseminated by this specific expression of a new, more militant supersessionism currently growing and capturing support across Evangelicalism, which demonises both Israel and those Christians who express the slightest theological support for her and the Jewish people.

Does This Issue Really Matter That Much?

Despite the polarised debate within the Church regarding Israel, there are some Christians who regard the whole subject as a peripheral issue, even an irritating distraction. In part such a response may be because getting to theological grips with this complex topic is costly both in the time and effort needed to reach a well-informed and biblically sustainable conclusion. And I am sure some such people are also reacting against some fringe Christian Zionists who seem to elevate Israel above all other biblical and theological issues. I would certainly agree that Israel is not a test of orthodoxy (a theological position which demonstrates whether someone is orthodox, or non-heretical in their beliefs). After all, we are saved through faith in Christ, not because we believe the Jews remain God's chosen people.

But as the above Scriptures indicate, neither is Israel or the continued role and purpose of the Jewish people in God's eternal plan a peripheral issue. Far from it. Meanwhile, this is a growing theological issue for many believers. In times past it divided the Church along hermeneutical (biblical interpretation) and theological lines. But now, as the current debate, which is beginning to trickle down to the local church level, becomes increasingly polarised and bitter as a direct result of the emergence of the new strain of supersessionism, I believe Israel as a theological topic will continue to grow in importance and become the focus of increasing attention.

Significantly (and somewhat ominously) the issue of Israel has also become a touch-paper – is symptomatic – of a wider ideological conflict which appears to be brewing within Evangelicalism, certainly here in the United Kingdom but perhaps elsewhere too. It mirrors the debate currently being played out in British society concerning how to respond to Islam, particularly growing Islamic radicalism. Arguably, several of the more vocal and polemical of the new supersessionists have crossed that line which separates legitimate criticism of Israel from intense dislike, even irrational hatred of the country. This kind of demonisation of the Jewish state, which can, when unchecked, come perilously close to anti-Semitism, also goes hand in hand with efforts by several Evangelicals to promote a sympathetic approach to hard-line Islam, glossing over Islamist extremes, or else explaining them as regrettable but wholly understandable reactions to Israel and the West (particularly the US). Thus we have a situation where several of the new supersessionists align themselves with extreme anti-Israel Islamic groups, speaking in Islamic centres against Israel and, significantly, criticising fellow believers in Christ on the basis that they are Christian Zionists, as well as aligning themselves with a rogue Islamic state such as Iran together with other anti-American political bed mates. Here is an important definer of the new supersessionism: a political agenda where the theology is made to fit, rather than the other way around.

One result has been that even Christians who do not openly support Israel but are nonetheless critical of Islam and what they perceive as an Islamist threat to the West are being singled out for criticism. A case in point is a situation near the time the first edition of this book was published. It involved Dr Patrick Sookhdeo, a former Muslim convert to

Christianity who leads the Barnabas Fund, a charity that speaks out on behalf of persecuted Christians worldwide, including those in Muslim lands. Criticism by some Christians who advocated a sympathetic approach to Islam drew Sookhdeo to the attention of extremist Islamist bloggers, while the serious nature of this Evangelical disagreement eventually reached the pages of the press.[1] Significantly, at least one of the Christians present at the meeting which allegedly criticised Sookhdeo's frank assessment of Islam is a supersessionist who is highly critical of Israel and Christian Zionism. Thus we see how the Israel issue is also symptomatic of a wider ideological struggle within British Evangelicalism. As such, it cannot be relegated to the periphery as an insignificant theological topic.

So how might Christians who generally reject supersessionism respond to this position in an effective and thoughtful manner? Many everyday Christians who, to varying degrees, take the view God has not finished with His people Israel are uneasy with an extreme form of Christian Zionism that takes an "Israel right or wrong" position. Such extremism is sometimes guilty of over-elevating Israel, ignoring how this is a secular country led predominantly by secular politicians. Moreover, much of modern Israel is a far cry from the divine expectations of holiness and sanctity as set out in the Torah (consider, for example, the many thousands of abortions carried out there each year, the active promotion and celebration of gay rights, youth dabbling in the occult, the intense social and legal difficulties faced by

---

[1] For a narrative see Melanie Phillips, "Beware the New Axis of Evangelicals and Islamists", 4 March 2009, *Spectator* website: www.spectator.co.uk/the-magazine/features/3409686/beware-the-new-axis-of-evangelicals-and-islamists.thtml (last accessed 21 April 2013).

Jewish believers in Jesus, and so on). By elevating Israel as they do, some within the Christian Zionist camp almost engage in a form idolatry (or "Israelolatry") of Israel, almost propagating their own form of replacement theology where the God of Israel is exchanged for the nation of Israel.

But such fringe elements are arguably a minority. Very often we hear from the new supersessionists how Christian Zionists are a numerous, mighty and dangerous crowd of people who hold tremendous sway over US foreign policy. The facts on the ground are somewhat different, and instead many intelligent lay Christians who by instinct support Israel seek a balanced approach to the issue while also challenging and effectively refuting the new supersessionism. This book is aimed at everyday Christians such as these who are looking for resources to draw upon as they debate these issues objectively and persuasively in their churches or among friends and family.

ABOUT THIS BOOK AND HOW IT IS STRUCTURED

There are several excellent academic treatments that roundly refute supersessionism (it is noteworthy that these books are rarely engaged with in much of the recent supersessionist literature). But such books are not always user-friendly or accessible to everyday Christians, often requiring a university background in theology.[2] Meanwhile, there are many popular books on the issue, yet notwithstanding some notable examples of solid exegesis, many pro-Israel popular books

---

[2] A notable recent exception is Michael Vlach's excellent *Has the Church Replaced Israel? A Theological Evaluation* (Nashville, TN: B&H, 2010). Apart from Vlach's biblical response, the authors of several chapters in this book have also produced valuable responses to supersessionism from different angles.

tend to lack a solid theological basis, relying on proof-texting or else spilling over into the very fringe Christian Zionist rhetoric that thoughtful non-supersessionists believers seek to avoid.

It was for these reasons that King's Evangelical Divinity School organised a weekend conference with a view to providing lay Christians with a range of theological resources aimed at equipping them to respond to the new supersessionism within a local context. A series of papers were presented which, while academic in tone, were designed to be accessible to everyday Christians. These were then adapted in light of question and answer sessions and debates which followed, resulting in the first edition of this book, which was pitched somewhere between the popular and academic levels.

When King's organised that conference I purposefully brought together a group of lecturers and writers on the basis of their expertise and what they could bring to the seminar (and eventually this volume). The original contributors not only represented a range of theological disciplines, they also came from across the Evangelical theological spectrum. This was deliberate, challenging disingenuous efforts by several new supersessionist commentators aimed at portraying all Christians broadly supportive of the view that God has not finished with Israel as a somehow narrow, peripheral and fanatical segment of the Church. So while all the original contributors were Evangelical, regarding the Bible as the inspired and authoritative word of God in all issues of faith and practice, and each rejecting supersessionism, they were quite a disparate bunch, counting Reformed, Arminian, Dispensationalist, Charismatic and others among them. As such, each person contributed solely as an individual, responsible only for his own paper, and not necessarily endorsing the theological tradition from which the others came.

Driven by an urgent desire to respond to growing anti-Israel sentiment and Christian anti-Zionism among some Evangelicals, the first edition was a fairly hurriedly assembled and somewhat short (and thus incomplete) volume. It was never intended to be anything more than a vehicle to transmit as widely and quickly as possible those 2008 conference papers to those non-supersessionists seeking resources to help them respond to the emerging new supersessionism at that time. However, the original book's popularity demonstrated the need to expand and re-publish the book at some stage, and a conference organised by King's Evangelical Divinity School and Chosen People Ministries (headed by Mitch Glaser), held at London School of Theology in late 2010, eventually provided us with additional resources to add to the first edition. Together with additional contributions from other authors who have published on this issue in their own right, all this has at last resulted in this re-worked and enlarged second edition.

There is still more which could be added to this volume, and this is a work in progress, with a third edition planned at some stage. Meanwhile, though the first edition was never designed to present anything other than a collection of autonomous resources which together responded generally to supersessionism (hence the first edition's subtitle "Resources for Christians", since dropped for this second edition), this new current edition offers a more structured, internally-coherent volume that focuses more sharply on the over-aching aim of a response to supersessionism, albeit still representing a collection self-contained, individual resources offered from a multi-disciplinary perspective.

The contributors range from academics to pastors to practitioners and observers, as reflected in the different styles and approaches across the book. Several of the essays are more popular in style than others employing academic language and standards such as footnotes. The focus has, in large part, been upon bringing together different voices from various walks of life, authors and people knowledgeable in the field so that readers can consider the issues from a range of angles. Throughout, there has also been a concerted effort to make the book accessible to as many people as possible. In short, it is hoped that there is something here for everyone, whether the layperson who either seeks to know how to respond to supersessionism or has not made up their mind on this issue, students embarking on their study of theology, or people already in ministry who encounter this issue frequently and seek material to assist them in developing a response.

This second edition adds six new essays, totally re-works several others, and sees much of the remaining material from the first edition re-visited and updated. The whole book is re-structured to contribute to added internal coherency and is divided into three sections, each exploring the issue of supersessionism from three separate angles: Church history, the Bible, and also the impact of supersessionism upon the Jewish people today.

Together, the various contributions, whether exploring historical supersessionism or the more recent variant, specifically seek to provide readers with material in order to assist responses to a new and militant expression of supersessionism. Together they respond to claims that many non-supersessionists are extremists and heretics, the issue of Jewish believers in Jesus and their wider relationship with the Church, as well as the impact of supersessionism upon

Jewish evangelism, Jewish perceptions of Christianity and Christians, and Jewish-Christian dialogue.

The first chapter by Steve Maltz, written in a popular style aimed at as a wide an audience as possible, seeks to provide readers with a general introduction to the philosophical roots underpinning supersessionism that later went on to influence the Church. In Chapter 2 Barry Horner takes up the theme of the growth of supersessionism within the Church with a detailed historical explanation of the process leading from a wholly Jewish New Testament church to one which was thoroughly Gentile and anti-Judaic, even anti-Semitic in part, just several centuries later. In Chapter 3 Colin Barnes offers a warning against the extremes of triumphalist supersessionism with a survey of how this theology ultimately underpinned the responses of many European churches to, and even collusion with, the Nazi intention (if not methods) of dealing with the "Jewish problem". This dismal historical section, however, ends on a high note with Paul Wilkinson's chapter examining how British churchmen and Christian politicians following a completely different theological line laid the foundations for an eventual Jewish homeland. His paper helps dispel the myth, favoured by some anti-Israel observers, that early Christian support for the establishment of a Jewish homeland was somehow the work of Zionist fanatics on the periphery of Evangelicalism. As Paul demonstrates this is far from the case, with many mainstream churchmen in nineteenth century Britain supporting and working towards a Jewish homeland.

Part 2 of the book explores and challenges supersessionism from a biblical theology perspective. In Chapter 5 Andy Cheung explores Israel from a linguistic aspect, challenging those who argue that the word "Israel" in the New Testament, especially Romans 9-11, does not refer to ethnic Israel. Next Ron Diprose explores and responds to the main New Testament passages cited by supersessionists in support of their view that God no longer retains a plan or purpose for the Jewish people and that they have been superseded by the Church (Chapter 6). In Chapter 7 I broaden the biblical theology focus further to trace Israel as a theme encompassing both Testaments and beyond, into the eschatological future. I also explore briefly and respond to new supersessionist biblical theology themes prevalent today, for example, the treatment of the alien. This is followed by Chapter 8 in which Jacob Prasch examines the issue from a hermeneutical perspective, highlighting not only how a spiritualised interpretation of the Bible gives rise to supersessionism, but also demonstrating how a rejection of the Jewish root of the Church is having a detrimental effect upon the interpretation of Scripture as a whole in such circles. Stephen Vantassel ends Part 2 with a combined biblical and systematic theology essay that moves beyond God's continued calling of the Jewish people to explore why Israel has a right to the land. Writing as a Calvinist he demonstrates how opinions on the issue of Israel and the Jewish people do not fall into neat categorisations that lack nuance so favoured by those seeking to draw a simplistic narrative of dispensational support for Israel with all others against.

The third section explores the effects of the new supersessionism upon the Jewish people today, whether Jewish believers in Jesus, those engaged in Jewish evangelism, or the wider Jewish world and their perceptions of Christianity. Brian Brewer begins this process in Chapter 10 with an Introduction to the Messianic movement – Jewish believers in Jesus – and the challenges they specifically face in light of the recent wave of recent anti-Israel supersessionism. This is followed by a paper from Richard Gibson, the leader of a Messianic fellowship who has been involved in working with the Jewish people for nearly two decades. He explores from a practitioner's perspective the very real damage triumphalist and anti-Israel versions of supersessionism are having upon Messianic congregations and more widely within the Jewish community. In Chapter 12 Tony Pearce, whose church is located in Golders Green (a predominantly Jewish area in London) discusses issues arising out of and approaches to Jewish evangelism. By including this chapter my aim is not only to challenge how some supersessionists view with suspicion efforts to evangelise the Jewish people, but also, just as importantly, to counter the doctrine espoused by some Christian Zionists of dual covenantalism, the view that postulates two ways of salvation, one for Jews through the Old Testament law, and another for Gentiles through Jesus Christ. I conclude Part three with an essay (Chapter 13) based on fieldwork in Israel. In it I challenge tired arguments claiming Israel severely maltreats Arab Christians and is solely to blame for the exodus of Christians from the Holy Land. Yet I also highlight how Israel is doing little to protect Messianic believers who face considerable opposition from religious Jews, demonstrating the dangers of pro-Israel Christians taking an "Israel right or wrong" position.

In the first edition we included a chapter by Howard Taylor offering an apologetic piece in support of Israel and God's continued purposes for the Jewish people. Sadly, Howard Taylor, who was a good friend of Israel, died earlier this year, and his chapter has therefore not undergone change or expansion like most of the others. It is published posthumously here in its original version as a fitting conclusion, setting out how God retains a plan and purpose for the Jewish people, how He has not finished with Israel.

One final point. In an attempt to make this book as user-friendly as possible we have sought to avoid using overly technical language, and from time to time include explanatory notes and definitions of theological terms in brackets and footnotes. Concerning terminology, in several chapters the terms Arab, Arab Israeli and Palestinian are used. These are not used interchangeably. The first refers to Arabs living anywhere in the Holy Land (or in neighbouring Arab countries, where specified). Arab Israelis, on the other hand, live within the State of Israel and hold Israeli citizenship. Palestinians are those Arabs who live in the so-called Palestinian Territories – the West Bank and Gaza – who do not hold Israeli citizenship. Of course, the reality is not as simple as that (for example, some Arab Israelis identify themselves first and foremost as Palestinians, not all Palestinians are Muslims, and so on). Inevitably, in a case where opinions are bitterly divided over such a conflict, whichever terms used will be seized upon by one side or the other as politically-biased or insensitive. I recognise this cannot be helped. In fact, they are simply included here for practical reasons, for the necessary purpose of differentiating one group from another.

Part 1

SUPERSESSIONISM AND THE CHURCH

CHAPTER 1

The Real Roots of Supersessionism

Steve Maltz

Something undeniably happened in 397 BC, when the final words of the Old Testament were written, then the book closed, because what followed was a four hundred year silence from the heavens. Until God opened the new book of the New Testament and instructed the angel Gabriel to appear to Zechariah in the Temple, there had been no universally accepted Holy Scripture, prophecy or divine visitations for four centuries.

Let us focus on that year, 397 BC. Malachi was the last great prophet of ancient Israel and, in Athens, Socrates, the first great philosopher of the modern age, was nearing the end of his controversial but influential life. Socrates was indeed influential, even for modern day thinkers. So key was he that all who preceded him were lumped together in a single classification, the "Presocratics", the string of warm-up acts preparing the audience for the main performer.

Plato was Socrates' disciple. He was Socrates' biographer and recorded his ideas and became, in his own right, perhaps the most influential of all Socrates' pupils. He founded a school in Akademia, a suburb of Athens, the very first "academy". There people were instructed in mathematics, geometry, law and the natural sciences, as well as philosophy. He also wrote much. Much of his early writings were expanding on the ideas of Socrates, who wrote no books himself.

Plato never realised it, but his ideas were to become almost as influential as Jesus in the development of Western Christianity. He said a lot of stuff, wrote an awful lot of stuff, but it is his *one big idea* that we are going to focus on because this was to become a tiny seed that somehow found its way into the fertile soil of early Christianity and grew and grew, until … you'll have to wait and see!

Plato's one big idea was *the Theory of Forms*. Here's the story…

We tend to label these clever Greek thinkers as cerebral giants, masters of thought and reason and defenders of human logic. We expect them to think through all matters of the inner world of the mind and body in terms of the natural world, of just what can be seen, heard and perceived by the senses. Actually, that is not true for this man. Plato was a man of ideas, but thought little of the world that surrounded him. He believed that there were two worlds, the obvious one that we live in and a "perfect" one, *somewhere else in the Universe*. I suppose this would be his concept of heaven and in this heaven exists what Plato called *Forms*.

To understand what these are, we need to think about everything that we see around us in our world, from actual objects like chairs and diamonds, to geometric shapes like squares and triangles, to concepts like beauty and goodness. Now you must realise that, according to Plato, all of these things are just imperfect copies of perfect chairs, diamonds, squares, triangles, beauty and goodness that exist in the other "perfect" world. These items of perfection are Plato's *Forms*.

Plato also believed that whereas most of us will never get to see these Forms, some of us would. These are the *guardians*, specially gifted and trained individuals (the philosophers of course!). Plato explained all of this in his analogy of the cave:

> Our lives are as prisoners deep inside a cave, where all we can see of objects are their shadows, projected on the wall by a fire. We believe that what we see is reality but we are mistaken. To see reality we have to leave the cave and see things as they really are, though most are content at just seeing the shadow shapes inside the cave. (*The Republic*)

According to Plato, the one who makes this step to leave the cave is the *guardian*, who is rewarded by viewing the "higher Good", the source of all truth and reason. Here is an idea that seems vaguely Christian, so perhaps here is the first clue as to how on earth this idea managed to find a home in the early development of Christian thought.

This "higher Good" is the ultimate Form, top of the Forms, Plato's concept of God, though not the personal God as we know Him. This "higher Good" is what we must aspire to. This "higher Good" is an eternal reality that exists in a higher realm and our physical senses are just not equipped enough to see any more than a pale reflection. Plato likens this concept to the sun in two ways. Both cause things to exist and grow and both are sources of light. As it is light that enables our eyes to have a partial sight of reality, then "the higher Good" enables our minds to have partial knowledge of what is real.

So there is space for the concept of God, albeit an *impersonal* one, in Plato's philosophy. Plato's God does not

21

answer prayers, or comfort those in distress, or teach his people or listen to the cries of the heart. Plato's God is most assuredly *not* our Father in Heaven.

Plato believed that there are absolute standards for such things as goodness, morality and truth, each of these existing as a perfect Form in this "second" world. He also believed in the eternal soul. So what is the problem with Plato? Well it all now starts to go downhill.

Plato believed that we are body and soul. He thought that these were totally separate entities, bound together temporarily during a person's lifetime. This was the concept of the *duality* of man. But, to Plato, the soul was the dominant, superior entity and it is immortal, being reborn again and again in different bodies, gaining in knowledge as it does so, like the concept of re-incarnation in Eastern religions. The soul is our seat of thought and knowledge, associated with the "second" perfect world. The body interacts through the five senses with our *imperfect* world and, to Plato, restricts the soul from attaining its full potential. So, in his view, the soul is good and the body is bad. Everything associated with the soul is good; everything associated with the body is bad. Fix this in your brain; it's the *Big Consequence* of Plato's "Big Idea". So, what's this got to do with the Church?

In the Apostolic Palace in the Vatican is a painting by Raphael. It is known as *The School of Athens* and features a whole gaggle of Greek philosophers. Clearly seen are Plato and Aristotle in conversation. Plato is pointing above to the heavens and Aristotle is pointing down to the earth. The question we need to ask is why they should be commemorated in the capital of the Roman Catholic Church?

Plato's Academy continued after he died, ensuring that his philosophy, *Platonism*, flourished. When Christianity spread westwards from Jerusalem to the lands to the east of the Mediterranean, it was Platonism that was encountered first. The early Church fathers had to make a decision: Do we ignore the prevailing culture, engage with it or learn from it?

It seems that engagement, as with Paul in the Areopagus, was the best way forwards, yet the Church Fathers took it much further than that. Trained in Greek thought, they saw no danger in constructing a Christian worldview in the light of the teachings of Plato. One of these teachers, Justin Martyr, had the view that Platonists would be so challenged by the similarities between their worldview and Christianity, that they may consider conversion. It seems that what may have started as engagement for the purposes of evangelism swiftly gave way to debate, then compromise, then finally assimilation. Christianity could be said to have become a subdivision of Platonism with added grace!

So how could this have happened? It all started with the Jews, strangely enough, or one in particular. Philo was his name and he lived in Alexandria in Egypt, one of the most famous cities in the world at that time. It was just after the time of Jesus.

Philo may have been a Jew but his education was thoroughly Greek, in common with all Jews living in the Egyptian capital. Yet he was a loyal and proud Jew and his life's ambition was to bring together his religious heritage and his philosophic tendencies. He believed he saw continuity between Moses and Plato. The problem of his day was that many Jews, trained in Greek ways, were rejecting Moses and the Bible and so Philo worked hard to create a compromise that would be acceptable. His main work was in the creation of Bible commentaries, mainly of the Book of Genesis, and he was the first to do so with one finger figuratively in the pages of the Bible and the other in the life and works of Plato.

We can start at the Creation story. To Plato (and to Philo), the Universe came into being through the work of the Demiurge, not quite God as we know Him, but a lesser god. Remember Plato's Big Consequence, that the soul is good, the body is bad, the concept of *dualism*. This can be simplified further in saying that anything of the physical world is *inferior* to anything of the spiritual world. So this Demiurge, responsible for the Creation of the physical Universe, just has to be an inferior god, from Plato's point of view.

The concept of the Demiurge is a consequence of Platonism. It is a fudge to support a faulty philosophy. That is the problem if your starting point is a falsehood. Everything that follows from it is also false and you are just sinking further and further into the mire. This is even the case with techniques used to implement your ideas. The technique that Philo used most of all when he turned to the Books of Moses is the same one already used in the study of Greek texts, such as those of Homer. This tool is known as allegory and the damage it did to the Biblical text is incalculable.

Allegory is a way of representing a situation, giving it a meaning that is not a literal meaning. Allegory and the Bible? Well, we know the author, God Himself. So when Philo went through the text of the early books of the Old Testament, he had to be sure that, if he saw allegory, then the author Himself would need to be in agreement. And, if He was not, then Philo was treading on dangerous ground indeed.

Why would Philo have to use allegory anyway and what's this to do with Plato? Well, it is back to Plato's "Big Idea", his *dualism*, and it is worth delving deeper to extract the core thinking behind it. When Plato says that the soul is good and the body is bad, he is declaring a basic principle that has many guises. In religious terms, he is saying that the physical world, the one in which we live, is bad (or evil) and the spiritual world (heaven and such places) is good, and therefore worth striving for.

Because of this, Philo was uncomfortable whenever, in the Bible, God (a spiritual being) mixes it with us on a human level (the material world), when He interacts with man personally, or shows human characteristics or emotions. When Philo wrote of such God-man interactions in his Bible commentaries, he would look beyond any literal interpretations of the verse for deeper meanings, *allegories*. In fact this became a regular feature of his work, looking for deeper "spiritual" meanings behind Bible verses that the author (God) meant just to be taken literally. Often he accepted that Bible verses could have both a literal and an allegorical meaning.

So what has all this to do with the Jews? Actually, it has everything to do with the Jews, as no other people have suffered more from allegorical thinking by the Church. And this thinking started very early, in fact shortly after the death of the last Jewish apostle, John the Evangelist.

We begin with Ignatius of Antioch, who was probably one of John's disciples. He wrote a letter to the Church in Magnesia, which included some comments about the Jews:

> Never allow yourselves to be led astray by false teachings and antiquated and useless fables. Nothing of any use can be got from them. If we are still living in the practice of Judaism, it is an admission that we have failed to receive the gift of grace ... To profess Jesus Christ while continuing to follow Jewish customs is an absurdity. The Christian faith does not look to Judaism,

but Judaism looks to Christianity. (*Epistle to the Magnesians*)

Now before we scream "anti-Semitism", we need to know the context of the letter. Ignatius was concerned with the Jewish folk in Magnesia who had become believers in Jesus, but were still clinging a little too much to the "old ways". Now this can be looked at in two ways. Either these Jews were adhering so much to the rules and regulations imposed by the Rabbis that they failed to make Jesus the centre of their worship, or they were simply living out their new faith in the best way they could, but in a Jewish context. Either way, it was clear that they were beginning to upset their Gentile Christian neighbours, so much so that they demanded instruction from one of the foremost Christian leaders of the day. Warning signs indeed of worse to come.

Justin Martyr, living early in the second century AD, was the first to provide the fuel for the unhappy days to follow. He wrote *Dialogue with Trypho*, a theological boxing match with a Jew, where the victor gets to write the book! It is a dangerous book, filled with naked attacks on both the Jews and their beliefs. He blames the Jews for the crucifixion and gloats at what he saw as their just punishment:

All this has happened to you rightly and well. For ye slew the Just One and His prophets before Him, and now ye reject, and ... dishonour those who set their hopes on Him, and God Almighty and Maker of the universe who sent Him... (*Dialogue with Trypho*)

So what do we make of this? Remember, the last of Jesus' Jewish apostles had died not too long earlier and the Jewish Christian community had dwindled by this time, to a negligible number. Justin had felt sufficiently confident in his reading of both the "Signs of the Times" and Holy Scripture to orchestrate such an attack on the Jews.

According to Justin and those who followed, the Jews had now blown it, had lost their *chosenness* and that this honour now belonged to the Church, the new "spiritual Israel". This is known as replacement theology, or supersessionism. Justin says as much in his *Dialogue with Trypho*:

> We have been led to God through this crucified Christ, and we are the true spiritual Israel, and the descendants of Judah, Jacob, Isaac, and Abraham, who, though uncircumcised, was approved and blessed by God because of his faith and was called the father of many nations. All this will be proved as we proceed with our discussion.

Spiritual Israel? Where does that come from? Is this in the Bible? It is not, unless you want it to be there. It suited the orderly Greek minds of the time to make assumptions and logical leaps, interpreting Holy Scripture in the light of their own ideas and expectations. This is called *eisegesis* and is a completely invalid way of reading the Bible. A better way would have been to read Holy Scripture as it is plainly written, in order to learn of the mind of God. Here is one they missed:

[handwritten margin note: Gal. 6 15,16 Roman 9.6. Romans 2 29]

> Lest you be wise in your own sight, I do not want you to be unaware of this mystery, brothers: a partial hardening has come upon Israel, until the fullness of the Gentiles has come in. And in this way all Israel will be saved. (Rom 11:25-26)

27

We will move on a century or so to the next major figure of our story, Origen. In common with Philo, he had a passion for interpreting the Bible but there was a major difference here. Although Philo looked to marry the orthodox Jewish interpretations with insights that he believed that he had from Greek philosophy, he always saw himself as a Jew first and his writings always reflected that fact. Origen was a Gentile Christian who was writing Bible commentaries for other Christians in the Greek-speaking world. For him, the Hebrew text and Jewish themes were just the raw data, to be processed using the tools of Greek understanding.

Origen was greatly influenced by both Philo and Plato but, in his approach to the Biblical texts, went a stage further than Philo. Whereas Philo often gave literal and allegorical interpretations of the Scriptures, Origen tended to dwell on allegory. As a Christian heavily influenced by Plato, he saw the spiritual dimension as all-important, so strained to find "deeper" meanings wherever he could. In fact Origen was responsible for making allegory the dominant form of Bible interpretation for centuries to come.

To Origen (and to Plato if he had still been alive), the Jews were *earthly* people, crude, hard-hearted, materialistic murderers. He would agree with what Justin Martyr had said:

> But you were never shown to be possessed of friendship or love either towards God, or towards the prophets, or towards yourselves, but, as is evident, you are ever found to be idolaters and murderers of righteous men, so that you laid hands even on Christ Himself; and to this very day you abide in your wickedness, execrating those who prove that this man

who was crucified by you is the Christ. (*Dialogue with Trypho*)

In Origen's mind, the physical, materialistic, law-strangled Jews were to be contrasted with the spiritually-minded grace-abounding Christians. Dualism in action, splitting the Bible in two and relegating the Jews to their role as the rejected people of the past.

Replacement theology is a perfect expression of the ideas of Plato, its followers should be proud of themselves for integrating pagan Greek philosophy into their Christian beliefs! Origen digs in the knife even further:

On account of their unbelief and other insults which they heaped upon Jesus, the Jews will not only suffer more than others in the judgment which is believed to impend over the world, but have even already endured such sufferings. For what nation is in exile from their own metropolis, and from the place sacred to the worship of their fathers, save the Jews alone? And the calamities they have suffered because they were a most wicked nation, which although guilty of many other sins, yet has been punished so severely for none as for those that were committed against our Jesus. (*Against Celsus*)

A favourite theme of his was to re-interpret the Old Testament in the light of the New Testament, using techniques from Greek philosophy, married with insights from early Christian tradition and other writings. His driving principle was that the Bible contained three levels of meaning, corresponding to the body, soul and spirit. You can see the influence of Plato here, particularly when he adds that the "body" level of meaning, the literal meaning of the text, is for the more simple minded whereas the "soul" and more particularly the "spirit" levels of meaning are for the *more enlightened* readers. If Origen discerned where a Bible passage spoke about Christ, then, for him, this *had to be* the original meaning of the text. This may have come from the noblest of motives, but is it correct, is this what God had in mind when He authored the text?

One target of this approach is the covenant with Abraham, re-interpreted in the light of the fact that Jesus Christ has since come into the world. Because of this, Origen would insist that some key themes of the Old Testament must be re-evaluated. This is an important issue and must not be underestimated. But neither must it be overestimated.

The problem is trying to decide exactly which parts of the Old Testament are affected by the coming of the Messiah. This is where we get differences in opinion because we are naturally departing from the safe haven of an objective literal reading of the text and we are moving into the subjective areas of allegorising or spiritualising the text. In other words, because we accept that Jesus changes everything, we have to accept that, for some people, some Bible texts now attract new meanings, determined by some scholars' understanding of how the Old Testament must be read in the light of the New Testament. We have the benefit of history to show us the results of such teachings.

The "uneducated" reader of the Old Testament is now told that s/he would be mistaken in reading parts of it as straight narrative, because we may not be getting the full story. But who sets the rules? Most of us simply do not have the training to be able to understand the theological complexities of this approach.

In some places we have little difficulty. For instance when we identify Jesus as the fulfilment of so many Old Testament promises and prophecies. We read such verses and even sing them, at Christmas time. This makes sense as these show the Old Testament pointing to the New Testament. But to have to read the Old Testament with one eye on the text and the other on a whole library of concordances and commentaries is beyond many ordinary Christians. They simply do not have the time. Surely reading the Bible was not meant to be *this* difficult?

So let us read the original wording of the covenant with Abraham (when he was just plain Abram):

> And I will make of you a great nation, and I will bless you and make your name great, so that you will be a blessing. I will bless those who bless you, and him who dishonors you I will curse, and in you all the families of the earth shall be blessed. (Gen 12:2-3)

> And I will give to you and to your offspring after you the land of your sojournings, all the land of Canaan, for an everlasting possession, and I will be their God. (Gen 17:8)

Now, not all Christians would read these scriptures in the same way. In fact, Christians tend to fall into one of two camps.

The first would take the plain meaning of the text, reading it literally, and take these promises to mean that there is a role for Abraham's descendants, the Jewish people - and the land of Israel - in the Christian age. For them, the descendants of Abraham - the Jews - are to become a great nation, living in a land promised to them by God as a permanent habitation and out of whom there would come great blessings to the world, through Jesus.

The second read the text symbolically or allegorically and say that there is absolutely no role at all for the Jewish people or the land of Israel in the Christian age. Whereas the first group tend to stress the continuity between the Old and New Testaments, the second group tend to elevate the New over the Old, saying that all things changed with the advent of Jesus the Messiah.

Even among themselves they would disagree about who exactly is the "great nation". Some appeal to the Book of Revelation, quoting from Revelation 7:4, the "144,000 from all the tribes of Israel", though not explaining who exactly is being referred to. Others are more specific, regarding all believers, Jew and Gentile, as this "great nation".

There is even more confusion among them about what is the "promised land". One popular scripture is Matthew 5:5, where they re-interpret "Blessed are the meek, for they will inherit the earth" as "Blessed are the meek, for they will inherit the *land*", remarking that the qualification for inheriting the physical "promised land" is meekness - a quality, they would say, that is displayed more by Christians than Jews. So in their view the land belongs to Christians. Others spiritualise the whole thing, saying that the "promised land" refers to heaven, or the Body of Christ, or the kingdom of God. Mathew Henry talks of a "heavenly Canaan" promised, again, to the *spiritual* descendants.

When answering the question "Whose God will He be?" they look forward to Revelation 7:9 to the "great multitude ... standing before the throne". The general consensus has God transferring His attention and love from Jews to the *spiritual* descendants, the Christians. Jews would now be no more loved or cared for than any other nation on earth.

Now these are all clever people, with a multitude of theological qualifications and decades of Christian service between them. But that does not make them infallible. Paul tells us in 1 Corinthians 1:27 "But God chose the foolish things of the world to shame the wise . . ." We must not be fazed by cleverness because, after all, most of the brightest brains of our age are still dead in their sins (i.e. they are non-Christians). Equally we must not neglect our brain cells out of laziness or neglect. Balance is what we need, head and heart, word and spirit.

This is the effect of Greek thinking, the tendency to rely on intellect and reason to read one's own ideas and imaginings *into* Scripture, rather than allowing the words of God to speak for themselves. It produces confusion and division, because once you forsake Biblical inspiration for intellectual debate, a debate and argument is what you get, with a myriad of possible interpretations. And, if there is even a smidgeon of anti-Semitism, not always acknowledged or even realised, then you have added personal agendas to the mix and you end up with something very dangerous indeed.

The ideas of Origen were taken up by Augustine of Hippo, one of the most important figures in the development of Western Christianity, for both Catholics and Protestants. The fact is that Augustine was just so influential in the subsequent development of the Western Church, that if we perceive any issues in the way he interpreted the Bible, then this is going to have great consequences. So his take on such matters as allegory versus literal readings of Scripture is crucial.

Suffice to say that he follows in the tradition started by Philo and refined by Origen, in using Platonic techniques to interpret Bible texts. Although Augustine was correct in declaring that Scriptures are inspired of God, he reinforced Origen's ideas that Christ needs to be shoe-horned all over the Old Testament, even where the fit is uncomfortable and that allegorical interpretations were given to passages he was unsure of or unhappy with. His approach was to say that, in the first instance, readers must look at the spirit *behind* the literal texts, to grasp the mind of God, through *spiritual* understandings.

Augustine was also convinced that the Church had replaced the Jews in God's plans. But he had a different slant on what to do about it. After hearing about the pogrom in Alexandria, when "Christians", fired up by the theological rabble-rousing by their Church leaders, slaughtered many Jews, Augustine said *no, don't kill the Jews!*

What's this? Had Christendom thrown up a true friend and protector of the Jews? Sadly, no; Augustine had a plan. He figured out that their punishment for their rejection of Jesus would be more effective if they were kept alive but never allowed to thrive. So perhaps the bittersweet survival of the Jews through the turbulent times of Christendom has been mainly down to Augustine!

The scene has now been firmly established that, because of the demands of the Platonic worldview in preferring the spiritual over the material, spiritual meanings were sought, even in Bible passages that were so obviously meant to be taken literally. A free-for-all was now created, allowing Christian teachers right up to the current day to be able to bend and coax God's word to say whatever they want it to say.

That is the legacy of the infiltration of Greek philosophy into Christian theology. The ideas of Plato, refined by Philo (for a Jewish audience) and Origen (for a Christian audience), became thoroughly entwined with God's revelation to us, thanks to Augustine, the father of the Western Church.

And that is where we are today. Replacement theology, supersessionism, is a consequence of allowing pagan Greek ideas into the Church. Everybody suffers, but none more than the Jewish people. Until Christians are aware of the root of this aberration and do something about it, the Church is never going to fulfil its true destiny.

CHAPTER 2

A Parting of the Ways:
Relations in the Post-Apostolic Period

Barry E. Horner

The Christian church, originating in Jerusalem, was thoroughly Jewish upon its founding. This is not surprising when one understands that Jesus Christ, up until His ascension, continued to be the quintessential Jew, even as the apostles were loyal Hebrews, and the available Word of God at that time was the Old Testament. The ministry of Jesus in the gospels, while initially directed toward "the house of Israel" (Matt 10:6), yet also reflected considerable compassion for Gentiles within Israel that also included the outlying regions of Galilee (Matt 8:1-13; 15:21-28). So He commenced, within Israel, a recovery of the established saving interest of His Father in "the nations," so "that all the ends of the earth may fear Him" (Ps 67:1-7).

JAMES, THE JERUSALEM COUNCIL AND
LEADERSHIP BEYOND

When Peter learned of the grace of God reaching out to the Gentile Cornelius, his report of this astonishing turn of events

37

at Jerusalem was well received. Hence the subsequent Council at Jerusalem, challenged by Judaisers, agreeably resolved the problem of the inclusion of the Gentiles so that the church at Antioch rejoiced at the liberty granted to it. Flourishing missionary activity there in the north did not reduce the established fact of Jerusalem remaining to be recognised as the mother church, with James, the brother of our Lord and author of the canonical epistle, as its first bishop. His leadership role, probably developed in conjunction with Peter, was certainly acknowledged by Paul (Acts 15:13-29; 21:18; Gal 1:19; 2:9).

The dominance of Jewish Christianity, emanating from Jerusalem at that time, continued for the next twenty years, that is until 70 AD when Titus destroyed most of Jerusalem and the Temple. Josephus tells us that part of a tower and wall were left to indicate the Temple's former glory. As a result, many Jews fled eastward to Pella beyond the Jordan, and other outlying areas. Then a further sixty-two years hence, a very severe Jewish uprising from more outlying regions, inspired by a messianic claimant identifying with Numbers 24:17, Bar Cochba, almost led to Roman defeat. However Hadrian responded with further Roman savagery upon Jerusalem in which, this time, it was totally ploughed and leveled, that is in 135 AD. On this occasion, a further 500,000 Jews were slaughtered.[1]

EUSEBIUS' RECORD OF THE JERUSALEM BISHOPS

It is important to notice that Eusebius, never a friend of Judaism, tells us that the first fifteen bishops of Jerusalem

---

[1] W. O. E. Oesterly, *A History of Israel*, II, 459-463. Also Joseph Adler, *Restoring the Jews to Their Homeland*, 6-8.

were Jewish, that is up to the 135 AD Roman triumph over the Bar Cochba rebellion and the prohibition of Jews being within sight of Jerusalem (the subsequent pagan city built on the ruins was called Aelia Capitolina after Hadrian). Hence it was almost inevitable that the next Bishop of Jerusalem would be Gentile.[2] This sequence would not change until a Protestant bishop, Michael Solomon Alexander, a former rabbi, was consecrated as Bishop of Jerusalem at Lambeth Palace, London, in November 1841.[3] Considerable significance is suggested here.

Listing of the fifteen Jewish bishops according to Eusebius

- James, "the Lord's brother" (Gal 1:19), first Bishop of Jerusalem. In the Epistle of James consider the explicit Jewishness of 1:1, "To the twelve tribes who are dispersed abroad." The meaning here plainly refers to Jewish or messianic Christians, the Christian Diaspora, not simply Christians in a more general or spiritual or homogenous sense.[4] This is made even more clear in 2:2, "For if a man comes into your assembly [NASB, ESV, NKJV], meeting [HCSB, NIV, better] synagogue [ASV, CJB, TCNT, συναγωγή, sunagōgē,] with a gold ring." Gentile exegesis has often failed here.

- Symeon, second Bishop of Jerusalem. Hegesippus, a Jewish Christian historian, indicates he was martyred at the age of 120. Eusebius concludes "he both saw and heard the Lord, in view of the length of his life and

---

[2] Eusebius, *The Church History*, 120-121, 167.
[3] Kelvin Crombie, *Restoring Israel 200 Years of the CMJ Story*, 59.
[4] R. V. G. Tasker, *The General Epistle of James*, 39-40; J. A. Motyer, 24; and E. M. Sidebottom, *New Century Bible Commentary: James*, 26.

39

reference in the Gospels to Mary, wife of Clopas whose son he was" [John 19:25].[5]

- Justus I, third Bishop of Jerusalem.
- Zacchaeus, fourth Bishop of Jerusalem.
- Tobias, fifth Bishop of Jerusalem. He was acquainted with Thaddeus who was involved in healing, being one of the Seventy (Luke 10:1, 17).[6]
- Benjamin, sixth Bishop of Jerusalem.
- John, seventh Bishop of Jerusalem.
- Matthias, eighth Bishop of Jerusalem.
- Philip, ninth Bishop of Jerusalem.
- Seneca, tenth Bishop of Jerusalem.
- Justus II, eleventh Bishop of Jerusalem.
- Levi, twelfth Bishop of Jerusalem.
- Ephres, thirteenth Bishop of Jerusalem.
- Joseph, fourteenth Bishop of Jerusalem.
- Judas, fifteenth Bishop of Jerusalem, was the last Jew to hold that office till modern times.

Listing of the fifteen (following) Gentile bishops

- Mark, sixteenth Bishop of Jerusalem, 135 AD.
- Cassian, seventeenth Bishop of Jerusalem
- Publiu, eighteenth Bishop of Jerusalem.
- Maximus I, nineteenth Bishop of Jerusalem.
- Julian I, twentieth Bishop of Jerusalem.
- Gaius I, twenty-first Bishop of Jerusalem

---

[5] Eusebius, *The Church History*, 106.
[6] Ibid., 46-47.

- Symmachus, twenty-second Bishop of Jerusalem.
- Gaius II, twenty-third Bishop of Jerusalem.
- Julian II, twenty-fourth Bishop of Jerusalem.
- Capito, twenty-fifth Bishop of Jerusalem.
- Maximus II, twenty-sixth Bishop of Jerusalem.
- Antonius, twenty-seventh Bishop of Jerusalem.
- Valens, twenty-eighth Bishop of Jerusalem.
- Dolichian, twenty-ninth Bishop of Jerusalem.
- Narcissus, thirtieth bishop of Jerusalem (c. 190 AD).

Thus, up to 135 AD, in the midst of great national conflict, the Jerusalem Church had been recognised with considerable respect as the dominant mother fellowship, even by the Gentile church at Antioch (Acts 15:1-2). Then followed unrelenting Gentile episcopacy from Jerusalem, and it is not unreasonable to speculate that this distinctive lineage was maintained in the light of developing supersessionism. With Christianity within Jerusalem denuded of is Judaic heritage, here was the perfect breeding ground whereby the adopted children were enabled to rise up and claim more of the inheritance of their mother than was their due. From now on the rich Jewish root would gradually be demeaned, except for that of the Jewish Saviour!

THE ESCHATOLOGY OF JUSTIN

Born of Gentile pagan parents c. 100 AD in Nablus, the ancient Shechem in Samaria, and after much philosophic searching, Justin professed Christianity c. 130 AD. He taught in Ephesus where he engaged in his famous disputation with Trypho the Jew, c. 135 AD, even when Jerusalem experienced

41

its climactic agony, and from then on Gentile leadership commenced dominance of the Christian Church. Later he formed a Christian school in Rome and there wrote his *First Apology*, c. 155, which was addressed to the Roman Emperor Titus. Soon after his *Dialogue with Trypho* was published. Then followed his *Second Apology*. Subsequently denounced as a Christian, he was scourged and beheaded c. 165 AD.

His millennial scenario
Justin is pivotal in the gradual move away from a Jewish centered eschatology toward a Gentile centered eschatology, that is within the early Church. So we focus upon his *Dialogue with Trypho,* that supposedly spanned two days, where it is plain that Justin was essentially premillennial in his convictions. So Trypho enquires of Justin:

> [D]o you really admit that this place, Jerusalem, shall be rebuilt; and do you expect your people to be gathered together, and made joyful with Christ and the patriarchs, and the prophets, both the men of our nation, and other proselytes who joined them before your Christ came? . . . I [Justin in reply] and many others are of this opinion, and [believe] that such will take place, as you assuredly are aware; but, on the other hand, I signified to you that many who belong to the pure and pious faith, and are true Christians, think otherwise. . . . But I and others, who are right-minded Christians on all points, are assured that there will be a resurrection of the dead, and a thousand years in Jerusalem, which will then be built, adorned, and enlarged, [as] the prophets Ezekiel and Isaiah and others declare. (5.80.1-5)

And further, there was a certain man with us, whose name was John, one of the apostles of Christ, who prophesied, by a revelation that was made to him, that those who believed in our Christ would dwell a thousand years in Jerusalem; and that thereafter the general, and, in short, the eternal resurrection and judgment of all men would likewise take place. Just as our Lord also said, "They shall neither marry nor be given in marriage, but shall be equal to the angels, the children of the God of the resurrection" [Matt 22:30]. (5.81.4)[7]

It is not unreasonable to believe that here Justin includes his expectation of a temple building at Jerusalem during the millennium. Even so, as we shall now see, he transitions us from earlier Jewish Christian distinctiveness, as reflected at Jerusalem and Antioch, to the conjoining of the Gentiles with Israel as one people of God, notwithstanding his millennial beliefs.[8]

His perspective on future Israel
In professing a moderate form of supersessionism, Justin believed that the Church was the true spiritual Israel, incorporating Jew and Gentile. The Gentiles, in being incorporated into Israel (Rom. 11:14), therefore participate in the Church as Israelites.

---

[7] Justin, *Dialogue with Tyrpho*, Christian Classic Ethereal Library, http://www.ccel.org. Accessed August, 2010.
[8] Refer to Ronad E. Diprose, *Israel and the Church*, 74-77; Dan Gruber, *The Church and the Jews: The Biblical Relationship*, 28-30; R. Kendall Soulen, *The God of Israel and Christian Theology*, 34-40.

[T]hose [Jews] who have persecuted and do persecute Christ, if they do not repent, shall not inherit anything on the holy mountain. But the Gentiles, who have believed on Him, and have repented of the sins which they have committed, they shall receive the inheritance along with the patriarchs and the prophets, and the just men who are descended from Jacob [Israel], even although they neither keep the Sabbath, nor are circumcised, nor observe the feasts. Assuredly they shall receive the holy inheritance of God. (25.6-26.1)[9]

Further, "therefore, Christ is the Israel and the Jacob, even so we, who have been quarried out from the bowels of Christ, are the true Israelitic race."[10] For the Gentiles, the New Israel has arrived while the Old Israel has faded into the background. Justin appears to be the father of this thought. This is the opinion expressed by Peter Richardson in his significant study, *Israel in the Apostolic Church*.[11] The tide has turned against Judaism.

THE ESCHATOLOGY OF IRENAEUS

Born of a Greek Christian family, probably in Smyrna, there as a boy he heard Polycarp preach, who was a direct pupil of the Apostle John. Subsequently he studied in Rome. Then, becoming a presbyter, he was eventually ordained as Bishop of Lyon, France, c. 178. Highly orthodox and influenced by

---

[9] Ibid., *Dialogue with Trypho*.
[10] Ibid., *Dialogue with Trypho*, 135. Diprose suggests that here we have the first association of "Israel" with "new" in a more supersessionist sense. *Israel and the Church*, 21, n. 26.
[11] Peter Richardson, *Israel in the Apostolic Church*, 9-14, 74.

Justin, he strenuously opposed Gnosticism as is evident in his major work, *Against Heresies*.

His millennial scenario

Irenaeus was probably the clearest exponent of a basic premillennial eschatology among the early church Fathers. It was a vital part of his response to Gnosticism. Millennialism, in embracing an earthy, spiritual materiality, became a telling antidote to elevated, more nebulous spirituality which at the same time demeaned materiality. We simply quote one of many passages that declare Irenaeus' basic premillennial eschatology:

> [W]hen this Antichrist shall have devastated all things in this world, he will reign for three years and six months, and sit in the temple at Jerusalem; and then the Lord will come from heaven in the clouds, in the glory of the Father, sending this man and those who follow him into the lake of fire; but bringing in for the righteous the times of the kingdom, that is, the rest, the hallowed seventh day [of one thousand years]; and restoring to Abraham the promised inheritance, in which kingdom the Lord declared, that "many coming from the east and from the west should sit down with Abraham, Isaac, and Jacob [Matt 8:11] (5.30.4).[12]

He further asserts that "these things [concerning the millennial creation, having been renovated and set free] are borne witness to in writing by Papias, the hearer of John, and a companion of Polycarp, in his fourth book" (5.33.4; cf.

---

[12] Irenaeus, *Against Heresies*, Christian Classic Ethereal Library, http://www.ccel.org. Accessed August 2010.

5.28.3).[13] However A. Skevington Wood explains with necessary clarification:

> It ought also to be borne in mind that the strong emphasis of Irenaeus on the literal fulfillment of the prophecies concerning the Millennium were no doubt conditioned to some degree by the fact that he was contending against the gnostic heretics, who denied the redeemability of the material. The millennial teaching of Irenaeus must not be isolated from the rest of his theology. It is all of a piece with it, and Irenaeus was the first to formulate (however embryonic an ally) a millennial - indeed premillennial - system of interpretation.[14]

Skevington Wood further explains that, like most of the Church prior to Origen, an earthly kingdom following the return of Christ is not merely what Revelation 20 teaches. It is also a central tenet of the faith because it functions to reinforce the central truths of Christianity—that there is one God who in love has created this world for us and us for it, who has personally entered this world in order to redeem us for a future in this world, and who will ultimately triumph in this world over the forces that are arrayed against him.[15]

His perspective on future Israel
In contrast with Justin, Irenaeus is, according to R. Kendall Soulen, far more advanced in his replacement theology:

---

[13] Ibid.
[14] A. Skevington Wood, "The Eschatology of Irenaeus," *Evangelical Quarterly* 40 (1968), 36.
[15] Ibid.

Because the Jews repudiated Christ, God granted their inheritance to the Gentiles alone (4.21.3). The Jews who boast of being Israel are in fact "disinherited from the grace of God" (3.21.1). Ireneaus' vision of the Christian story is profoundly supercessionist.[16]

And this is in the face of his strong belief in an earthly millennium. Moreover, Ronald Diprose draws attention to Irenaeus' understanding of Isaiah 26:19, Ezekiel 36:24-25; 37:12-14, and Jeremiah 23:6-7, which passages have been commonly understood, in context, with regard to the eschatological restoration of Israel. So Diprose explains:

> Irenaeus finds the fulfillment of all these passages in the salvation of people from Gentiles nations. By so doing he disinherits Israel of promises which are clearly addressed to her and at the same time manifestly makes the Church the new or true Israel. In other words he bases his exegesis on the assumption that the Old Testament should be read in light of what we have called replacement theology, which he apparently considered to be a part of orthodox Christian thought.[17]

THE ESCHATOLOGY OF ORIGEN

Born and raised in Alexandria c. 185 AD, and consequently indebted to Philo, Origen was also destined to follow in the steps of Clement in upholding the allegorical school of biblical interpretation. As a voluminous biblical scholar and commentator, along with considerable derived status, his

---

[16] R. Kendall Soulen, *The God of Israel and Christian Theology*, 48.
[17] Ronald E. Diprose, *Israel and the Church*, 77-78.

allegorical hermeneutic led to not only wide-spread spiritualisation, but also more vigour to the ongoing acceptance and anti-Judaic consequences of replacement theology.

His millennial scenario

Directed by Platonic presuppositions, Origin believed a literal, future millennial kingdom, as described by the prophets, to be carnal rather than spiritual. So:

> Certain persons, then, refusing the labor of thinking, and adopting a superficial view of the letter of the law, and yielding rather in some measure to the indulgence of their own desires and lusts, being disciples of the letter alone, are of the opinion that the fulfillment of the promises of the future are to be looked for in bodily pleasure and luxury. . . . [T]hey say, that after the resurrection . . . the earthly city of Jerusalem is to be rebuilt. . . . [T]hey [the Jews] think that the natives of other countries are to be given them as the ministers of their pleasures, whom they are to employ either as tillers of the field or builders of walls, and by whom their ruined and fallen city is again to be raised up; and they think that they are to receive the wealth of the nations to live on, and that they will have control over their riches; that even the camels of Midian and Kedar will come, and bring to them gold, and incense, and precious stones. . . . And from the New Testament also they quote the saying of the Savior, in which He makes a promise to His disciples concerning the joy of wine, saying, "Henceforth I shall not drink of this cup, until I drink it with you new in My Father's kingdom" (Matt 26-29).

Such are the views of those who, while believing in Christ, understand the divine Scriptures in a sort of Jewish sense, drawing from them nothing worthy of the divine promises.[18]

His perspective on future Israel

Following recollection that in the past Israel had been re-gathered after divine discipline, yet Origen indicates his irrevocable supersessionism as follows:

[T]hey [the Jews] will never be restored to their former condition. For they committed a crime of the most unhallowed kind, in conspiring against the Savior of the human race in that city where they offered up to God a worship containing the symbols of mighty mysteries. It accordingly behoved that city where Jesus underwent these sufferings to perish utterly, and the Jewish nation to be overthrown, and the invitation to happiness offered them by God to pass to others,—the Christians.[19]

Further he explains:

[W]hen they [the Jews] heard Him [Jesus Christ], they did not understand from His words the divinity that was in Him, and which transferred God's providential care, hitherto exercised over the Jews, to His converts from the heathen. Therefore we may see, that after the advent of Jesus the Jews were altogether abandoned, and possess now none of what were considered their

---

[18] Origen, *De Principiis*, 11.2.
[19] Origen, *Against Celsus*, 4:22.

ancient glories, so that there is no indication of any Divinity abiding amongst them.[20]

THE ESCHATOLOGY OF CHRYSOSTOM

Born in Antioch c. 347 AD and educated for law, John Chrysostom later studied theology under the leadership of the more literal Antiochene school. Subsequently he became Bishop of Constantinople. His expository skill in preaching gained for him the title of "golden-mouthed," and this gained for him popularity amongst the common people. Unfortunately his anti-Judaism, rooted in his theology, was shameful. Honesty and tactlessness eventually led to his banishment from Constantinople.

His millennial scenario
Chrysostom had been educated according to the standard curriculum of the Hellenised world. He was best known for delivering expository biblical homilies with great passion rather than writing profoundly as a theologian. While expressing more Semi-Pelagian convictions,[21] in modern terms with regard to eschatology, he would be considered amillennial, that is believing that the church is the new spiritual Israel, with the Jewish people, as a distinct covenant nation, having been disenfranchised forever. He comments on Galatians 6:16:

For they [Gentiles] who pursue these things [concerning a new creation, v. 15] shall enjoy peace and amity, and may properly be called by the name of

---

[20] Ibid., 2:8.
[21] Otto W. Heik, A History of Christian Thought, I.

"Israel." While they who hold contrary sentiments, although they be [physically] descended from him (Israel) and bear his appellation, have yet fallen away from all these things, both the relationship and the name itself. But it is in their power to be true Israelites, who keep this rule, who desist from the old ways, and follow after grace.[22]

His perspective on future Israel

Chrysostom's notorious eight sermons (homilies) against the Jews titled "Against the Jews/Judaising Christians," were delivered during his first two years of preaching activity in Antioch (386–387). Some have suggested he was responding against a very large and active Jewish community. Consequently he prohibited Christians from having social intercourse with Jews, though one wonders how making them jealous, according to Paul's admonition (Rom 11:11-14, 18-20), was possible in these circumstances! Chrysostom had imbibed the mainstream anti-Judaism of Christendom. Doubtless it was evident in his whole demeanor which manifestly lacked a winsome disposition.[23]

a.   Homily I. [T]hey [the Jews] became dogs, and we became the children. . . . Although such beasts [Jews as untamed calves] are unfit for work, they are fit for killing. And this is what happened to the Jews: while they were making themselves unfit for work, they grew fit for slaughter. . . . the synagogue is not only a brothel and a

---

[22] Chrysostom, *Commentary on Galatians.*
http://www.ccel.org/ccel/schaff/npnf113.iii.iii.vi.html.
[23] John Chrysostom, *Against the Jews.*
http://www.fordham.edu/halsall/source/chrysostom-jews6.html. Accessed August 2010.

theater; it also is a den of robbers and a lodging for wild beasts.

b.   Homily II. Now then, let me strip down for the fight against the Jews themselves, so that the victory may be more glorious—so that you will learn that they are abominable and lawless and murderous and enemies of God. . . . But may it never be that any of the children of the churches be found in the gathering-place of those murderous people—not now, not ever!

c.   Homily VI. Suppose the Jews should plead their sins as an excuse. Suppose they should say: "We sinned against God and offended him. This is the reason why we are not recovering our homeland. We did treat shamelessly the prophets" . . . You did slay Christ, you did lift violent hands against the Master, you did spill his precious blood. This is why you have no chance for atonement, excuse, or defense. . . . God is not reconciled to you on this account [concerning repentance in Sabbath breaking]. Since that sin of yours [in crucifying Christ] surpassed all sins, it is useless to say your sins are keeping you from recovering your homeland. You are in the grip of your present sufferings not because of the sins committed in the rest of your lives but because of that one reckless act.

While it is to be hoped that preaching has consequences, yet in the instances referenced here concerning Chrysostom, James Carroll rightly concludes:

Such words inevitably led to actions: assaults on synagogues, the exclusion of Jews from public office, expulsions. . . . Should we be surprised that not long after these sermons were preached, there were several violent outbursts against Jews in Antioch.[24]

It is not going to excess in claiming that for the likes of Chrysostom, such anti-Judaism extended to a virulent and spiritual illness. John Gager explains:

While he [Chrysostom] does not advocate the use of force against the Jews, he is not opposed to it as a means of recovering a fellow Christian from the fellowship of "the Christ killers" (I. 4). At another point he admits that he has come to lust for combat against the Jews (IV. 1).

Clearly this [Chrysostom] is an extreme case. And yet, how far removed are we from Cyril, bishop of Alexandria in 412, or Ambrose, bishop of Milan from 374? Cyril, shortly after having ascended his Episcopal throne, expelled the large Jewish community from the city of Alexandria.[25]

Surely Paul would be outraged at such an attitude and behavior, especially their erroneous doctrinal roots.

THE ESCHATOLOGY OF JEROME

Jerome was born c. 342 AD near the border of Italy and Yugoslavia. Having studied in Rome, he followed ascetic interests and, after some wandering, settled in Bethlehem where he ruled a monastery and, to the end of his life, pursued biblical studies, especially in the field of linguistics. Most notably he produced the Latin Vulgate version of the

---

[24] James Carroll, *Constantine's Sword*, 191, 213.
[25] John Gager, *The Origins of Anti-Semitism*, 120.

Old Testament, and being capable in Hebrew and Greek, he did not need to depend so much upon the Septuagint. He held the apocryphal books in low regard. Having been an admirer of Origen, later he turned against Origenism as heresy. Perhaps it was the Hebrew influence in Palestine that led to a more literal approach in interpretation.

His millennial scenario

Jerome's amillennialism is quite plain when commenting on Daniel 7:17-18. He writes: "But the saints shall never possess an earthly kingdom, but only a heavenly. Away, then, with the fable about a millennium!"[26] So Wayne House comments: "Jerome rarely passed up the opportunity to ridicule millenarianism and the idea of the reconstruction of the temple."[27]

His perspective on future Israel

Jerome was plainly committed to replacement theology. "The Jewish people perished in their pride, for while they claimed the chief seats and salutations in the market place, they were superseded by the Gentiles." (Letter to Antony, Monk).[28] Robert Wistrich describes the animosity that this Augustinian theology aroused. Jerome "denounced the [Antioch] synagogue in these terms. 'If you call it a brothel, a den of

---

[26] Jerome, *Commentary on Daniel*, Translated by Gleason L. Archer, Jr. http://www.ccel.org/ccel/pearse/morefathers/files/jerome_daniel_01_intro. htm. Accessed August 2010.
[27] H. Wayne House, Gen. Ed., "The Church's Appropriation of Israel's Blessings," *Israel: the Land and the People*, 101. In support House references Bellarmino Bagatti, *The Church from the Circumcision*, 90-91.
[28] Jerome, *Letter to Antony, Monk.* http://www.ccel.org/ccel/schaff/npnf206.v.XII.html Accessed August, 2010.

vice, the Devil's refuge, Satan's fortress, a place to deprave the soul . . . you are still saying less than it deserves.'"[29]

THE ESCHATOLOGY OF AUGUSTINE

Aurelius Augustine was born in Tagaste (Algeria), 354 AD. Following his profligate university life at Carthage, and entanglement with Manichaeism, he became professor of rhetoric at Milan. Upon hearing the appealing preaching of Bishop Ambrose, he was attracted to his reconciliation of the Old Testament with allegorical method and Platonist, esoteric spirituality. Ambrose was also decidedly anti-Judaic.

Augustine's conversion, based upon Romans 13:13-14, led to a more ascetic lifestyle and much writing, specially against the Manicheans. Baptised in 386 AD, he returned to North Africa and was ordained as a priest at Hippo. In 396 AD he became Bishop of Hippo until his death in 430 AD. While his *Confessions* and work on *The Trinity* were significant, yet his largest work *The City of God*, will best reveal Augustine's understanding of Israel and the Church. So with good reason he became the most influential theologian through subsequent centuries since the Apostle Paul.

His millennial scenario
In his *The City of God*, Augustine confesses that he was once a carnal Chiliast or millenarian, but now has become a spiritual Chiliast or amillennarian:

---

[29] Robert S. Wistrich, *Antisemitism: The Longest Hatred*, 17. He references Friederich Heer, God's First Love, 50.

[T]his opinion would not be objectionable if it were believed that the joys of the saints in that Sabbath will be spiritual, and consequent on the presence of God; for I myself, too, held this opinion. But, as they assert that those who then rise again shall enjoy the leisure of immoderate carnal banquets, furnished with an amount of meat and drink such as not only to shock the feeling of the temperate, but even to surpass the measure of credulity itself, such assertions can be believer only by the carnal.[30]

So this highly influential theologian formally established amillennialism which became the official eschatology of not only the Roman Catholic Church, but also the Lutheran and Reformed movements originating with the Reformation. Of course there were exceptions to this overwhelming thrust that were reinforced by the dominant power of the Roman Catholic Magisterium. The result was the pervasive belief that the Church had become the new spiritual Israel. So Augustine writes:

For if we hold with a firm heart the grace of God which hath been given us, we are Israel, the seed of Abraham: unto us the Apostle saith, "Therefore are ye the seed of Abraham." Let therefore no Christian consider himself alien to the name of Israel. . . . The Christian people then is rather Israel.[31]

The inevitable result has been the negation of any ethnic, national or territorial prospects for Israel according to God's

[30] Aurelius Augustine, *The City of God*, II, 20. 7.
[31] Aurelius Augustine, *Exposition on the Book of Psalms*, Ps. 114.3.

covenantal revelation. While the amillennial school has often expressed a desire for the Jews' salvation, the hoped for end result is that following conversion, absorption into the church will result in the forfeiture of all Jewish identity. Over the centuries, the Roman Catholic Church has been severe in its maintenance of this doctrine.

His perspective on future Israel

Because of the deep influence of Ambrose of Milan c. 339-37, upon the young Augustine, we briefly make reference to the extreme anti-Judaism of this popular preacher. Malcolm Hay explains:

> When St. Ambrose told his congregation that the Jewish synagogue was "a house of impiety, a receptacle of folly, which God himself has condemned," no one was surprised when the people went off and set fire to one. St. Ambrose accepted responsibility for the outrage. "I declare that I set fire to the synagogue, or at least I ordered those who did it, that there might not be a place where Christ is denied. If it be objected to me that I did not set the synagogue on fire here, I answer that it began to be burnt by the judgment of God."[32]

For Augustine, national Israel has no future. Rather the Christian church has superseded the distinctive Old Testament people of God. So Peter Gorday explains:

> Some Jews have believed in Christ, and they are the remnant of the natural olive tree and fulfillment of the

---

[32] Malcolm Hay, *Thy Brother's Blood: The Roots of Christian Anti-Semitism*, 25.

divine promises to historical Israel. . . . The "Israel" that will ultimately be saved are the predestined elect, drawn into a unity out of Jews and Gentiles. . . . Judaism is simply relegated to the latter [non-elect] category, and its status in salvation-history assigned to the pre-Christian past.[33]

However, what then of the visible Jews over the centuries and up to the present? How are they to be regarded? It is here that Augustine establishes a novel principle that, if not as pernicious as Chrysostom and Ambrose, yet results in centuries of demeaning treatment oscillating between mortal violence and insulting ostracism. Commenting on Psalm 59:11 we read:

For a prophecy about this thing [concerning the Jewish people] was sent before in the Psalms, which they [the Jews] also read, where it is written. "My God, His mercy shall prevent [meet/go before] me. My God hath shown me concerning mine enemies, that Thou shalt not slay them, lest they should at last forget Thy law; disperse them in Thy might.

But it was not enough that he should say, "Slay them not, lest they should at last forget Thy law," unless had had also added, "Disperse them;" because if they had only been in their own land with that testimony of the Scriptures, and not everywhere, certainly the Church which is everywhere could not

---

[33] Peter Gorday, *Principles of Patristic Exegesis: Romans 9-11 in Origen, John Chrysostom and Augustine*, 171, 333.

have had them as witnesses among all nations to the prophecies which were sent before concerning Christ.[34]

The exegetical arbitrariness here is astonishing. Doubtless it is associated with Augustine's inherited Neoplatonism as well as his more allegorical hermeneutic. There are no contextual grounds upon which Augustine can claim that here we have a "prophecy" concerning the future treatment of the "Jews" which, of course, he would be instrumental in overseeing. Clearly, as a Jew, David is here inveighing against "my enemies, O my God." While maintaining innocence, vs. 3-4, it seems that some of his enemies are Gentiles, vs. 5, 8.[35] So Augustine appears to ignore Paul when, in Romans 11:17-20, he explicitly admonishes the Gentile Christian to treat the Jews, both believing and unbelieving, with respect and fear.

CONCLUSION

The martyrdom of Stephen c. 35 AD ushered in an eruption of persecution against "the church in Jerusalem, [especially as orchestrated by the Jewish leadership (Acts 9:1-2)], so that they [Messianic Jews] were all scattered throughout the regions of Judea and Samaria, except the apostles" (Acts 8:1).

---

[34] Augustine, *The City of God*, II, 278-279. According to James Carroll, it was much later that Bernard of Clairvaux reproduced Augustine's understanding of Psalm 59:11. *Constantine's Sword*, 270.

[35] As a Lutheran, E. W. Hengstenberg, offers no support for Augustine's exegesis, yet he comments: "Christian expositors have all along drawn attention to the fact, that the substance of our verse [Ps. 59:11], as that also of vs. 6, 14, has gone into fulfillment on the Jews." *Works: The Psalms*, VI, 271.

Hence those who remained in the mother church in Jerusalem suffered material impoverishment to which Paul was moved to respond with aid. Yet in those early days, the apostolic response of Peter and John in Jerusalem was: "For truly in this city there were gathered together against Your holy servant Jesus, whom You anointed, both Herod and Pontius Pilate, along with the Gentiles and the peoples of Israel, to do whatever Your hand and Your purpose predestined to occur. And now, Lord, take note of their threats, and grant that Your bond-servants may speak Your word with all confidence" (Acts 4:27-29).

It would have been unthinkable for the Christians of that time to rise up and physically abuse the unbelieving Jews. According to verses 26-27, Peter and John describe both Jewish and Gentile opposition as the violent rejection of "His [the LORD'S] Christ." It involved both "the Gentiles and the peoples of Israel" (v. 27).

Yet following the destruction of Jerusalem, 70 AD and 135 AD, it is obvious that a parting of the ways has gradually developed between Jew and Gentile. The former amicable relationship, as reflected between the mother church in Jerusalem and her adopted daughter in Antioch (Acts 14:19-32), is fading. Incongruous as it may seem, the assailed mother becomes looked down upon by an arrogant, ungrateful, engrafted, unnatural progeny (Rom 11:17). Now the Jews, as distinct from the Gentiles, were to be perpetually demeaned because they were Christ-killers! Implicit was the false biblical conclusion that the Gentiles were more moderate sinners while the Jews were great sinners (Rom 3:9; Acts 4:27). So following the consolidation of vigorous supersessionism via Ambrose and Augustine during the close of the fourth century, the growing authority of the Roman Catholic Church ensured that no other eschatology would be tolerated. Rather, from then on and even to the present time, the global humiliation of the Jewish people was assured.

There is another related factor that needs to be considered at this juncture and it concerns advance in the politicising and secularising of biblical Christianity, and especially its formal manifestation during the Constantinian revolution. As a result church and state were wedded with the church eventually becoming dominant by means of an increasingly authoritarian Magisterium, along with supporting military development and the employment of coercion.[36] The more independent ecclesiology of Acts was almost lost so that by the time of Ambrose and Augustine, not only have numerous doctrinal barnacles adhered to, and begun to impede, the barque of Christ, but also an imperious clergy has led to the increasing dominance of the papacy!

Following conversion to Christianity c. 312, Constantine's intent was to wed the Christian Church to the secular state. The subtlety here was:

What the Emperor said had great weight. After all, Constantine was the one who had ended the persecution of the churches. He was the founder of the Holy Roman Empire. He openly, personally professed the Christian faith. He had convened the council [of Nicea, 325 AD]. The churches, therefore were more than willing to hear whatever he had to say to them.[37]

But what did he say? In addressing the Council of Nicaea, Constantine declared that there was agreement concerning

---

[36] Leonard Verduin, *The Anatomy of a Hybrid*, 103-104, 107,
[37] Dan Gruber, *The Church and the Jews*, 33.

61

there being no association of the Jewish Passover, on   the 14th of Nissan, with the Christian celebration on Easter Sunday. Following the Council he circulated a personal exhortation to all the churches. His tone, heartily approved of by Eusebius, is shamefully anti-Judaic:

> When the question relative to the sacred festival of Easter arose, it was universally thought that it would be convenient that all should keep the feast on one day. . . . It was declared to be particularly unworthy for this, the holiest of all festivals, to follow the custom [the calculation] of the Jews, who had soiled their hands with the most fearful of crimes, and whose minds were blinded. . . . We ought not, therefore, to have anything in common with the Jews. . . [W]e desire, dearest brethren, to separate ourselves from the detestable company of the Jews. . . . [It is] your duty not to tarnish your soul by communications with such wicked people[the Jews].[38]

Hence prior to Chrysostom and Jerome and Ambrose and Augustine, the cancer of anti-Judaism was already metastasising. It was the foremost theologians and scholars who subsequently agreed with the proclamation of Nicea and Constantine. Their formulations on behalf of the state church provided impetus which gathered steam and rolled on through the centuries. The Reformation provided some gospel relief, yet it continued to perpetuate the Augustinian eschatology which ultimately led to the horrific slaughter of

---

[38] Eusebius, *Vita Const.*, Lib. iii., 18-20.
http://www.fordham.edu/halsall/source/const1-easter.html. Accessed August 2010.

the Jews during the twentieth century. As Leonard Verduin
has put it:

> In a word, the sons of God [the Church] and the
> daughters of men [the State] had given birth to an
> illegitimate hybrid, an ungainly and ugly creature but,
> as is often the case with hybrids, a rugged one. It
> promised to be on the scene for a long time to come.[39]

Of course this hybrid is with us today with all of its attending
superficiality, carnality, tyranny, and perpetuated anti-Judaic
heritage. Today we need an eschatological revival, beginning
with heartfelt repentance concerning a shameful past, and
then a fresh return to the Word of God that focuses upon
establishing rapport with unbelieving Jews and prayerfully
endeavors to arouse jealousy when they learn of the grace of
God in the Gospel. Of course the assumption here is that
individually we glory and boast in that grace which we
proclaim.

Finally, it needs to be understood that the God of the
Bible is not some abstract, spiritual deity who, according to
supersessionist Christianity, has in fact taken flight from
biblical history and sullied His covenantal and elective
integrity. As Soulen puts it quite plainly:

> Apart from a relationship to the God of Israel, no
> relationship to the God of Israel is possible. God is the
> Creator and Ruler of the universe, but God does not
> draw near as the conclusion of cosmological or
> ontological proofs for the existence of God. God draws
> near as the God of Abraham who took the people Israel

---

[39] Verduin, *The Anatomy of a Hybrid*, 101.

out of the land of Egypt and who remains this nation's God to the end of time.[40]

Yes, even Chrysostom and Augustine offered limited patronage toward the Jewish people in expressing a token desire that they be saved. So today supersessionists say the same thing. However, while employing the term "Jew" without distinction, they eventually envisage the loss of Jewish identity upon conversion. Hence Soulen puts his finger on a most important point here.

In short, the problem of supersessionism turns on the Church's capacity to acknowledge the *abiding* [emphasis added] religious significance of Israel's corporeal election and hence the *abiding* [emphasis added] religious significance of the distinction between Gentile and Jew.[41]

It is this eternal dimension that must be vigorously upheld today. As Paul declares: "[I]t is not as though the Word of God has failed" (Rom 9:6). For this reason, it remains true that the Jewish people "are [and will continue to be] beloved for the sake of the fathers" (Rom 11:28).

---

[40] R. Kendall Soulen, *The God of Israel and Christian Theology*, 8.

[41] Ibid., 11. By way of example, in John Murray's *Commentary on Romans*, especially concerning 11:16-32, he writes of an eschatological mass conversion of ethnic Israel, "the restoration of Israel to gospel favor and blessing," 98, yet the word "nation" is never employed, and certainly not "land." Further, he never defines the eschatological prospects of this mass conversion. It seems assumed that absorption into the Church is envisaged without any ongoing Jewish identity. *Romans*, II, 84-103.

CHAPTER 3

Denouement of Supersessionist Triumphalism: European Churches and the Holocaust

Colin Barnes

Hard (or punitive) supersessionism especially carries within it a clear theological understanding of the Jewish people. It states that the covenants God made with the Jews were invalidated by Jewish unfaithfulness, and therefore, as a result of that Jewish unfaithfulness, those covenants now belong to the Church. These doctrines were taught and strengthened by reference both to Jewish wickedness (Jews being the "children of Judas", etc.) and to Jewish misery. Jewish wickedness proved that God was just in taking the covenants from them, while Jewish suffering proved that they were indeed under his judgment. This triumphalist version of supersessionism is therefore predisposed to anti-Semitism, as evidenced throughout much of the Church's history.

So too several militant supersessionists today highlight any perceived wickedness in Israel, believing this strengthens their position theologically. Clearly, there are individuals who hold to this doctrine without being anti-Semitic, but by seeing divine purpose in Jewish wickedness and suffering, the doctrine of punitive supersessionism, as such, potentially encourages the church to lean towards anti-Semitic views and acts. As Clark Williamson writes:

> The church's theological understanding of itself in relation to Jews and Judaism was never mere theorizing. Theory, interpretation, always has a practical moment. The church's anti-Judaism reflects and reinforces anti-Jewish practice, whether that practice is internal to the church in how it talks about Jews and Judaism and itself, in the ideas and attitudes that people adopt toward Jews, or whether it finds its ramifications in more visible and public forms, such as legislation or a willingness to tolerate violence or discrimination against Jews.[1]

Such harsh supersessionism is, arguably, anti-Christian. Jesus told his followers to love and do good to their enemies. Paul tells us that love does not keep a record of the other's wrongs. Yet a Church often claiming exclusive possession of Jewish covenants (and Scriptures) committed itself to proving, in word and deed, that this theft was justified, and that the Jewish people were rightly damned. According to Eckardt, "the primary causal agent in western anti-Semitism is the Christian message and the Christian church ... [this] has become a truism of historical, psychological and theological scholarship"[2] As Hay commented: "Hatred was the product of clerical propaganda."[3]

---

[1] C. W. Williamson, *A Guest in the House of Israel: Post-Holocaust Church Theology* (Louisville: Westminster/John Knox Press, 1993), 7.
[2] A. Eckardt, "The Nemesis of Christian Antisemitism" in *Church and*

Such triumphalist supersessionism, then, very often emanated from within the upper echelons of the Church. Perhaps nowhere is this more graphically illustrated than in Europe in the first half of the twentieth century where, in the lead-up to and during the Second World War, many European Christians and churches were complicit in the persecution of the Jewish people. That is not to say all supersessionists are anti-Semitic or were involved in the horrors of the Holocaust's genocide. Nonetheless, triumphalist supersessionist sentiment over the centuries, melded with other factors, helped contribute to an anti-Jewish mindset, which made the Holocaust possible. Often, Christian complicity in the Holocaust focuses on Roman Catholicism in Europe. Yet some Protestant churches – and not only in Germany – played their part too. This chapter seeks to highlight briefly how the European churches and denominations, shaped by punitive supersessionist tendencies, contributed to, even legitimised, Nazi Germany's Jewish policy.

ENCOURAGING ANTI-SEMITIC VIEWS BY TEACHING: THE NEED FOR THE JEWS TO BE WICKED

The consequences of this are clearly seen in the teaching and actions of the European churches in the years leading to and during the Holocaust. "Then desire when it has conceived gives birth to sin, and sin when it is fully grown brings forth death" (Jas 1:15). In the years leading to and during the Holocaust, the churches of Europe, for their own theological

---

State, 13-2 (1971): 227-244, 229. See also his extensive bibliographic footnote to this statement.

[3] M. Hay, *Thy Brother's Blood* (New York: Hart, 1975), 35.

COLIN BARNES

reasons, in self-conscious conformity to their own history and doctrines, continued to demonise the Jews to the point where the collaboration or acquiescence of the European population made the Nazi goals possible.

During the Second Reich, segments of the German Catholic press portrayed the Jews as "shameless intrigants, swindlers, venal, unscrupulous exploiters who lived off their hosts like parasites and who seduced, and slandered all except their coreligionists".[4] During the Weimar years, 70 to 80% of Protestant pastors were members of the anti-Semitic German National People's Party (the DVNP). The DNVP fought its first election "against the Jewish predominance in public life."[5]

In 1935, it was a periodical serving Catholic Bavarian priests which "exposed" the role of Jews in the German defeat of 1918 (the "stab in the back", or *Dolchstoss*), and traced Jewish "treason" during that war back to 1914.[6] On the same basis, the French Catholic Church had committed itself to the guilt of Dreyfus a generation earlier. In 1941, the Protestant Churches of Thuringia, Saxony, Nassau-Hesse, Schleswig-Holstein, Anstalt and Lübeck publicly stated that they believed that the Jews were responsible for the war, and that they themselves "stood in the van of the historic defensive action against the Jews".[7]

Again, these were the direct fruits of these churches' own doctrinal positions. The Jew was a natural traitor. Jerome, for

---

[4] U. Tal, *Christians and Jews in Germany: Religion, politics and ideology in the Second Reich, 1870-1914* (Ithaca: Cornell Univ. Press, 1975), 92-3.
[5] R. Gutteridge, *Open Thy mouth for the Dumb: The German Evangelical Church and the Jews 1879-1950* (Oxford: Basil Blackwell, 1976), 36.
[6] D. Dietrich, "Catholic Theologians in Hitler's Reich: Adaptation and Critique" in *Journal of Church and State* 29.1 (1987), 19-46, 25.
[7] Gutteridge, 253.

instance, writing in his Homily on Psalm 108, had stated that; "the Jews take their name, not from Judah who was a holy man, but from the betrayer. From the former we (Christians) are spiritual Jews, from the traitor come the carnal Jews". This was supersessionism in practice. The Jews were traitors according to the doctrines of the church, and the church acted upon and propagated those doctrines. In all this, the churches and the Nazi Party drew disturbingly close. Indeed, after viewing the three hundredth anniversary performance of the Oberammergau Passion Play in 1934, Hitler praised it as "a precious tool" in the war against the Jews.[8]

Turning to the Scriptures, which the Church also claimed as an exclusive possession, when the Old Testament came under attack as being Jewish, it was defended by reference to Jewish sin. That is, Jewish sin was a necessary component/defence of supersessionist Christian doctrine. In his famous Advent sermons of 1933, Cardinal Fulhaber stated; "By accepting these books [those of the Old Testament], Christianity does not become a Jewish religion. These books were not written by Jews; they are inspired by the Holy Ghost, and are therefore the word of God, they are God's books".[9] Likewise, the 1937 papal Encyclical of Pius XI *Mit Brennender Sorge*[10] (originally drafted by Faulhaber[11]),

---

[8] Jonathan Broder and Igal Avidan, "Oberammergau Cleans Up Its Act" in *The Jerusalem Report* (May 8, 2000).

[9] M. Macina, "Cardinal Faulhaber and Nazi anti-Semitism in the Thirties" English translation of the French publication: M.R. Macina, "Le cardinal Faulhaber et l'antisémitisme nazi des années trente" in *Bulletin Trimestriel de la Fondation Auschwitz*, n° 64, juillet-septembre 1999, Bruxelles, pp. 63-74. French version available at http://www.upjf.org/fr/846.html [last accessed 12/5/13].

[10] Pius XI, *Mit Brennender Sorge*. Available at:
http://www.vatican.va/holy_father/pius_xi/encyclicals/documents/hf_p-xi_enc_14031937_mit-brennender-sorge_en.html [last viewed 14/6/03].

states in paragraph fifteen: "The sacred books of the Old Testament are exclusively the word of God". Indeed, the canon was defended in an explicitly anti-Semitic fashion. Faulhaber's sermons continued: "People of Israel, this did not grow in your own garden of your own planting. This condemnation of usurious land-grabbing, this war against the oppression of the farmer by debt, this is not the product of your spirit!" The encyclical similarly states that the Old Testament contains the "record of the story of the chosen people, bearers of Revelation and Promise, repeatedly straying from God and turning to the world." and continues in paragraph sixteen: "Whoever wishes to see banished ... the Old Testament, blasphemes the name of God ... he denies his faith in the true Christ ... the Christ who took His nature from a people that was to crucify Him". Both documents present a profoundly orthodox defence of the Old Testament, defended as a Christian possession, by reference to Jewish failings. The only references to the Jews are as land-grabbing Christ killers. As Faulhaber twice commented: "antagonism to the Jews of today must not be extended to the books of pre-Christian Judaism".

In 1937, an article in *Junge Kirche* (the paper of the Protestant Confessing Church) by Gerhard Schmidt, a pastor in the Confessing Church, enlisted the support of Martin Luther to make the same point, that defence of the Old Testament in no way required the Church to defend the present day Jewish community. "Exactly at the point where Martin Luther criticises the insolence and impertinence of contemporary Jews, he commits himself with all his power on behalf of the Old Testament ... He does not reject the Old

---

[11] H. Wolf, *Pope and Devil: The Vatican's Archives and the Third Reich*, trans. Kenneth Kronenberg (Cambridge, MA: Belknap Press, 2010), 266.

Testament because of the Jews, but rather the other way around: Because of the Old Testament, he rejects the Jews".[12]

ENCOURAGING ANTI-SEMITIC VIEWS BY DEED: THE NEED FOR THE JEWS TO BE PUNISHED

Just as Jewish wickedness was a theological imperative, so to was Jewish misery. As Pascal put it:

The condition in which one sees the Jews is moreover, a great proof of the Religion. For it is an astonishing thing to see that people subsisting for so many years, and to see them always in a state of misery; it being necessary for the proof of Jesus Christ, both that they subsist as a proof, and that they be wretched, because they crucified him.[13]

Here also a clear blueprint for how Jews "ought" to live was derived from supersessionist doctrine. Church doctrine taught that the Jews were under God's curse, and that doctrine was proved by Jewish misery. They were fundamentally different to others, and their degradation revealed their true nature and protected Christians from the threat they posed. At the Fourth Lateran Council, (AD 1215) it was decreed that Jews must wear a distinctive badge on their clothing (similar rules would later apply to lepers and prostitutes). Flannery cites "numerous reiterations of the prescription by councils, popes and civil rulers".[14] In France,

---

[12] W. Gerlach, *And the Witnesses were Silent,* trans. V. J. Barnett (Lincoln: University of Nebraska Press, 2000), 112.
[13] M. Hay, *op. cit.,* 172.
[14] E. Flannery, *The Anguish of the Jews* (Mahwah, NJ: Paulist Press, 1985), 103.

Jews had to wear a yellow badge, in Germany, a "Judenhut",[15] in Poland, a pointed hat, in Sicily, Jewish shops were marked with a circle. "By these measures the Church impressed on the population the conviction that the Jews were a race of outcasts, branded with the mark of Cain ... treated at all times as if they were beings of an inferior species".[16]

For example, on March 5, 1233, Pope Gregory XI wrote to the archbishops and bishops of Germany complaining that the German Jews were not living in "the state of complete misery to which they had been condemned by God".[17] The exclusion of Jews from professions, schools, land ownership and handicrafts, boycotts of their businesses and the requirements that they wear distinctive dress or badges so as to more easily set them apart, were all church objectives pursued by church leaders acting in their official capacity. The English bishops of Oxford in 1222 issued an injunction forbidding Christians, under pain of excommunication, to sell any provisions to the Jews; but the king refused to sanction this proposal.[18] Nor was it the Church, through its own self examination and understanding that had ended these practices, rather this accompanied the spread of the secular Enlightenment. It is therefore unsurprising that no church in Germany objected to the Nazi laws discriminating against Jews.

In 1874, Alban Stolz, a Catholic theologian and popular writer, wrote that Catholics needed to counter the

---

[15] "Jew-hat", *Ibid.*, 103.
[16] Hay, 87.
[17] Ibid., 106.
[18] Ibid., 90. The Polish kings likewise refused to allow boycotts and exclusions of Poland's Jews.

"pernicious influence" of Judaism on Christian life.[19] In 1875, the major German Catholic daily, *Germania* demanded a boycott of Jewish firms.[20] A popular theme within Catholic anti-Semitic writers at this time was that the church had always promoted the segregation of Jews.[21] In 1934, the *Civilta Cattolica* commented on the Nazi exclusions, noting with regret that the Nazi anti-Semitism

> did not stem from the religious convictions, nor from the Christian conscience ... but from the desire to upset the order of religion and society ... We could understand them, or even praise them, if their policy were restricted within acceptable bounds of defence against the Jewish organizations and institutions.[22]

The semi-official Vatican paper thus thought that, if it stemmed from a Christian conscience, legislation against Jews could be termed praiseworthy.

In the immediate aftermath of the passing of the Nuremberg Laws, the Third Confessing Synod was held at Steglitz also in September 1935. The Synod was presented with a detailed report on the situation of the Jews in Germany by Marga Meusel.[23] In it, she set out in detail the persecutions being suffered by the Jews. Indeed, she already

---

[19] Tal, *op. cit.*, 91.

[20] Dietrich, *op. cit.*, 14.

[21] D. Niewyk, "Solving the 'Jewish Problem': Continuity and Change in German Antisemitism, 1871-1945" in *Leo Baeck Institute Yearbook* 35:1 (1990): 335-370, 349.

[22] G. Lewy, *The Catholic Church and Nazi Germany* (New York: McGraw Hill, 1965), 296.

[23] O. Chadwick, "The Present Stage of the 'Kirchenkampf' Inquiry" in *Journal of Ecclesiastical History* 24.1 (1973), 33-50, 47; W. Gerlach, *op. cit.*, 85.

spoke of "the attempt to annihilate the Jews." In the face of this, her church stood idle and mute. Her report concluded:

> What should one say in response to all the desperate, bitter questions and accusations: Why does the church do nothing? Why does it tolerate this unspeakable injustice? How can it repeatedly make jubilant declarations to the National Socialist state, which are political declarations directed against the lives of its own members? Why does it not protect at least the children? Should then everything that is absolutely incompatible with the humanity so despised today be compatible with Christianity? And if the church can do nothing in many cases today because of the threat to its own existence, why does it not at least admit its guilt? Why does it not pray for those who are afflicted by this undeserved suffering and persecution? Why are there not worship services of intercession, as there were for the imprisoned pastors? The church makes it bitterly difficult for one to defend it ...[24] What shall we answer to the question, where is thy brother Able? The only answer that will be left to us as well as to the Confessing Church is the answer of Cain.[25]

In 1933, Bishop Rendtorff (who would later become a leader in the Confessing Church) had questioned the whole assumption that the state's behaviour towards the Jews was "unevangelical". For 1700 years, he noted, the church had

---

[24] Gerlach, *op. cit.*, 85. Her statement also noted that Jewish Christians received more help from Jewish aid organizations than they did from their own churches. Cf. also Gutteridge, *op. cit.*, 242.
[25] D. Goldhagen, *Hitler's Willing Executioners: Ordinary Germans and the Holocaust* (London: Little, Brown and Co., 1996), 438.

fully approved of restrictive laws against Jews. Emancipation was an idea of the enlightenment, and should not be identified as an evangelical norm.[26] Wilhelm Halfmann, the spiritual director of the Confessing Church in Schleswig-Holstein, and Bishop of Holstein after 1946, wrote in 1936 that, because of "legitimate" Christian anti-Semitism, it was not the church's duty "to interfere in the state's Jewish legislation:

> Far more, we of the church must say, based upon two thousand years' experience with the Jews: the state is right. It is attempting to protect the German people ... with the approval of the Christian church".[27]

Likewise, the Brethren *Die Tenne* spoke of the "accursed" nature of the Jews, and of "the cleansing of Germany from ... Jewish immigrants". On June 18, 1933, *Licht und Leben* carried an article by the Chairman of the Gnadau Association to Promote Fellowship and Evangelisation, Walter Michaelis, stating that he and his organisation "had nothing against stemming Jewish influence, and treating Jews as non Germans." From a Biblical point of view, "nothing could be said against this," and it was indeed, "part of the divine plan for them."[28] Concerning the Nuremberg Laws, the Baptist *Wahrheitszeuge* "told its readers not to forget that the hearts of Jews had been hardened by God following their rejection of the Messiah. Under God's judgment, they had become a

---

[26] Gutteridge, *op. cit.*, 81.
[27] Gerlach, *op. cit.*, 105.
[28] N. Railton, *The German Evangelical Alliance and the Third Reich: An analysis of the "Evangelisches Allianzblatt"* (Berne: European Academic Publishers, 1998), 174.

curse for the world."[29] Likewise, the founder of the Elim Pentecostal church in Germany stated that he had "warmly welcomed" the Nuremberg Laws and knew that they did not violate God's Word "in any way".[30]

In Poland, during 1936, Monsignor Trzeciak addressed a large audience on the topic "The Jewish problem in the light of Christian ethics". He stated:

> Saint Jerome hated the Jews and Pope Pius V expelled all Jews from the Papal domain. Poland should follow this example: Jews should be destroyed, exterminated and expelled from Poland ... Noble are those Christians who refuse to sit with Jews on the same bench at university ... every Polish woman who buys from a Jew is a traitor. The Christian religion imposes a penalty for dealing with Jews.[31]

The fruits of supersessionism in the above material are clear. Anti-Jewish legislation is approved of by these churches, based on "2,000 years" of Church history, the "accursed" nature of the Jews, the "divine plan" for them and "God's word." Jewish suffering was officially promoted by these churches based on their own doctrines. The churches could have behaved like the Israelites in 2 Chronicles 28:13-15, or like David in 1 Samuel 26:11. Instead, they behaved like Babylon in Isaiah 47:6, not understanding Isaiah 54:7-8. This official support for the boycott and exclusion of Jews dispersed across Europe finds its ugly parallel in today's supersessionist Christian support for the boycott,

---

[29] Ibid., 181.
[30] Ibid.
[31] L. Cooper, *In the Shadow of the Polish Eagle: The Poles, the Holocaust and Beyond* (Houndsmill: Palgrave, 2000), 78.

disinvestment and sanctions aimed at the ingathered Jews in the state of Israel.

The same pattern of Church support based on supersessionism held true for the next step towards genocide, the expulsion of the Jews from Western and central Europe. For the churches, the ideological background to these actions was the mythology of the Jew as an alien, a stranger doomed to wander, never finding a home. Pope Innocent III had written:

The Lord made Cain a wanderer and a fugitive over the earth, but set a mark upon him, making his head to shake, lest any who find him should slay him. Thus the Jews, against whom the blood of Jesus Christ calls out, although they ought not to be killed, lest the Christian people forget the divine law, yet as wanderers ought to remain upon the earth, until their countenance be filled with shame and they seek the name of Jesus Christ the Lord.[32]

As well as recommending expulsions, Luther praised the Catholic King of Spain for the above expulsion of the Spanish Jews. Jews were also expelled from the Calvinistic Palatinate in 1575, where upon it was declared "Jew free".[33]

The move to view Jews as aliens, or non-Germans, was given a symbolic expression in the program of the Free Churches 1933 Prayer Week, published before Hitler took office. In this program, the traditional prayer for the Jews was

---

[32] A. Davies, *Anti-Semitism and the Christian Mind* (New York: Seabury, 1969), 69-70.
[33] P. Johnson, *A History of the Jews* (Phoenix: London, 1993), 243; E. Barnavi, *A Historical Atlas of the Jewish People: From the Time of the Patriarchs to the Present* (New York: Alfred A. Knopf, Inc., 1992), 138.

moved from the "home" missions to the "missionary endeavours among foreigners" section. This change was due to internal pressure to distance the Evangelicals from the Jews.[34] The top Lutheran theologian Gerhard Kittel had stated in the 1930's: "Authentic Judaism abides in the symbol of the stranger wandering restless and homeless on the face of the earth".[35] Niemöller preached in 1937: "We speak of the "eternal Jew" and conjure up the picture of a restless wanderer who has no home and cannot find peace".[36] Cardinal Faulhaber agreed: "the daughters of Zion received their bill of divorce and from that time forth wanders, forever restless, over the face of the earth."[37] So, when the deportations started, no voices of protest came from the churches-because *that was what was supposed to happen to Jews.* Speaking of the climate such sentiments created, in 1938, an American writer wrote:

What is to be done with these people, with the millions who are clawing like frantic beasts at the dark walls of the suffocating chambers where they are imprisoned? The Christian world has practically abandoned them, and sits by with hardly an observable twinge of conscience in the midst of this terrible tragedy.[38]

In February 1942, the German Catholic bishops received a report detailing the conditions of the deportees in the Lodz

[34] N. Railton, 1998: 106.
[35] M. Brown, *Our Hands are Stained with Blood* (Shippensburg, PA: Destiny Image, 1992), 16.
[36] D. Goldhagen, *op. cit.,* 112.
[37] S. Friedländer, *Nazi Germany and the Jews: Vol 1; The years of persecution 1933-39* (London: Weidenfeld and Nicolson, 1997), 48.
[38] Hay, *op. cit.,* 5.

Ghetto, where over 20,000 Jews from Germany and Austria had already been resettled. It read in part:

> Housing in unheated rooms. Between 32 and 80 persons to a room ... Sustenance: about 200 grams of bread a day, together with a watery soup once or twice a day ... Indescribable cold. No possibility to change clothes. No flushing toilets; no running water. Huge epidemics. Death rate in the first weeks was 35 a day, and, according to one man, 200 a day in January.[39]

The bishops made no response to this report for over a year. A petition was then presented to them, which called for humane camps, rather than for the return of the deportees. Even this call was rejected by the bishops. Jesuit Alfred Dlep spoke at this conference, asking "has the Church forgotten how to say 'thou shalt not?' Has the church lost sight of the commandments".[40] Again, the doctrine of supersessionism stated that "authentic Judaism" was a "restless wanderer" with "no home", who "cannot find peace", for she had "received her bill of divorce" from God. How could the churches protest what they believed was God's will?

In similar manner, when a Jew who had escaped from the death camp at Majdanek asked for help from a Pole, the Pole replied: "if God takes no pity on your people, how can you expect pity from a human being?"[41] The Pole then shut his door. The wording of such sentiments makes it clear that this sentiment did not come from Nazi propaganda, but from the

---

[39] M. Phayer, *The Catholic Church and the Holocaust, 1930-1965* (Bloomington: Indiana University Press, 2000), 69.

[40] Lewy, *op. cit.,* 307.

[41] D. Gushee, *The Righteous Gentiles of the Holocaust: A Christian Interpretation* (Minneapolis: Fortress Press, 1994), 118.

churches. Consider also the account of David Rodman, who was hidden by the Polish Catholic, Lech Sarna:

Essentially a highly moral and good person, he changed after each visit to Church. At such times, he would grumble, swear and scream at his wife. 'I am sure to loose in both worlds. They will kill me for keeping Jews and then I will lose heaven for helping Jews.'[42]

Similarly, when Leopold Socha, a Lvov Gentile who had been involved in the rescue of Jews, was accidentally run over by a truck shortly after the war, Halina Wind, one of those who had been rescued by Socha, reported: "As he lay on the pavement with his blood dripping into the sewers, the Poles crossed themselves and said it was God's punishment for hiding Jews".[43]

In 1938, the Polish Jesuits published a pamphlet which quoted Thomas Aquinas, who said that "Jews should be expelled from Christian societies".[44] Concerning this, the *Mlodziez Katolicka* wrote: "like Jesus, Poles must drive away Satan and all those who aided him".[45] On April 26, 1942 the Slovakian Catholic episcopate issued a pastoral letter

---

[42] Ibid., 165. One must also ask, how many potential rescuers were put off, not by the Nazis, but by preaching such as this man endured?
[43] Ibid., 118. See J. Gross, *Neighbors: The Destruction of the Jewish Community in Jedwabne* (Princeton: Princeton University Press, 2001), 131, 158-161; N. Tec, *When Darkness Pierced the Light: Christian rescue of Jews in Nazi-occupied Poland* (New York: Oxford University Press, 1986), 58-59; for still more rescuers killed or turned on after the war by "Christians", not Nazis.
[44] R. Modras, *The Catholic Church and Antisemitism, Poland, 1933-1939* (Jerusalem: Harwood Academic Publishers, 1994), 284.
[45] Ibid., 320.

concerning the deportation of Jews to Poland.[46] It declared that the Jews were a cursed people because of their deicide:

> Also, in our eyes has the influence of the Jews been pernicious. ... Not only economically, but also in the cultural and moral spheres, they have harmed our people. The church cannot be opposed, therefore, if the state with legal actions eradicates the dangerous influence of the Jews.[47]

When in 1942, Archbishop Kametko of Slovakia was approached by the Nitra Rebbe, asking for the church to intervene to try and halt the deportations, he reportedly stated:

> This is no mere expulsion. You will not die there of hunger and disease. They will slaughter all of you there, young and old alike, women and children, at once. It is the punishment that you deserve for the death of our Lord and Redeemer, Jesus Christ.[48]

Turning to Hungary, as early as 1920 a pamphlet of the United National Christian League had stated that:

---

[46] L. Rothkirchen, "The Churches and the 'Final Solution' in Slovakia" in *Judaism and Christianity under the Impact of National Socialism,* O. Dov Kulka, P. Mendes-Flohr, ed. (Jerusalem: The Historical Society of Israel, 1987): 413-422, 417.

[47] J. Morley, *Vatican Diplomacy and the Jews during the Holocaust, 1939-1943* (New York: Ktav, 1980), 85; L. Rothkirchen, *Ibid*; P. Blet, *Pius XII and the Second World War: According to the Archives of the Vatican* (New Jersey: Paulist Press, 1999), 171.

[48] D. Gushee, *op. cit.,*117-88; and W. Nicholls, *Christian Antisemitism: A History of Hate* (Northvale, NJ: Jason Aronson Inc., 1993), 357-358.

There is no possibility of maintaining legislation in the Christian spirit and Christian education in a region infected by Judaism. Thus, we must burn out the abominable Jewish nest, the roosting region of all moral and cultural poison.[49]

On June 29, 1944, after the majority of Hungary's Jews had been deported to Auschwitz, the head of the Catholic Church in Hungary, Cardinal Seredi, released the following letter:

We do not deny that a number of Jews exercised a wicked, destructive influence upon Hungarian economic, social and moral life ... We do not doubt that the Jewish question must be solved in a legal and just manner. And so, we do not voice any opposition to the steps which have been taken against them until now in the economic field in the interests of the state. Similarly, we lodge no protest against the eradication of their undesirable influence. On the contrary, we would like to see it disappear.[50]

He had previously called for the "removing of the Jewish spirit from public and economic areas as well as from additional walks of life," and had spoken of the need "to eliminate the Jewish spirit".[51] In a newspaper interview on August 12, 1944, a priest declared: "Ever since the Jews crucified Jesus, they have been the foes of Christianity. May the Jews be expelled from Hungary, and then the church too,

---

[49] M. Herczl, *Christianity and the Holocaust of Hungarian Jewry* (New York: New York University Press, 1993), 38.
[50] Ibid., 207.
[51] Ibid., 189-190.

will be able to breathe more freely".[52] A newspaper article written by a Catholic monk and reprinted in a Catholic journal in the summer of 1944 (during the deportations) stated that, "the Christian doctrine of brotherly love is not violated by what is being done at present with the Jews. On the contrary, it is realised by means of those deeds".[53]

For many, deportations led directly to death. For others, they led initially to ghettoes. As with the boycotts (deportations, etc.), ghettoes were originally a Christian idea, again based on a clear supersessionist doctrine of Jewish identity. Augustine had written: "Jews were bound until the end of time to serve as witnesses to the Church's teaching as slaves". Thomas Aquinas had agreed with this, and preached the idea that Jews must be compelled to live in perpetual slavery.[54] Pope Innocent III re-stated this in a letter to the Archbishop of Seus and the Bishop of Paris (15 July 1205): "The Jews are condemned to eternal slavery".[55] A Papal legate presided over the Council of Breslau in 1266. This council decreed that Jews must not live side by side with Christians, and advised special quarters for Jews who must also wear pointed hats and a red badge. A year later, in 1267 the Council of Vienna urged the total separation of Jews from society. Their exclusion from the common law of humanity was explicitly affirmed in 1268, by the Jewry-law of Brünn, where it was written: "The Jews are deprived of their natural rights and condemned to eternal misery for their sins".[56] In 1516, the first Ghetto was established in Venice. In 1555, Pope

[52] Ibid., 190.
[53] Ibid., 233.
[54] Flannery, op. cit., 96.
[55] F. Heer, God's First Love: Christians and Jews over Two Thousand Years, trans. Geoffrey Skelton (London: Trinity Press, 1967), 73.
[56] Hay, op. cit., 109.

Paul IV, confirming that Jews had been condemned by God to eternal slavery, issued the bull *Cum nimis absurdum,* which decreed the establishment of "Ghettos" throughout Europe.[57]

In 1823, one of the first acts of the new Pope, Leo XII, was to order the Jews back into the ghetto: "to overcome the evil consequences of the freedom [they] have enjoyed".[58] Leo also asked the Office of the Inquisition to make sure that all of the ancient restrictions on Jews were being enforced. Following their report, the Vatican issued orders that Jews were not to be permitted to leave the ghetto for even a single day without a written permit from the Criminal Tribunal. Fear of disease led in 1836 to the public health commission sending Prince Odescalchi to investigate conditions within the ghetto of Rome. He reported that the inhabitants lived in "untold misery."[59] There was no hospital in the ghetto, and Jews were not allowed by the Vatican to become doctors. They were also forbidden to open bookstores, or go to public schools. In 1843, Prince Metternich of Austria, whose troops had helped the Vatican retake the Papal States, asked the Pope if he could cease his policy of re-ghettoisation. Coming from such an important backer, the prince's request was answered by the Pope himself:

The prohibitions on the Jews, forbidding them from employing Christian servants or wetnurses, from owning real estate ... from living outside [ghetto] walls mixed in and confused with Christians, are prohibitions

---

[57] A. Rubin, *Scattered Among the Nations* (New Jersey: Jason Aronson Inc., 1995), 61.
[58] D. Kertzer, *The Popes Against the Jews: The Vatican's Role in the Rise of Modern Anti-Semitism* (New York: Alfred A. Knopf, 2001), 63 and 73.
[59] Ibid.

founded in the sacred Canon. These ... command the separation of Christians and Jews.

The Pope went on to note "the scandal of seeing Jews pretending to be living the same as others". Jews living outside of the ghetto, the Pope concluded: "cannot be tolerated in the Ecclesiastical State, because they are openly contrary to the most sacrosanct principles of the Ecclesiastical laws".[60]

In 1870, the Pope was forced to retreat into the Vatican, and Rome's Jews were finally emancipated. In 1871, the Pope told a Catholic women's organization that Jews were "dogs". He continued: "We have today in Rome unfortunately too many of these dogs, and we hear them barking in all the streets, and going around molesting people everywhere".[61] *L'Osservatore Romano* wrote in 1898 that Jews "cannot and must not live among others".[62] In 1937, four years after Hitler came to power, the Jesuit periodical *Civilta Cattolica*[63] again recommended the reimposition of segregation as their preferred solution to the Jewish problem.[64]

From Germany, as early as 1878, conservative Protestant voices and publications were also calling for the rolling back of emancipation.[65] In 1886 the Protestant bishop H. Martensen also went into print to warn of the dangers of Jewish emancipation.[66] Ten years after the Emancipation in

---

[60] Ibid., 82-83.
[61] Ibid., 130.
[62] Ibid., 149.
[63] Lewy, *op. cit.,* 296.
[64] S. Zuccotti, *Under His Very Windows: The Vatican and the Holocaust in Italy* (New Haven: Yale University Press, 2000) 13.
[65] Niewyk, *op. cit.,* 348.
[66] Tal, *op. cit.,* 91. His work was entitled "*Die christliche Ethik*".

Hungary, in 1883, a petition draw up by Reformed priests calling for their reintroduction was presented to parliament.[67] In 1938, an article in the Polish Catholic press likewise called for the disenfranchisement of the Jews and for the reintroduction of ghettos.[68]

CONCLUSION: A CONTRADICTORY MINDSET

Even Jewish deaths were a doctrinal concern for the churches. The relationship was formulated by Augustine. Unlike heretics and pagans, they were to be allowed to survive, but as a theological construction. They were to be a witness people, both their survival and their misfortune witnessing to their own evil and the Christian truth. "Like Cain, they carry a sign, but are not to be killed".[69] "Killed" here applies not so much to the individual, as to the community. For example, after large numbers of Jewish men, women and children were killed in Rouen, Orleans, Limoges and Mainz in 611, the chronicler of the time recorded that a few managed to escape: "because it is necessary that some should remain alive to provide a constant proof of their crime, and to bear witness to the blood of Christ".[70] As St. Bernard affirmed:

> Consult the pages of Holy Writ. I know what is written in the Psalms as prophecy about the Jews: God hath shown me, saith the church, thou shalt not slay my enemies, neither shall my people ever be forgotten.

---

[67] Herczl, *op. cit.*,14.
[68] Modras, *op. cit.*, 154.
[69] Flannery, *op. cit.*, 53.
[70] Hay, *op. cit.*, 37.

They are living signs to us, representing the Lord's Passion. For this reason they are dispersed to all regions, that they may pay the penalty of so great a crime, that they may be the witnesses of our redemption.[71]

The church thus committed itself both to their degradation and to their survival. These aims were to an extent contradictory. On one hand, church resources were allocated to demonising the Jews, to stirring up feelings of fear and hatred towards them, to showing the flock that they represented a very real threat, both spiritual and physical, to them. However, while the natural reaction to such a threat would be to eliminate it, here the church stepped in as their protector. They should be feared and hated, but not killed.

This subtlety often lay beyond the flocks to which they preached. To be both persecutor and protector was difficult, and to be able to persecute in love was held up as a sign of true spirituality. *Civilta Cattolica* wrote of the anti-Semitic policies in Germany, that they should be practiced "without hatred ... in a spirit of Christian charity".[72] Clearly, the two aims were incompatible. The desire to persecute could not help but weaken the desire to protect, or to treat lovingly. One finds in Christian history a very casual[73] attitude towards violence directed towards Jews. As friendly relations between Jews and Christians were protested, so anti-Jewish violence could even be regarded favourably, as a sign that the population generally had the right idea.

It should be noted that for other Christians, Jewish

---

[71] Ibid., 44.

[72] W. Perl, *The Holocaust Conspiracy: An International Policy of Genocide* (New York: Shapolsky Publishers, 1989), 206.

[73] Hay, *op. cit.*, 36.

survival would also be attributed to the divine will, but here it would be viewed as proof of God's continuing faithfulness and love, and of evidence of the blessed hope, when all Israel would be saved. As such, it would be viewed as an encouragement to acts of Christian mercy and love.

During the war, Pastor Walter Hochstadter printed the following declaration in secret and sent it to over 1,000 soldiers at the front:

> Today the blood of millions of slaughtered Jews, of men, women and children, cries to heaven. The Church is not permitted to be silent.... Nor is the church permitted to say that the just punishment for the sins of the Jews has come to pass in the present time ... The Christian cannot have an indifferent attitude on this question. There is no moderate Christian anti-Semitism ... This, the Church, the community of Jesus Christ, must acknowledge. If she does not do it, then she will have failed ... The Church ought to live of love ... Woe to it if it does not do this! Woe to it if it becomes implicated in worldly outbursts of hate through keeping silent or through all sorts of dubious excuses! ... Love knows no compromise; love knows no bounds. It comes from the truth of faith.[74]

While the churches ignored this protest, it deserves careful attention. Indeed, there is no "moderate Christian anti-Semitism." The church is called to love, and any doctrine which finds solace in Jewish wickedness, and vindication in Jewish suffering, is condemned. Jesus said that a tree is judged by its fruit, and after 2,000 years, the churches are

---

[74] Goldhagen, *op. cit.*, 431-2; and Gerlach, *op. cit.*, 218.

clearly in a place to condemn a doctrine which has caused and rejoiced in so much suffering.

This chapter draws upon the author's extensive postgraduate research exploring the roles of the European churches in the Holocaust, which he seeks to publish in full. However, over a four-year period none of the many Christian publishers approached concerning the publication of this disturbing research would even view the manuscript.

Clearly the topic is of immense importance to the Church (though Christians will not relish reading it). For this reason King's Evangelical Divinity School's Centre for Jewish-Christian Studies is seeking to publish the research in its entirety, or else assist its publication elsewhere. If you would be willing to donate towards the book's publication, or are interested in exploring the possibility of becoming the book's patron, please contact the Administrator of the Centre. We would also be interesting in making contact with ministries and Christian networks willing to promote the book upon its publication.

CHAPTER 4

Jealous For Zion: Evangelicals, Zionism and the Restoration of Israel

Paul Richard Wilkinson

And the word of the Lord of hosts came, saying, "Thus says the Lord of hosts: I am jealous for Zion with great jealousy, and I am jealous for her with great wrath. Thus says the Lord: I have returned to Zion and will dwell in the midst of Jerusalem, and Jerusalem shall be called the faithful city, and the mountain of the Lord of hosts, the holy mountain". (Zech 8:1-3)

According to Edward Flannery, without Christian support for Zionism "it is highly unlikely that the present State of Israel would have come into being so rapidly as it did".[1] Lawrence Epstein concurs, suggesting that too few people appreciate "how much Christians have contributed to the

---

[1] Edward H. Flannery, "Christian Zionist Ethos should be Revived" in *Providence Journal-Bulletin* (26 April 1996).

Zionist movement and to the nation of Israel".[2] In 1985, Israel's ambassador to the United Nations, Benjamin Netanyahu, gave the following tribute at a prayer breakfast in Washington DC:

> I suggest that for those who know the history of Christian involvement in Zionism, there is nothing either surprising nor new about the steadfast support given to Israel by believing Christians all over the world. For what, after all, is Zionism but the fulfilment of ancient prophecies?...There was an ancient yearning in our common tradition for the return of the Jews to the Land of Israel. And this dream, smouldering through two millennia, first burst forth in the Christian Zionism of the 19th Century – a movement that paralleled and reinforced modern Jewish Zionism...Thus it was the impact of Christian Zionism on Western Statesmen that helped modern Jewish Zionism achieve the rebirth of Israel.[3]

In a letter to the *Jerusalem Post* dated 26 October 1975, G. Douglas Young, founder of the Jerusalem-based Israel-American Institute of Biblical Studies (1959) and the Bridges for Peace ministry of reconciliation (1976), wrote the following:

> Sir, – I have been accused of being a Zionist – a Christian Zionist – by some of my co-religionists in

---

[2] Lawrence J. Epstein, *Zion's Call: Christian Contributions to the Origins and Development of Israel* (London: Univ. Press of America, 1984), ix.
[3] Benjamin Netanyahu, "Christian Zionism and the Jewish Restoration", www.internationalwallofprayer.org/A-091-Christian-Zionism-and-the-Jewish-Restoration.html (last accessed 28 October 2008).

Israel and in the administered areas. I would like to take this means of thanking them for this compliment. In spite of being a Christian, my Jewish friends in Israel and elsewhere have labelled me a Christian Zionist and for this I want to thank them too...I feel sorry for my Christian friends, and apologise for some of them, who are silent and have not yet identified publicly with Zionism, perhaps because they do not understand it or because they fear other consequences.[4]

Though well attested and eulogised by Jewish and non-Jewish commentators alike, Christian support for the modern State of Israel continues to arouse strong, and sometimes furious, opposition from many quarters. Such hostility emanates not only from fanatics like Mahmoud Ahmadinejad, and the international community which has consistently failed to denounce his anti-Semitic tirades, but also, more disturbingly, from within the Church. A growing number of theologians, clergymen, and parachurch organisations have been outraged by the Christian Zionist claim that Israel's re-establishment on 14 May 1948 ought to be attributed to the fulfilment of Biblical prophecy, and therefore to the hand of God. Their response has been to rally behind and promote the Palestinian/Arab agenda, by campaigning for divestment from Israel and by supporting the boycott of Israeli goods and universities.[5] There can be no doubt: "Israel" has become a watershed issue for the Church.

---

[4] Quoted in Calvin B. Hanson, *A Gentile, With the Heart of a Jew* (Nyack, NY: Parson Publishing, 1979), 294-295.

[5] For a comprehensive survey of the "Christian Palestinianist" movement, see Paul Richard Wilkinson, *For Zion's Sake: Christian Zionism and the Role of John Nelson Darby* (Milton Keynes: Paternoster, 2007), 48-66.

In this chapter we will consider how Evangelical belief in the promised restoration of Israel prepared the ground theologically *and* politically for the establishment of the modern State of Israel. I will emphasise the role played by a number of prominent Evangelical leaders in Britain and the United States, and draw particular attention to the key motivating factor behind their Zionist endeavours: belief in the *imminent* return of the Lord Jesus Christ.

WILLIAM E. BLACKSTONE AND THE
BALFOUR DECLARATION

Following a meeting of British Prime Minister Lloyd George's cabinet on 31 October 1917, a letter was written on their behalf by then Foreign Secretary Arthur James Balfour. Dated 2 November 1917, the letter declared the "sympathy" of the British government with "Jewish Zionist aspirations". Viewing with favour "the establishment in Palestine of a national home for the Jewish people", the British government resolved to "use their best endeavours to facilitate the achievement of this object". The letter was addressed to Lord Rothschild, a leader of the Jewish community in Britain, for the attention of the Zionist Federation. Despite the British government's subsequent, and well-documented, betrayal of the Jewish people, which was sealed on 17 March 1939 following the publication of its "reprehensible"[6] and "unconscionable"[7] White Paper (which severely restricted Jewish immigration into "Palestine"), the *Balfour Declaration* paved the way for Israel's re-establishment in 1948. However,

---

[6] Douglas J. Culver, *Albion and Ariel: British Puritanism and the Birth of Political Zionism* (New York: Peter Lang, 1995), 24.
[7] Dave Hunt, *Judgment Day! Islam, Israel and the Nations*, 2nd edn (Bend, OR: The Berean Call, 2006), 94.

without the official approval of U.S. President Woodrow Wilson, "powerful forces in London"[8] which were opposed to the *Declaration* might have prevailed.

The Blackstone Memorial

On 30 June 1917, Thomas Woodrow Wilson (1856-1924), a "son of the (Presbyterian) manse" from Staunton, Virginia, was presented with a petition which had originally been drawn up in November 1890, during a conference on "The Past, Present and Future of Israel". This unprecedented gathering of Christian and Jewish leaders at the First Methodist Episcopal Church in Chicago had been organised by William Eugene Blackstone (1841-1935), founder of the Hebrew Chicago Mission and a successful businessman turned lay preacher who had converted to Christ at the age of ten. What became known as the *Blackstone Memorial* was signed by over four hundred of America's most notable politicians, industrialists, newspaper editors, journalists, and religious leaders, and was presented to President Benjamin Harrison on 5 March 1891. The petition called upon the American administration to persuade its European counterparts to convene an international conference on behalf of the Jews. Such a conference, Blackstone maintained, would seek to alleviate the suffering of European Jewry, especially in the wake of the Russian pogroms, and consider what he believed to be the rightful claim of the Jewish people to "Palestine" as "their home, an inalienable possession from which they were expelled by force"[9] during the Roman occupation.

---

[8] Rufus Learsi, *The Jews in America: A History* (New York: The World Publishing Company, 1954), 257.
[9] "Palestine for the Jews: Copy of Memorial presented to President

95

Although Blackstone's petition ultimately failed, it struck a chord some years later with one of America's leading Zionists, and close confidant of Woodrow Wilson, Supreme Court Justice Louis D. Brandeis (1856-1941). The *Memorial* was brought to the attention of Brandeis, and on 8 May 1916 a letter was sent on his behalf to Blackstone by New York businessman Nathan Straus. It included the following personal, and remarkable, tribute:

> Mr Brandeis is perfectly infatuated with the work that you have done along the lines of Zionism. It would have done your heart good to have heard him assert what a valuable contribution to the cause your document is. In fact he agrees with me that you are the Father of Zionism, as your work antedates Herzl. (Emphasis mine).

In July 1916, Blackstone was the guest of honour at a large Zionist meeting in Philadelphia, where Brandeis introduced him as "a most important ally which Zionism has in America outside the Jewish rank".[10]

Following a meeting in April 1917 with British Foreign Secretary Balfour, Brandeis decided that the best way to convince President Wilson of the need to support the British proposal for a Jewish homeland was to appeal to his "biblically based Christian faith".[11] Brandeis contacted William Blackstone and urged him to re-present his petition. The revised *Memorial* was finally presented on Blackstone's

---

Harrison, March 5th, 1891", in *Christian Protagonists for Jewish Restoration* (New York: Arno Press, 1977), 1-2.
[10] Quoted in Paul C. Merkley, *The Politics of Christian Zionism 1891-1948* (London: Frank Cass, 1998), 89, 61.
[11] Merkley, *The Politics of Christian Zionism*, 89.

behalf to the President on 30 June 1917. Although Woodrow Wilson withheld his public endorsement of the petition on the grounds of political expediency, he nevertheless authorised Brandeis to convey to Balfour and the British cabinet his "entire sympathy"[12] with their proposal.

It is not without cause, then, that William Blackstone has been described as "one of a handful of the most influential American actors in the story leading to the achievement of the state of Israel".[13] As E. Schuyler English declared in a 1943 edition of *Our Hope* magazine, "The best friend that the Jew has is the Christian, who knows God's Word, His love for His Chosen People, and their place in the prophetic plan."[14] Blackstone was such a Christian. He is described in the *Encyclopaedia Judaica* as the "most famous of the Zionist millenarians in the United States",[15] and in 1956 the Israeli government paid their own tribute by naming a forest in his honour.

Despite such acclaim Blackstone's Zionist legacy must be set in its proper context. The zeal he had for Zion stemmed from his zeal for the God of Zion, whose Son, he believed, was soon to return.

Jesus is Coming

In 1878, Blackstone published a 96-page pamphlet entitled, *Jesus is Coming*, which was later expanded, revised, and translated into over forty languages. In what became "the

[12] David Brog, *Standing with Israel: Why Christians Support the Jewish State* (Lake Mary, FL: FrontLine, 2006), 116-118.
[13] Merkley, *The Politics of Christian Zionism*, 60.
[14] Quoted in Arno C. Gaebelein, *The Conflict of the Ages*, Revised edn (Neptune, NJ: Loizeaux Brothers, 1983), xv.
[15] *Encyclopaedia Judaica* (Jerusalem: Keter Publishing House Ltd, c.1971), 16, 1154.

most widely read premillennialist book of its time",[16] Blackstone demonstrated from the Scriptures how the physical and spiritual restoration of Israel was not only "an incontrovertible fact" of Biblical prophecy, but also one that was "intimately connected with our Lord's appearing". To detractors in the Church he made the following appeal:

> But, perhaps, you say: 'I don't believe the Israelites are to be restored to Canaan, and Jerusalem rebuilt.' Dear reader! have you read the declarations of God's word about it? Surely nothing is more plainly stated in the Scriptures...We beg of you to read them thoroughly. Divest yourself of prejudice and preconceived notions, and let the Holy Spirit show you, from His word, the glorious future of God's chosen people, "who are beloved" (Rom.11:28), and dear unto Him as "the apple of His eye." (Zech.2:8)[17]

In front of a large Zionist gathering in Los Angeles on 27 January 1918, Blackstone explained that his solidarity with the Zionist movement was based on his firm belief that "true Zionism is founded on the plan, purpose, and fiat of the everlasting and omnipotent God, as prophetically recorded in His Holy Word, the Bible."[18] Some years earlier he had despaired at Theodor Herzl's indifference towards "Palestine", when Herzl was seeking to secure a viable

---

[16] Timothy P. Weber, *Living in the Shadow of the Second Coming: American Premillennialism, 1875-1982* (Chicago, IL: University of Chicago Press, 1987), 137.
[17] William E. Blackstone, *Jesus is Coming* (Chicago, IL: Fleming H. Revell Company, 1932), 176, 162.
[18] David A. Rausch, *Zionism within early American Fundamentalism 1878-1918* (New York: The Edwin Mellen Press, 1979), 268.

homeland for the Jewish people. Blackstone duly sent Herzl a Bible, with all the prophecies pertaining to the Land of Israel clearly marked for his attention. By 1932, Blackstone was in no doubt: "God's hand is in this [Zionist] movement".

Despite his Biblical convictions and his solidarity with the Jewish people, Blackstone's focus was not on Israel, however dear to God and central to His purposes he understood that nation to be. It is precisely because his focus lay not on Zion, but on the God of Zion, that he was able to articulate a clear and appropriate *Christian* response to the question of Israel's national future, and play such a crucial role in the securing of a national home for the Jewish people. Blackstone's attention was firmly fixed on the Second Coming of Jesus Christ, who, he believed, would first appear to catch away His Church (1 Thess 4:15-18), before returning, at least seven years later, to take up His earthly throne as King in Zion (*cf.* Ps 2:6-7; Is 9:6-7; Zech 9:9). Time was short, he believed, both for unbelievers who had thus far rejected Christ, *and* for those in the Church who had lost sight of His return. As he wrote in the opening pages of his book:

> Reader, do you know that Jesus is coming again? He said, 'I will come again' (John 14:3) and His word endureth forever, for He is the truth...Perhaps you are not a Christian, and say – 'I don't care anything about it.' Then, dear friend, we point you to the crucified Saviour as the only hope of salvation...He is coming, and we know neither the day, nor the hour, when He may come. What if He should come now? Would you be found of Him in peace, or would you be left behind to endure the terrible things which shall come upon the world, while the church is with Christ in the air?

In the same way that faithful Jews like Simeon and Anna had been watching and waiting immediately prior to Christ's *first* advent (Luke 2:25-39), so in Blackstone's day "many of the most devout and faithful of God's people...in this and foreign lands" had become "seriously impressed with the conviction, that the coming of the Lord is near".[19] As we shall see in due course, the man Blackstone was perhaps indebted to more than any other for his premillennial understanding of Israel's restoration and his pretribulational understanding of Christ's return, was an "Irish clergyman"[20] by the name of John Nelson Darby.

THE CHURCH'S DUTY TO ISRAEL

During the nineteenth century a number of Evangelicals in Britain were instrumental in recovering the Church's historic, *premillennial* faith, after centuries of amillennial and postmillennial heterodoxy. The theological seed had been sown by a number of English Puritans during the seventeenth century, including Sir Henry Finch (c 1558-1625), whose book, *The Worlds Great Restauration, or The Calling of the Jewes, and with them of all the Nations and Kingdomes of the Earth, to the Faith of Christ* (1621), sent shockwaves throughout the political and ecclesiastical world because of its emphasis on Israel's *national* restoration. The seed was subsequently watered during the Evangelical Revival of the eighteenth century, when John and Charles Wesley led the way in reviving interest in Biblical prophecy, and with it, concern for the present and future prospect of the Jewish people.

---

[19] Blackstone, *Jesus is Coming*, 242, 11-13, 213.
[20] Francis W. Newman, *Phases of Faith* (London: Trübner & Co., 1881), 17.

However, it was not until a period of unprecedented political and economic upheaval in Europe inspired premillennialist scholars such as James Bicheno, James Hatley Frere, and George Stanley Faber to turn the attention of the Church back to Biblical prophecy, that Israel's place on the theological and eschatological map came into sharper focus.[21]

On 17 November 1839, following his return from a Church of Scotland mission of inquiry to "Palestine", the young Presbyterian minister, Robert Murray McCheyne (1813-1843), preached a sermon entitled, "Our Duty to Israel". Based on his key text, Rom. 1:16, McCheyne stressed how critically important it was for the Church not only to preach the Gospel "first to the Jew", but also to experience God's compassion for His ancient covenant people. He gave the following impassioned plea to the Church, which resonated throughout much of the Evangelical world during the nineteenth century:

The cloud of indignation and wrath that is even now gathering above the lost will break first upon the head of guilty, unhappy, unbelieving Israel. And have you none of the bowels of Christ in you, that you will not run first to them that are in so sad a case?...It is like God to care first for the Jews. It is the chief glory and joy of a soul to be like God...But the whole Bible shows that God has a peculiar affection for Israel...Strange, sovereign, most peculiar love! He loved them because He loved them...Now the simple question for each of you is, and for our beloved Church, Should we not share with God in His peculiar affection for Israel? If we are filled with the Spirit of God, should we not love

---

[21] See Wilkinson, *For Zion's Sake*, 135-201.

as He loves? Should we not grave Israel upon the palms of our hands, and resolve that through our mercy they also may obtain mercy?[22]

The hub of this burgeoning, philo-Semitic, Restorationist movement was the London Society for the Promotion of Christianity amongst the Jews (LSPCJ). Founded in 1809, the London Jews Society, as it was more commonly known, drew into its fold such notable Evangelicals as William Wilberforce, Lewis Way, Alexander McCaul, Charles Simeon, Hugh McNeile, J.C. Ryle, and Alfred Edersheim. Another long-time advocate, and future president of the LSPCJ, was the eminent Christian philanthropist and seventh Earl of Shaftesbury, Anthony Ashley Cooper (1801-1885).

CONSCIOUS OF HIS COMING

Shaftesbury was convinced that Britain had been sovereignly appointed by God to help the Jewish exiles return to their promised land. He successfully persuaded his stepfather-in-law, Lord Palmerston, to establish a British consulate in Jerusalem, and was instrumental in the establishment of the first Protestant Bishopric in that city. The appointment of the converted Rabbi, Michael Solomon Alexander, as first Anglican Bishop of Jerusalem, owed much to Shaftesbury's influence.[23] According to an article which appeared in *The Times* newspaper in 1839, Lord Shaftesbury "turned public attention to the claims which the Jewish people still have

---

[22] Andrew A. Bonar, *Memoir and Remains of Robert Murray McCheyne* (Edinburgh: The Banner of Truth Trust, 1978), 490-493.
[23] See Wilkinson, *For Zion's Sake*, 211-216.

upon the land of Israel as their rightful inheritance".[24] As one biographer records,

> 'Oh, pray for the peace of Jerusalem!' were the words engraven on the ring he always wore on his right hand – the words, too, that were engraven on his heart. His study of the prophetic Scriptures led him to associate the return of the Jews with the Second Advent of our Lord, and this was the hope that animated every other.[25]

As Hodder's quote suggests, Shaftesbury's zeal for Zion cannot be understood in isolation, for it was the hope of Christ's return that motivated his Zionist endeavours. As he himself confessed towards the end of his life,

> I think I can say that, for the last forty years, I have not lived one conscious hour that was not influenced by 'the Hope' of the Coming again of the Lord Jesus Christ.[26]

Shaftesbury was not alone. Another respected churchman who understood the centrality to the Christian faith of Christ's return and Israel's restoration was the first Anglican Bishop of Liverpool, J.C. Ryle (1816-1900). In his sermon, "Scattered Israel to be Gathered", Ryle declared that the denial of these two truths was "as astonishing and incomprehensible to my own mind as the denial of the

---

[24] *The Times*, 24 January (1839), 3.
[25] Edwin Hodder, *The Life and Work of the Seventh Earl of Shaftesbury, K.G., Vol. II* (London: Cassell & Company Ltd., 1886), 477.
[26] Quoted in Maud E. Powell, *"Maranatha" (Our Lord is Coming)*, 2nd edn (London: Samuel E. Roberts, 1913), 13.

divinity of Christ". There was, however, an order of priority for the Church, as Ryle explained:

> The one point on which I desire to fix the eyes of my own soul, is the second personal coming of my Lord and Saviour Jesus Christ. To that "blessed and glorious appearing", I wish, by God's help, to direct all who read this volume.

In his sermon, "What time is it?" he gave the following exhortation:

> Live as if you thought Christ might come at any time. Do everything as if you did it for the last time. Say everything as if you said it for the last time. Read every chapter in the Bible as if you did not know whether you would be allowed to read it again. Pray every prayer as if you felt it might be your last opportunity...This is the way to be found ready. This is the way to turn Christ's second appearing to good account.[27]

ALBURY, POWERSCOURT, AND THE RAPTURE

During the second quarter of the nineteenth century a number of Evangelicals came together to discuss Biblical prophecy, at a time when "the majority of what was called the Religious World disbelieved that the Jews were to be restored to their own land, and that the Lord Jesus Christ was to return and reign in person on this earth".[28] One of the most

---

[27] J.C. Ryle, *Are You Ready for the End of Time?* (Fearn: Christian Focus Publications, 2001), 112, 11, 80.
[28] Henry Drummond, *Narrative of the Circumstances which led to the setting up of the Church of Christ at Albury* (1834), 7.

important venues for such gatherings was Albury Park in Surrey, the home of the wealthy landowner and Member of Parliament, Henry Drummond. The first of five annual conferences at Albury Park was inaugurated in November 1826. Those invited included Hugh McNeile, Charles Hawtrey, Edward Irving, William Cuninghame, James Haldane Stewart, Spencer Perceval (Jr.), Alexander Haldane, and William "Millennial" Marsh.

No sooner had the Albury meetings concluded than another series of prophecy conferences commenced, this time at the home of Lady Theodosia Powerscourt near Dublin. Lady Powerscourt had herself attended the inaugural Albury conference in 1826. On 4 October 1831, a number of invited clergymen and lay people, who were "distressed at the condition of the Church ... and ... convinced that the hope of Christ's return should figure more prominently in the thinking of Christians",[29] assembled at Powerscourt House. The question of Israel again occupied much of their discussion. Among those who met at Powerscourt were some of the pioneers of the emerging Plymouth Brethren movement, including Benjamin Wills Newton, George Müller, and John Nelson Darby.

The Eye of the Believer

John Nelson Darby (1800-1882) was the London-born son of an English merchant, the godson of Admiral Horatio Lord Nelson, a Classics graduate of Trinity College, Dublin, a trained barrister, a one-time curate and priest in the Church of Ireland, and the principal architect of Plymouth Brethrenism. His legacy, though largely misunderstood and

---

[29] Harold H. Rowdon, *The Origins of the Brethren 1825-1850* (London: Pickering & Inglis, 1967), 2.

misrepresented by historians and churchmen to this day, is considerable, and is based on his unwavering devotion to Christ, his adherence to the authority of God's Word, his literal interpretation of the Scriptures, his *futurist* approach to prophecy, and his understanding of the distinction between Israel and the Church, all of which today underpin Dispensationalism and Christian Zionism.[30]

In stark contrast to the *historicist* school of Biblical interpretation, which associates of Albury Park and the LSPCJ subscribed to, Darby maintained that apocalyptic events recorded in the book of Revelation related to a *future* period of time, and were not to be viewed retrospectively. Accordingly, the prophetic "days", "weeks", "months", and "years" of Daniel and Revelation were to be interpreted in their plain, literal, natural, and common sense, and not symbolically, as *historicists* had done since the time of the Protestant Reformation. Darby's futurist approach enabled him to successfully challenge and overturn the historicist school, which, for all its achievements in awakening the Church to the importance of Israel and the centrality of Christ's return, had failed to properly distinguish between the *earthly* inheritance of Israel (to be realised *after* the Great Tribulation) and the *heavenly* inheritance of the Church (to be realised *before* the Great Tribulation). The historicist school inevitably fell into disrepute because of its propensity to date-set not only the return of the Jews to the Land, but also, more disturbingly, the return of Jesus to Jerusalem.

---

[30] This is the principal thesis of my book, *For Zion's Sake: Christian Zionism and the Role of John Nelson Darby* (Milton Keynes: Paternoster, 2007).

In 1840, Darby observed with great anticipation how "all the thoughts of the politicians of this world"[31] were beginning to focus on a land which, according to indisputable first-hand accounts, lay "buried deep under the accumulated ruins of centuries".[32] Although the Jewish people had been forcibly expelled from their land during the Roman occupation, they had remained "ever and unchangeably loved as a people" by virtue of the *everlasting* covenant God had cut with Abraham and his descendants (Gen 17:7-8; Ps 105:8-11). As Darby declared in his exposition of Romans 11:25-32,

> God's covenant to take away Israel's sins is sure. It shall be accomplished when Christ comes; for, note, the apostle speaks of Christ in Zion in a time yet to come; for God's gifts and calling suffer no change or setting aside, and Israel is His, by gift and calling, as a people...The final restoration of Israel will be on the ground of the promises made to the fathers, 'for his mercy endureth for ever.'[33]

Although Darby's understanding of Israel was rooted in Scripture, it was his devotion to Christ and his focus on the coming of Christ *for the Church*, which enabled him to set Israel in her proper theological, and eschatological, context.

---

[31] John Nelson Darby, "The Hopes of the Church of God, in Connection with the Destiny of the Jews and the Nations as Revealed in Prophecy (1840)" in *The Collected Writings of J.N. Darby*, ed. by William Kelly (Kingston-on-Thames: Stow Hill Bible & Tract Depot, n.d.), 2:342.
[32] Alfred Edersheim, *Sketches of Jewish Social Life in the Days of Christ* (Grand Rapids, MI: Wm. B. Eerdmans Publishing Company, 1982), 7.
[33] Darby, "Exposition of the Epistle to the Romans" (1871), in Kelly (ed.), *Collected Writings*, 26:186.

As he declared in 1828, "Let the almighty doctrine of the cross be testified to all men, and let the eye of the believer be directed to the coming of the Lord."[34] Although men like Shaftesbury, Ryle, and the Albury Park circle all emphasised the centrality of the Second Coming, they were less clear and emphatic on the Rapture of the Church and, in particular, on its timing. This may be explained, in part, by the prevailing historicist tradition, which had misled students of Biblical prophecy for generations.

In his *Reflections upon the Prophetic Inquiry* (1829), Darby observed how, in every New Testament letter, "the coming of the Lord Jesus is...made the prominent object of the faith and hope of believers".[35] He drew particular inspiration from the Thessalonians, who had turned to God from idols "to wait for His Son from heaven" (1 Thess 1:10). The problem in the Church of his day was not so much "the denial of the Lord's coming", but "the loss of the sense and present expectation of it."[36] The teaching that Jesus could not come for His Bride until certain prophetic events had taken place had forced the Church into prophecies relating to the time of *Jacob's* trouble (Jer 30:7; Dan 12:1; Matt 24:21). As a consequence, the Rapture of the Church had been set back by at least seven years. Darby's response was unequivocal:

The Lord considers it important that the saints should be always expecting [His return] as a present thing, and wishing for it as a present thing...And, indeed, were I to

---

[34] Darby, "Considerations on the Nature and Unity of the Church of Christ" (1828), in Kelly (ed.), *Collected Writings*, 1:30.

[35] Darby, "Reflections upon the Prophetic Inquiry and the Views advanced in it (1829)", in Kelly (ed.), *Collected Writings*, 2:25.

[36] Darby, "The Rapture of the Saints and the Character of the Jewish Remnant", in Kelly (ed.), *Collected Writings*, 11:156.

adopt the system proposed to me, I should not expect the Lord at all until a time when I was able to fix the day of His appearing...I say fix the day, for I cannot expect His coming until the abomination of desolation is set up at Jerusalem, and then I can say, Now in twelve hundred and sixty days the Lord will be here. And this fixing by signs and dates, I am told, is the sober way of waiting. But it is quite clear that it is contrary to the way the Lord Himself has taught me to expect Him. It is clear that, if these signs are to be expected for the church, I have nothing to expect till they are fulfilled. I may expect them, and have my mind fixed on them, but not on Christ's coming. And, when one particular one happens, I can name to a day His coming. This is not what Christ has taught me, and therefore I do not receive it.[37]

The impact of Darby's re-statement and clarification of the doctrine of the Second Coming, with the inclusion of the "precious truth"[38] of the Rapture as the first *stage* of Christ's return, was felt not only in Britain but also across North America, where a new generation of believers took up Darby's mantle.

A PROPHETIC WITNESS IN BRITAIN

Upon receiving news of the Balfour Declaration in November 1917, one of the country's most respected preachers, F.B. Meyer (1847-1929), invited a number of his fellow Christian

---

[37] Darby, "A Few Brief Remarks on 'A Letter on Revelation 12'", in Kelly (ed.), *Collected Writings*, 11:25-27.
[38] H.A. Ironside, *A Historical Sketch of the Brethren Movement* (Neptune, NJ: Loizeaux Brothers, 1985), 23.

leaders to a prayer breakfast in London. The purpose was to consider how the wider Church could be alerted to the significance of this historic development. A seven-point manifesto was subsequently drawn up and published just six days after Balfour's letter was issued. Entitled, "The Significance of the Hour", points 1-4 of the manifesto read as follows:

1. That the signs of the times point towards the close of the Times of the Gentiles.
2. That the return of our Lord may be expected at any moment when He will be manifested as evidently as to His disciples on the evening of His resurrection.
3. That the completed church will be translated to meet the Lord in the air, and to be forever with the Lord.
4. That Israel will be restored to their own land in unbelief, and afterwards converted by the manifestation of Christ as their Messiah.

Darby's legacy can clearly be seen, even if it was not explicitly acknowledged. The manifesto was released to the national press, and public meetings were planned by F.B. Meyer and his associates, to be held on 13 December 1917 at the Queen's Hall in London.[39] In his address that day, F.S. Webster spoke of the joy felt by all speakers over news of Allenby's liberation of Jerusalem, which had been secured just four days earlier. However, Webster's joy for Israel was tempered with sadness over the spiritual state of the Church. As he explained,

---

[39] Colin Le Noury, *In the Steps of F.B. Meyer: 90 Years of Prophetic Witness* (Belfast: Ambassador Productions, 2008), 19-20.

The chief fault of Christians today is that they do not make enough of the Lord Jesus Christ...It is good and right to preach Christ incarnate, Christ crucified, Christ risen, Christ ascended, but if we would be true to the Scripture we must add one more note – Christ returning, Christ coming again...Now the danger of the present day...is this, that just because the Lord delayeth His coming...people have let slip the blessed hope of His coming again...If we really belong to Him, if we really believe in Him, we shall love His appearing, we shall long for His coming again.[40]

The Advent Testimony Movement was launched shortly after. Later renamed the Advent Testimony and Preparation Movement, it continues to proclaim the any-moment coming of Christ under the name Prophetic Witness Movement International. Among those who emerged as its early leaders and speakers were General Sir William Dobbie, Bishop Handley Moule, Revd W. Graham Scroggie, and Dr Frederick Tatford, all of whom "kept continual watch on happenings in the Middle East, in the firm belief that the nation of Israel would one day be re-established"[41] and that Christ would soon appear.

AN AMERICAN AWAKENING

In the years preceding the American Civil War (1861-1865), a number of books were published which helped trigger a premillennial revival in the largely postmillennial American

---

[40] *Advent Testimony Addresses delivered at the Meetings at Queen's Hall, London, W.C., December 13th, 1917* (London: Chas. J. Thynne, 1918), 84-88.
[41] Le Noury, *In the Steps of F.B. Meyer*, 85.

Church. Such books included Edward Winthrop's *Lectures on the Second Advent* (1843), Jacob Janeway's *Hope for the Jews* (1853), John Cumming's *Signs of the Times* (1854), and Joseph Seiss's *The Last Times* (1856). However, it was the visit of John Nelson Darby to the United States in 1862 which proved to be of greater significance.

Between 1862 and 1877, Darby crossed the continent of North America seven times, travelling "on the skirts of the [American Civil] war" in 1863. He recalled in a letter from Toronto that year that he had travelled "about 2,000 miles in the last four weeks".[42] Wherever he went his mission remained the same, namely "to present Christ and the truth, accomplished salvation, and His coming".[43] Chicago pastor and evangelist, Dwight L. Moody (1837-1899), was among the many Church leaders who were inspired by Darby's devotion to Scripture, and his "uncompromising belief in the imminent, bodily, and premillennial return of the Lord Jesus Christ".[44] Another was James Hall Brookes (1830-1897), who heard Darby speak in St. Louis "with great pleasure and profit".[45] Brookes was the driving force behind the Bible and Prophecy Conference Movement, which propagated and popularised the dispensationalist message.[46] According to C. Norman Kraus, "there can be little room for doubt that Darby and other early Plymouth Brethren preachers gave direct

---

[42] Darby, "Letter to Mr Pollock (Toronto, 27 May 1863)" in J.N. Darby, *Letters of J.N.D.* (Kingston-on-Thames: Stow Hill Bible & Tract Depot, n.d.), 1:351-352.
[43] Darby, "Letter to G. Biava (New York, 1873)" in Darby, *Letters of J.N.D.*, 2:212.
[44] Lyle W. Dorsett, *A Passion for Souls: The Life of D.L. Moody* (Chicago, IL: Moody Publishers, 1997), 136.
[45] Quoted in R.A. Huebner, *Elements of Dispensational Truth: Vol. I*, 2nd edn (Morganville, NJ: Present Truth Publishers, 1998), 20.
[46] See Wilkinson, *For Zion's Sake*, 247-251.

stimulus and at least indirect guidance to the movement."[47] In his final letter from America, written in June 1877, Darby made the following observation: "The truth is spreading...For some time the coming of the Lord has wrought in souls far and wide, and the doctrine is spreading wonderfully."[48]

CONCLUSION

Shortly after Darby's death on 29 April 1882, the following tribute appeared in *The Christian Commonwealth*:

There has recently passed away one of the most remarkable servants of Christ that this country has produced. We refer to Mr. John Nelson Darby...It would have been too much to expect that any lengthened notice of this remarkable man should have a place in the daily papers, or that he should find a sepulchre amongst the great men of our national history. Nevertheless, it is true to say that the movement of which he was, at once, one of the principal leaders, was most distinguished for vitality, force, and widespread influence.

At Darby's funeral, a member of the Brethren read John 14:1-3 and 1 Thess 4:15-18, and spoke of the "precious" and "distinctive truths" concerning the "coming of the Lord to take His Church", which had become "familiar to thousands, and perhaps tens of thousands in the Church of God". He proceeded to speak of "the great goodness of our God and

---

[47] C. Norman Kraus, *Dispensationalism in America* (Richmond, VA: John Knox Press, 1958), 79.
[48] Darby, "Letter to Mr. Brockhaus (7 June 1877)" in Darby, *Letters of J.N.D.*, 2:395.

Father in using our beloved departed brother as His vessel to restore these and other blessed truths to the Church", and prayed that "the coming of the Lord, as the *immediate* hope of believers...might more than ever be a living and operative truth in our souls."[49]

One man who was deeply indebted to John Nelson Darby was William Blackstone, whose petition influenced Woodrow Wilson at such a crucial moment in history. In his book, *Jesus is Coming*, Blackstone included several stanzas from a hymn penned by Hannah K. Burlingham, who was a member of the Plymouth Brethren. Entitled, "I'm Waiting For Thee, Lord", the hymn was included by the Brethren in their *Hymns and Spiritual Songs for the Little Flock*, and inspired Darby to write his own version, "The Soul's Desire" (1881), shortly before his death. Blackstone included Burlingham's hymn to highlight not only the doctrine of Christ's *any-moment* return, but also the longing for His return which Christ looks for in the heart of every believer. The opening verse of the hymn reads as follows:

I'm waiting for Thee, Lord,
Thy beauty to see, Lord,
I'm waiting for Thee,
For Thy coming again.
Thou'rt gone over there, Lord,
A place to prepare, Lord,
Thy home I shall share
At Thy coming again.[50]

[49] *The Last Days of J.N.D. (John Nelson Darby) From March 3rd to April 29th, 1882, With Portrait*, 2nd edn (Christchurch: N.C.M. Turner, 1925), 26, 22-23.
[50] Blackstone, *Jesus is Coming*, p. 215; cf. J.N. Darby, *Spiritual Songs* (Lancing: Kingston Bible Trust, 1974), 71.

To men like Darby and Blackstone, the Second Coming was far more than a doctrine to be preached and expounded; it was a blessed hope that needed to burn brightly in the heart of every believer, as it had once done in the heart of the Apostle Paul and the early Church (2 Tim 4:8). The return of the Jewish people to their homeland, after nearly two millennia in exile, not only vindicated nineteenth-century Evangelicals who faithfully proclaimed that God had "by no means" rejected or replaced His people Israel (Rom 11:1), but convinced many that Christ's return was near. Following the liberation of Jerusalem on 9 December 1917, Sir Robert Anderson (1841-1918), the Assistant Commissioner at Scotland Yard for thirteen years, a member of the Plymouth Brethren, a friend of John Nelson Darby, and an associate of the Advent Testimony Movement, expressed his personal conviction that Allenby's triumph

> gives hope that we are nearing the age in which they [the Jews] will be restored to favour, and therefore that the Lord's coming for us [the Church], which must precede that restoration, may be close at hand.[51]

Anderson's conviction is conspicuous by its absence in what we may loosely term "the pro-Israel Church" today, where the priority for many believers lies in expressing solidarity with the Jewish people and the Jewish State, rather than in exclaiming the midnight cry, "Behold, the Bridegroom!" (Matt 25:6). The Church in this country appears to have forsaken not only the prophetic witness of many of its Evangelical forebears, but her first love (Rev 2:4). In *Jesus is*

---

[51] Sir Robert Anderson, *Unfulfilled Prophecy; and The Hope of the Church*, 2nd edn (London: James Nisbet & Co. Ltd., 1918), vii.

Coming, William Blackstone included the following letter, which had been sent to him by a "dear brother" in Christ. May it serve to stir the hearts of many in the Church today, so that all true believers might look, with eager longing and expectation, for the coming of the Heavenly Bridegroom:

> I find so many who are willing to receive the truth of the Second Coming, but it is generally those who are passing through affliction, or those living very near the Lord. Those who are enjoying the well watered plains of this world, seem to care very little about seeing the Owner of the Estate. But He will come. Hallelujah! He will come. Yes! He is coming. The bride who knows the Bridegroom, and is true, says, He is coming. 'Come Lord Jesus,' Come! Come!! Come!!! Come!!!! A poor cursed earth (Rom. 8:19-22) groans out Come! Thank heaven, He speaks: 'SURELY I COME QUICKLY.' Rev. 22:20.[52]

---

[52] Blackstone, *Jesus is Coming*, 215.

Part 2

SUPERSESSIONISM AND THE BIBLE

CHAPTER 5

Who is the "Israel" of Romans 11:26?

Andy Cheung

For Evangelicals, sound theology and solid exegesis rest ultimately on a capacity to understand the underlying text. So while other Christian groups may prefer to base doctrines on historical patterns or particular authorities, Evangelicals insist upon correctly handling the written word. Accordingly, in approaching the question of the place of Israel in Christian theology, it is paramount that Evangelicals begin with some straightforward linguistics. The question at hand concerns the meaning of "Israel". This apparently simple question is not at all easy when one considers its usage in early Christian writings in general and the New Testament in particular. The term Israel in early Christian writings can include Gentiles, so we must be careful with it when we find it in Scripture. The goal in this chapter is to explore the meaning of "Israel" in Romans 11:26, a study that I suggest is of value to all Evangelicals, no matter what particular theological stance is held on the question of Israel.

Of particular concern in this paper is the usage of Israel in Romans 11:26, but before concentrating on this one verse, we would be wise to consider a few relevant, necessary questions first:

• What does Israel mean in 11:25-26?
• What does Israel mean in Romans 9-11, and in Romans generally?
• What does Israel mean in the New Testament?
• What does Israel mean in early Christian literature?

We will begin in reverse order, but first some preliminary words on why this question matters at all.

WHY IS A STUDY OF ROMANS 11:26 IMPORTANT?

The verse is uniquely important in discussions concerning God's purpose for ethnic, historic Israel. Romans 11:26 reads, "And in this way all Israel will be saved" (ESV). Here we have a promise that there will be a future salvation for a group of people called Israel. But to whom does Israel refer in this verse? It either refers to historic, ethnic Israel or to a "new Israel" representing the Church of Gentiles and Jews.

If we take this verse to refer to ethnic Israel, it means we have a unique New Testament promise that there will be some kind of future salvation for all Jews (I will explore what is meant by the term "all" later). On the other hand, if Israel here is a synonym for the Church of Gentiles and Jews, then we have no such promise. Indeed, nowhere else in the New Testament is there a verse that potentially says as much as 11:26. Either God uniquely promises here a future salvation for ethnic Israel or no such promise exists at all. For this reason, Romans 11:26 demands closer study.

Is this question under debate?

For centuries, Christians have disagreed on the meaning of Israel in this verse. Modern scholarship seems to be moving towards a consensus that Israel in this verse refers to ethnic Jews: there are few modern commentaries on Romans that would deny this. However, there are still a number of scholars who believe that the term Israel refers to the Church of Gentiles and Jews.

Why engage in a linguistic study?

Most discussion of the place of Israel is necessarily theological. Questions such as "does Israel still have a place in God's purposes?" "Does the land of Israel still belong to the Jews?" "How do we understand the differences between the Old and New Testament with respect to Israel?" are all theological questions. But we cannot answer these without looking at the words of Scripture. Theology, it must always be remembered, is a second-order task that follows exegetical and linguistic study.

WHAT DOES "ISRAEL" MEAN IN EARLY CHRISTIAN LITERATURE?

It is very clear that in early Christian literature, the term Israel was often used to refer to Christians generally, whether Jew or Gentile. We see this in Irenaeus, Clement of Alexandria, Theodore of Mopsuestia, Theodoret, Augustine, and Origen. The earliest definite application of the term Israel to Gentiles was by Justin Martyr (100–165) who wrote that the Church is "the true spiritual Israel" in Dialogue 11.5, dated to around AD 150.

It is therefore beyond dispute that in the early Church, the term Israel is a valid synonym for the Church of Gentiles and Jews. But does this evidence require us to understand Israel in such ways in the New Testament? After all, the New Testament was completed at least 50 years before Justin Martyr's Dialogue. The other church fathers used the term Israel in later periods still. We may need to differentiate between the use of the word Israel in the early Church and its use in the New Testament. Peter Richardson for example has argued in his book, *Israel in the Apostolic Church*, that a new meaning was applied to Israel after the New Testament was written. In other words, Scripture would appear to be extremely careful and ethnically restrictive in its use of the term Israel.

If Richardson is right, then the evidence of the early Church is not directly relevant to understanding the meaning of Israel in Romans 11:26. Even if Israel is used as a synonym for the Gentile and Jewish church in early Christian history, it does not follow that the same pattern of usage is necessarily the case in the earlier documents of the New Testament. It may be wise to differentiate between the use of the word Israel by early church fathers and its use in the New Testament.

WHAT DOES "ISRAEL" MEAN IN THE NEW TESTAMENT?

In this section, we consider the term Israel in the New Testament. The word appears 68 times with the related word Israelite appearing nine times. There does not appear to be any doubt that the latter means a physical Jewish descendant so we focus our discussion on the term Israel only. The term appears as follows:

12 times in Matthew
2 times in Mark
12 times in Luke
4 times in John
15 times in Acts
11 times in Romans
1 time in 1 Corinthians
2 times in 2 Corinthians
1 time in Galatians
1 time in Ephesians
1 time in Philippians
3 times in Hebrews
3 times in Revelation

Most of the above instances undoubtedly refer to ethnic Israel, for example Luke 9:25 which reads, "there were many widows in Israel in the days of Elijah" (ESV). Such usage as found here poses no theological or lexical difficulty since the term can only refer to the historical land of Israel. But the situation is not so simple in certain New Testament verses whereupon the term Israel is used in a manner that may suggest a wider meaning. Indeed, four verses have sometimes been used to suggest that Israel can refer to the Church (made up of Gentiles and Jews). One of these verses of course is Romans 11:26, our key discussion point, but it will be fruitful and necessary for an examination of the other three verses (Gal 6:16, 1 Cor 10:18 and Rom 9:6).

The use of the term Israel in Galatians 6:16
In this verse, scholars are divided over whether the apostle Paul uses the term Israel to refer to ethnic Israel or to the Church of Gentiles and Jews. Deciding which is the case is notoriously difficult because the Greek is ambiguous and

could be understood either way. Most commentators make use of Paul's running theological themes in Galatians to determine the most likely answer but this in itself tends to raise different interpretations. We begin with a brief discussion of the original Greek.

The ESV translation of this verse reads, "and as for all who walk by this rule, peace and mercy be upon them, and upon the Israel of God." The English Standard Version (ESV) is an essentially literal translation and to an extent retains the ambiguity of the Greek. The apostle's blessing upon "all who walk by this rule" is understood by all sides of the debate to be a reference to the Church. But when the apostle subsequently follows this with the ambiguous "and upon the Israel of God", is he now addressing ethnic Israel, a separate group to the Church, or is he identifying the Church as the Israel of God?

The difference between these two is considerable: is Paul blessing just one group, the Israel of God made up of all Jewish and Gentile believers? Or is he placing a blessing upon two groups, the Church on the one hand, and ethnic Israel on the other? The difference between these two meanings is made clear when we consider two translations that adopt differing stances. Following are the respective renderings of the New Living Translation (NLT) and the Holman Christian Standard Bible (HCSB):

> May God's peace and mercy be upon all who live by this principle; they are the new people of God. (NLT)

> May peace be on all those who follow this rule, and mercy also be on the Israel of God! (HCSB)

What is the difference between the two? In the NLT, Israel is understood as the "new people of God" and they, the Church, are seen as the recipients of the apostle's blessing of "peace and mercy". In contrast, the HCSB has the apostle asking for peace upon the Church on the one hand, but then also mercy upon Israel. Since the HCSB separates the two groups, it is most likely that it considers Israel to be an ethnic entity separate from the Church.

LINGUISTIC, EXEGETICAL AND THEOLOGICAL ANALYSIS

We now turn to a brief discussion of the major viewpoints offered by commentators in their attempts to resolve this issue. The debate hinges on the Greek word for "and" (*kai*) in the phrase "and also the Israel of God" (ESV). There are two possibilities for understanding this. The first approach is to take an appositional or explicative meaning in which Paul directs his words to one group only. The second approach has Paul extending his words to two separate groups and hence would give a meaning along the lines of, "and additionally the Israel of God". The first approach would produce a meaning such as, "who are indeed the Israel of God".

It is rather difficult to choose between the two, especially since the Greek is vague. Also, analysing the words is not helpful since "Israel of God" is found nowhere else in the New Testament or indeed any of the writings of Second Temple Judaism or later rabbinic writings. It is therefore unsurprising that most commentators seek to find a solution by looking at theological clues from the epistle itself. Alternatively, rhetorical analysis is often used. For example, one might be inclined to ask whether Paul would really have described his contemporary ethnic Jews as the Israel of God, especially since as a nation they largely rejected the Gospel. And as we shall see, there are some who believe that 1 Corinthians 10:18 ("Israel according to the flesh") reflects better Paul's preferred term for unbelieving Israel.[1] A counter argument to this can be found in Romans 11 where Paul asks the question "has God rejected his people?" (ESV) The apostle has no apparent problem with referring to unbelieving ethnic Israel as "his people" and that being so, it seems reasonable for him to refer to them also as the Israel of God.

One approach that is sometimes taken is the matter of Paul's general theme in Galatians: it is thought possible to discern which meaning of Israel would be a contextually better fit. For example, if Paul has been arguing throughout the epistle that the promise of Abraham is for both Jews and Gentiles in Christ, would it not be somewhat strange for him at the end of the letter to suddenly separate his blessings between separate groups? Yet this seemingly valid argument is problematic because were Paul to identify Gentile Christians as Israel, he would therefore be conceding a major point of discussion between him and his Judaising opponents.

Such attempts to interpret the apostle's mind by trying to infer his likely intentions are largely unhelpful. Attempts to predict his likely train of argument produce alternative viewpoints none of which can be satisfactorily proven. It might be more fruitful to avoid rhetorical analyses and return to linguistic and exegetical approaches and here we are aided by one ancient text that may underlie the enigmatic phrase

---

[1] The matter of the choice of words in 1 Corinthians 10:18 will be dealt with later.

"and upon the Israel of God". The text in question is the 19th of the Jewish benedictions, particularly the "blessing of peace" of the Babylonian Recension which reads: "bestow peace, happiness and blessing, grace and loving-kindness and mercy upon us and upon all Israel, your people". This ancient prayer is of uncertain age but is generally considered to have been in existence at the time of Paul. The wording, especially in Greek, is similar enough to Galatians 6:16 that it or something similar to it may have been in Paul's mind.

Interestingly, Frank Matera, a professor of New Testament at the Catholic University of America, believes that the majority of commentators support this second view (that is, that Paul speaks to two different groups).[2] It is doubtful whether that is true generally across Church history but it may well be the case that in recent years there has been a gradual move towards it by Greek scholars.

How does the second approach deal with the words, "and as for all who walk by this rule, peace and mercy be upon them, and upon the Israel of God"? The first group is clearly the Church (containing Jews and Gentiles) and they are addressed as "all who walk by this rule" while "the Israel of God" are understood as a second group altogether. But it is not enough to simply conclude that it refers to Israel for we ought to be more specific.

Seeking a more specific definition of "Israel"
If we grant that Israel refers to ethnic Jews, there remains further consideration: are they unbelieving Jews? Believing Jews? Or a mixture of both? The preference among scholars is

---

[2] Frank J. Matera, *Galatians, Sacra Pagina 9* (Collegeville, MA: Liturgical Press, 1992), 232.

to understand the verse as referring to Jewish Christians[3] but I prefer to understand the verse as referring to unbelieving Jews. The HCSB translation quoted above is a satisfactory rendering of the Greek and importantly, it makes exegetical and theological sense for Paul to pray for "peace" upon Christians yet "mercy" for unbelieving Jews. After all, it would be unnecessary to extend a separate blessing upon believing Jews when they are already accounted for in Paul's initial prayer for "all who follow this rule". The second, separate blessing should be seen as directed to another group, non-Christians, and specifically Jewish non-Christians. There is also good reason for Paul to pray for *mercy* upon his unbelieving fellow Jews. Consider his anguish over Jewish unbelievers in Romans 9:1-5, but especially these verses from Romans 11:30-32 where Paul also speaks of the *mercy* that is due to unbelieving Israel:

> For just as you were at one time disobedient to God but now have received mercy because of their disobedience, so they too have now been disobedient in order that by the mercy shown to you they also may now receive mercy. For God has consigned all to disobedience, that he may have mercy on all. (ESV)

The use of the term Israel in 1 Corinthians 10:18
This verse occasionally solicits comment because it could imply that there are two Israels: a fleshly Israel, and a spiritual Israel. This idea springs from Paul's words,

---

[3] See for instance Robert Keith Rapa, "Galatians" in Tremper Longman III and David E. Garland, eds. *The Expositor's Bible Commentary Revised Edition, volume 11 Romans-Galatians* (Grand Rapids, MI: Zondervan, 2008), 638-639.

"consider Israel according to the flesh" which could be taken to mean there is such a thing as an "Israel according to the Spirit".[4] But these words occur in the midst of discussion on idolatry and Paul's intention is to discuss the Israel of ancient times and although the assertion by Fee is possible, it is more likely that *kata sarka* (according to the flesh) refers to earthly descent, and is therefore not about spirituality. Paul is not describing an unbelieving Jewish group but rather an ethnic group of descendants. That is how the ESV understands it by rightly translating, "Consider the people of Israel". There does not seem to be any linguistic or exegetical reason for inferring the existence of an "Israel according to the Spirit". Furthermore, there is also no reason to suppose that "Israel according to the flesh" requires also an "Israel according to the Spirit", a term that is found nowhere in the New Testament.

The use of the term Israel in Romans 9:6

We turn now to a much quoted verse which seems to imply that the term Israel can be used to refer to Gentiles as well as Jews. The ESV translates thus: "But it is not as though the word of God has failed. For not all who are descended from Israel belong to Israel." There is no disagreement with the first usage of the term Israel in this passage: all are agreed that it concerns ethnic Israel. But what does the second Israel mean? There are two possibilities: either it means the Church or it means a spiritual remnant within Israel. If we paraphrase the statement with these two alternative ideas in mind we must choose between either:

---

[4] This is the view of Gordon Fee, *The First Epistle to the Corinthians* (Grand Rapids, MI: W.B. Eerdmans, 1987), 470f.

1) Not all who are descended from Israel *belong to the Church*.

2) Not all who are descended from Israel *belong to the spiritual remnant within Israel*.

The difference between these two is significant. The first option *widens* the meaning of Israel from ethnic Jews to the entire Church of Gentiles and Jews. The second option *narrows* the meaning of Israel from ethnic Jews to a spiritual remnant within Israel.[5] There are two exegetical reasons for preferring the second interpretation.

Firstly, the meaning of Israel in this verse must be tied to the use of the term Israelites in 9:4-5. These two verses are part of the opening statements that Paul begins to explain in 9:6. In other words, there is a direct, indissoluble connection between 9:6 and 9:4-5. Moreover, it is clear from the context that the Israelites of 9:4-5 refers to ethnic Jews. Indeed, the word Israelite appears nine times in the New Testament and is never used for Gentiles. Since the term Israelite is restricted in its usage to ethnic Jews, it is therefore more likely for Israel in 9:6 to be likewise restrictive.

Secondly, 9:7-13 focuses on God's winnowing process whereby through successive generations of Abraham, Isaac and Jacob, God narrows his chosen people to a spiritual remnant. This winnowing, a theme of the remnant, fits perfectly with the idea that Israel in 9:6 refers to a spiritual remnant of Israel within the larger ethnic group of Jews generally. Hence, 9:6 teaches that not every Jew is a part of God's selected remnant of believing Jews.

---

[5] Scholars are divided on this and among those who prefer the first option are N. T. Wright and Eugene Nida. Among those who prefer the second are Thomas Schreiner, Douglas Moo and Charles Cranfield.

WHAT DOES "ISRAEL" MEAN IN ROMANS 9-11, AND IN ROMANS GENERALLY?

A few brief remarks on the theme of Romans may be useful. The purpose behind Paul's writing of the great epistle is disputed which is unsurprising given that the apostle does not explain his purposes. A steady stream of theories have been proposed over the years[6] but in my view the best course of reasoning is one that follows approximately a path originally struck by F. C. Baur[7] in 1876 who proposed that Gentile/Jewish divisions at the church in Rome necessitated Paul's desire to set right a growing and dangerous disharmony in a congregation that was splitting along ethnic lines. There is insufficient space in this article to pursue this idea but I do think that the disunity between Gentile and Jewish believers is one of the main causes of Paul's writing of Romans and especially chapters 9-11.

The relevance of this to our present discussion is that if part of Paul's reason for writing Romans emanates from a need to resolve conflicts between Gentile and Jewish Christians, it follows that 11:26 is just one important part of an ongoing discussion and hence we should avoid isolating it from the rest of the epistle. In Romans, the word Israel appears 11 times and Israelite two times. The only occurrence that is debated is 11:26 but if the theme of Israel is so important throughout the letter, why would Paul adopt a different meaning in this one verse? It seems more likely that

---

[6] The best single volume collection of essays is K. P. Donfried, *The Romans Debate – Expanded Edition* (Peabody, MA: Hendrickson Publishers, 1991).
[7] F. C. Baur, *Paul the Apostle of Jesus Christ, His Life and Work, His Epistles and His Doctrine. A Contribution to a Critical History of Primitive Christianity* (London: Williams and Norgate, 1876).

in a letter dominated by Gentile and Jewish relations, and especially in the section of the epistle (chapters 9-11) that focuses particularly on these themes, the apostle would not modify his normal usage of the term Israel.

One other item is worthy of remark at this point. The word Jew appears 11 times in the epistle and I consider every instance to refer to an ethnic Israelite. But Romans 2:28-29 is sometimes interpreted to describe a "true Jew", a Christian who may be Gentile or Jewish. The pertinent verses are as follows:

> For no one is a Jew who is merely one outwardly, nor is circumcision outward and physical. But a Jew is one inwardly, and circumcision is a matter of the heart, by the Spirit, not by the letter. His praise is not from man but from God. (ESV)

All interpreters agree on the following: Paul argues that mere circumcision does not make someone a "true Jew." True spirituality is a matter of the heart and not a matter of outward law keeping. So far so good but the error often made is to assume that anybody, Gentile or Jew, who finds faith in Christ is therefore a Jew inwardly. But this is not what Paul means. Rather, he is restricting the traditional definition of Jew to an ethnic Israelite who has faith in Christ. So instead of *widening* the meaning of Jew to embrace all Gentile believers, the apostle is *narrowing* the meaning of Jew to only those Israelites who have found faith in Christ. The approach to this verse is similar to that taken in Romans 9:6 where I argued that the meaning of Israel was not being widened to include Gentiles, but narrowed to a spiritual remnant within Israel.

WHAT DOES "ISRAEL" MEAN IN 11:25-26?

Having laid the groundwork, we come now to our main subject, the meaning of Israel in Romans 11:26 which is best considered by looking also at the preceding verse 11:25. The link between the two verses is clear from the words "and in this way" at the beginning of verse 26 and which demonstrate the connection between the two verses.[8]

Lest you be wise in your own conceits, I want you to understand this mystery, brothers: a partial hardening has come upon Israel until the fullness of the Gentiles has come in. And in this way all Israel will be saved. (ESV)

How should we understand the term Israel in the expression "all Israel will be saved"? It is occasionally suggested that here the term Israel refers to the Church[9] and is therefore a promise that God will save all Christians. But as we shall see, it is far more likely that the term Israel excludes Gentiles.

The immediate context of these two verses is the theme of Israel's ingrafting. In Romans 11:17-24, Paul writes about the natural branches being grafted back into their own olive tree. Accordingly we ought to interpret verse 25 against the backdrop of this metaphor of wild and cultivated olive tree: a discourse that nobody doubts is concerned with ethnic Israel and Gentiles. Moreover, verse 25 also references ethnic Israel

---

[8] A few translations treat verse 26 as beginning a new sentence but this is most unlikely. The standard Greek editions, UBS[4] and NA[27] connect it with verse 25, a view shared by the majority of Greek exegetes.
[9] Most recently claimed by Christopher R. Bruno, "The Deliverer from Zion: The Source(s) and Function of Paul's Citation in Romans 11:26-27" in *Tyndale Bulletin*, 59.1, 2008, 119-134.

by discussing their partial hardening. Once again, there is no doubt among any commentator that verse 25 refers only to ethnic Israel. When we consider verse 26 against this, we can isolate three distinct clauses between the two verses:

[11:25] A partial hardening has come upon Israel
      until the fullness of the Gentiles has come in
  [26] and in this manner all Israel will be saved.

It would be linguistically naive to assume that Paul changes the meaning of Israel upon commencing verse 26. The strong words of John Murray do not seem to be an overstatement:

> It should be apparent from both the proximate and less proximate contexts in this portion of the epistle that it is exegetically impossible to give to 'Israel' in this verse any other denotation than that which belongs to the term throughout this chapter. There is the sustained contrast between Israel and the Gentiles ... What other denotation could be given to Israel in the preceding verse? It is of ethnic Israel Paul is speaking and Israel could not possibly include Gentiles. In that event the preceding verse would be reduced to absurdity and since verse 26 is a parallel or correlative statement the denotation of 'Israel' must be the same as in verse 25.[10]

To Whom Does "All Israel" Refer?
The previous section demonstrated that "all Israel" is best understood as representing ethnic Israel but we need to be

---

[10] John Murray, *The Epistle to the Romans, the English Text with Introduction, Exposition and Notes.* Volume 2 (Grand Rapids, MI: Eerdmans, 1965), 96.

more specific. For instance, by "all Israel" do we mean every individual Jew? Or do we mean the nation as a whole generally? There are three possibilities:

1. All Israel refers to every Jewish Christian.
2. All Israel refers to every individual Israelite.
3. All Israel refers to ethnic Israel as a whole.

The first option is possible but may be discarded because such a statement would be redundant. In effect it would leave Paul saying that all Jews who have been saved will be saved. Such a statement is unnecessary and thereby renders this option unlikely. The second option has attracted some considerable support[11] for it enables the word "all" to be taken literally, even if this might pose considerable soteriological questions.

But there are two reasons for preferring the third option by which "all Israel" refers to ethnic Israel as a whole. Paul is not saying that every individual Jew will one day be saved but rather that the nation generally, as an ethnic identity, will find salvation in the Messiah. The fact is that the Greek term behind "all Israel" is not the most obvious way of referring to every individual Jew. Better options exist which might produce English equivalents such as "all Israelites" or "all Jews" but as it stands "all Israel" has an ambiguity evident as much in English as in Greek. As a phrase, "all Israel will be saved" is not strong enough to indicate every living individual.

---

[11] Such as Robert Jewett, *Romans : A Commentary (Hermeneia, a Critical and Historical Commentary on the Bible)* (Minneapolis, MN: Fortress Press, 2007), 701-702.

Secondly, there is a biblical basis for understanding "all Israel" to mean ethnic Israel as a whole. For this, we must turn to the Septuagint, an ancient translation of the Hebrew Bible into Greek. Its precise date of emergence is disputed but certainly arrived long before the New Testament which quotes from it frequently. Undoubtedly, Greek speaking Jews (such as the apostle Paul) were acquainted with it and their vocabulary was shaped by it.

In the Septuagint, we find some examples of "all Israel" which refer not to every individual Israelite but to the people generally, as a whole. In Numbers 16 there is the description of Korah's rebellion where a group of rebels turned against Moses and Aaron by challenging their authority. But their evil actions brought upon God's judgement and the ground swallowed them up. Then in 16:34 it says that "all Israel who were around them fled their cries". The point here is that the people as a whole, as a group, sought refuge from the disaster. It is not stating that every individual Jew fled but merely those "who were around them".

Another example can be found in Joshua 7. Following the defeat at Ai, Achan is discovered to have sinned against the Lord by stealing possessions and defaming God's glory. In the ensuing judgement, we read that "all Israel stoned him with stones" (Joshua 7:25). It is of course unlikely that every single living Israelite took part in the actual stoning. Rather, it was the actions of a representative group of Israelites, acting on behalf of Israel as a whole.

A final example of a generic "all Israel" can be found in 2 Samuel 16 which describes the events following Absalom's revolt. At one point he takes his father's concubines onto the roof of the palace whereupon we read, "And Absalom went into his father's concubines in the sight of all Israel" (2 Sam 16:22). Once again there are the words "all Israel" and again it does not literally mean every single Israelite. Rather, it means that Israel generally, as a corporate nation, witnessed Absalom's taking of his father's concubines.

Accordingly, when Romans 11:26 states that all Israel will be saved, it is best understood that ethnic Israel will as a whole receive salvation even if the promise is not extended to every single individual Jew.

CONCLUSION

The following points are crucial in our understanding of the meaning of Israel in Romans 11:26. Firstly, the term Israel is ambiguous in early Christian literature which at times uses the term as a synonym for the Church, but other times reserves the usage for ethnic Israelites only. But although this practice is apparent among second century writers and beyond, the New Testament appears to be far more restrictive in its usage of the term.

There are four New Testament verses in which the term Israel appears to have a meaning that includes Gentiles. This is certainly the view of a number of commentators, but close analysis suggests that at best, such interpretation is uncertain and it is more likely that these four passages restrict the meaning of Israel to ethnic Jews alone. The weight of evidence suggests that every single instance of the term Israel in the New Testament refers to the ethnic nation alone. That being the case, Romans 11:26 should be seen as a declaration that God will one day bring salvation to "all Israel", a term that refers to the nation generally, as a whole.

CHAPTER 6

The New Testament and Supersessionism

Ronald E. Diprose

When I began research into the origins of supersessionism, I planned to focus my attention on the patristic writings. However Dr Donald Moreland observed that according to many scholars, the idea that in God's plan the Church has taken the place of God's elect people Israel, has its roots in the New Testament writings. Accordingly he suggested that I begin my research by examining New Testament passages commonly thought to support the view that the Church can be legitimately called the *new* or *true* Israel and that ethnic Israel no longer has special significance in the working out of the divine plan. The issue is of crucial importance: if it could be demonstrated that the New Testament itself teaches the cessation of Israel's special election, now that God is calling a people for his name from the nations, that would require us to either become supersessionists or adopt a critical attitude towards the New Testament writings themselves.

I accepted this challenge and proceeded to examine the passages which supersessionists most commonly appeal to in support of their view. I strived to give due attention both to the various contexts of each passage and to what each passage actually affirms (or, in cases like 1 Peter 2:9-10, what interpreters attribute to the passages but which, in fact, differs from what the biblical text actually affirms).

My purpose in this chapter is to share what I learned from my examination of these passages. However I will begin by summarising the contrasting opinions of scholars concerning the link between the New Testament and the development of supersessionism and anti-Semitism.

CONFLICTING VIEWS

According to Robert Osborn, Christianity has suffered from a "persistent, chronic strain of hostility to Jews and Judaism"[1] and this is partly because the New Testament designates God's covenant with Israel as something "old"[2] and makes Jews as such responsible for Jesus' death and the persecution of early Christians.[3] Rabbi Eliezer Berkovits' indictment is more severe. He writes: "Christianity's New Testament has been the most dangerous anti-Semitic tract in history. Its

---

[1] Robert T. Osborn, "The Christian Blasphemy: A Non-Jewish Jesus," in *Jews and Christians,* James H. Charlesworth, Frank X. Blisard and Jeffrey S. Siker, eds. (New York: Crossroad, 1990), 211.

[2] Defining God's former covenant with Israel as "Old," cannot properly be considered anti-Judaic, as such a definition is suggested by Jeremiah's prophecy concerning a *new* covenant and his description of the limitations of the covenant which God stipulated with his people at the time of the Exodus (Jer 31:31-34).

[3] Robert T. Osborn, op. cit., *ibid.* Actually the New Testament lays the blame for Jesus' death with Gentiles as well as with Jews but sees it supremely as the working out of God's plan (see Acts 4:27-28). It is a simple fact that non Christian Jews did persecute the followers of Jesus (Acts chapters 6-9, 13-14, 17-18, 21-26; 1 Thess 2:14-16). But so did non-believing Gentiles (Acts 19:23-41; 1 Thess 2:14; 1 Pet 4:14-16; 5:8).

hatred-charged diatribes against the "Pharisees" and the Jews have poisoned the hearts and minds of millions and millions of Christians for almost two millenia now... Without Christianity's New Testament, Hitler's *Mein Kampf* could never have been written".[4]

According to Gregory Baum the problem is not so much the New Testament itself but rather the way it was used by Christian writers in later centuries. He writes:

Christian authors have covered the mystery of Israel with theological embroidery that has contributed to the contempt and the debasement of the Jewish people and these theories have become so much entangled with the Church's teaching that they have formed the mentality of generations, of whole centuries, even to our own day.[5]

The idea that Christian anti-Semitism has roots in the New Testament received new impetus in 1974 with the publication of Rosemary Ruether's monograph *Faith and Fratricide*.[6] She writes: "In the synoptic tradition, messianic and anti-Judaic midrashim arose as two sides of the same development."[7] Contrasting reactions to Ruether's work are contained in a series of essays published under the title *Anti-Semitism and the Foundations of Christianity*.[8] In his Preface, James Parkes

---

[4] Eliezer Berkovits, "Facing the Truth" in *Judaism* 27 (1978), 324-325.

[5] Gregory Baum O.S.A., *Is the New Testament Anti-Semitic?* (Glen Rock, NJ: Paulist Press, 1960, Revised ed. 1965), 17.

[6] Rosemary R. Ruether, *Faith and Fratricide: The Theological Roots of Anti-Semitism* (New York: Seabury Press, 1974), see especially 64-116.

[7] Ibid., 64.

[8] Alan T. Davies (ed), *AntiSemitism and the Foundations of Christianity* (New York: Paulist Press, 1979). The work was presented to James Parkes, on the occasion of his eightieth birthday.

challenges Christendom to "accept the appalling fact that the foundations of antisemitism, and the responsibility for the holocaust, lie ultimately in the New Testament."[9] However John Meagher, author of the first essay, does not agree. While admitting that there was something very amiss in Christian theology's understanding of the Jews, he believes that its function was "to whitewash and justify an antagonism that sprang mainly from other sources."[10] The author of the fifth essay, Monika K. Hellwig,[11] also disagrees with Ruether's thesis. She attributes it to "a series of unquestioned ethnocentric assumptions arising out of the particular patterns of our history (anachronistically) read back into the story of Jesus and into the doctrine that he is Christ and Lord [and that this implies] a divinely ordained ending of the covenant of Israel, giving way to the new era of the covenant of Christians."[12]

Similarly, Lloyd Gaston hesitates to place blame with the New Testament. Writing of Paul's relationship to the Torah,[13] he suggests that Paul was "concerned to argue for equal rights of gentiles as members of the people of God... [but this] need not at all imply something negative about Israel and the Torah."[14] Gaston suggests that there may be room in

---

[9] Ibid., x.
[10] John C. Meagher, "As the Twig was Bent: Antisemitism in Greco-Roman and Earliest Christian Times," in Alan T. Davis, ed. *Antisemitism and the Foundations of Christianity* (New York: Paulist Press, 1979), 23.
[11] Monika K. Hellwig, "From the Jesus of Story to the Christ of Dogma," ibid., 118-136.
[12] Ibid, 132.
[13] Lloyd Gaston, "Paul and the Torah," ibid., 48-71.
[14] Ibid., 67.

Pauline thought for such a concept as "two religions, two chosen people".[15]

On the other hand, according to John Townsend,[16] the writer of the fourth Gospel actually "proclaims a replacement theology". This assertion is based on such passages as John 1:17, 2:6-10, 18-22, 4:12-24, 5:39-40, 8:39-40 and 15:1-17.[17]

Our investigation will begin with John 8:39-40 without which a supersessionist interpretation of the other Johannine passages mentioned would be groundless.

JOHN 8:30-47

In his insightful work, *The Partings of the Ways*, James Dunn has this to say concerning Jesus' statements in this passage:

> We should certainly be slow to let our own sensitivities dictate a verdict of anti-Judaism or anti-semitism on those whose world of discourse was so very different from our own. [18]

On the other hand Jeffrey S. Siker deduces from this passage that, according to John's Gospel, unbelieving Jews have no legitimate claim to being "children of Abraham" but rather are "children of the Devil" (8:44) while anyone who meets the conditions of 1:12, whether a physical descendant of

---

[15] Ibid.

[16] John T. Townsend, "The Gospel of John and the Jews," ibid., 72-97.

[17] Ibid., 72.

[18] James D.G. Dunn, *The Partings of the Ways* (London: SCM, 1991), 161.

Abraham or not, becomes both a child of God and a child of Abraham.[19]

Some comment is called for here. The Greek text of John 8:44, which links Jesus' Jewish opponents with the Devil, does not contain the word *tekna* ("children"), as Siker avers.[20] The text reads literally: "out of your father the devil you are". Moreover, it is not true that Jesus denies that Abraham is the father of these Jews "in any meaningful way".[21] Although the Jews who opposed Jesus were not, according to John, "children of God" (1:12) and could not be described as *spiritual* "children of Abraham", there still was a sense in which they could legitimately call Abraham their father (8:56).

It is important to remember that Jesus' denial of the status of "children of God" to his Jewish opponents was no novelty. In Deuteronomy 14:1-29 Moses makes it clear that being children of God implies obedience to the covenant, while in the "Song of Moses" we read: "They have dealt corruptly with him; they are no longer his children because they are blemished, they are a crooked and twisted generation" (Deut 32:5). So the issue turns not on language but rather on whether Jesus is really the Christ, as the writer of the fourth Gospel has set out to demonstrate (John 20:30-31). If he is, those who fail to recognise this fact are disobedient and thus cannot be considered children of God according to Deuteronomy 32:5 (cf. 1 John 3:21-23).

[19] Jeffrey S. Siker, *Disinheriting the Jews; Abraham in early Christian Controversy* (Louisville, KY: Westminster/John Knox Press, 1991), 136-139.
[20] Ibid., 139.
[21] Ibid., 136.

As for Jesus' words: "you are of your father, the devil" (John 8:44), if read out of context they could be seen to favor a theology of contempt in relation to the Jewish nation.[22] But if we take into account the Jewish way of speaking in Jesus' time, the same words no longer appear to be anti-Judaic, much less a sign that unbelieving Israel has been repudiated by God. In fact, a little later in the same conversation Jesus' Jewish opponents express the conviction that *he* has a demon (v. 52). Moreover in 1 John 3:9-10 *all* of humanity, not just the Jewish people, are divided into "children of God" and "children of the devil", to indicate those who are born of God and those who are not. Further on in the same letter, John affirms: "We know we are from God, and that the whole world lies in the power of the evil one" (5:19).

It is faulty exegesis to take the phrase "you belong to your father, the devil" used by Jesus in isolation and read anti-Judaic attitudes into it, while failing to consider the parallel expressions used elsewhere in John's writings. Clearly the words "children of the devil" used in 1 John 3:10 do not have anti-Judaic connotations. Neither is John the only one to report Jesus' use of similar language. It is Matthew who records Jesus' use of "Satan" to describe not his opponents, but no less a follower than Peter (Matt 16:23). Nor are all John's references to "the Jews" negative. While some statements put "the Jews" in a bad light (10:31-39; 12:37-40; 18:12-40), others are positive (10:41-42; 11:19, 31, 33, 36, 45; 12:11, 17-19).[23] Moreover, the attention given to theological

---

[22] Cf. Siker's discussion (op cit., 136-143). Rosemary Ruether uses John 8:43-47 (op. cit., 113-114) to argue that the NT teaches the rejection of the Jews.

[23] Charles H. Dodd and James Dunn observe that, in order to understand the negative references to "the Jews" in John's Gospel, it is necessary to bear in mind the theme of *krisis*, (separation, judgment), in 3:19; 5:22, 24,

debate between Jesus and "the Jews" in the fourth Gospel suggests that the evangelisation of the Jewish people was an important part of John's purpose (20:31).[24]

The most significant references to "the Jews" in John's Gospel, and perhaps in the whole of the New Testament, are those found in chapter four. Here Jesus himself features as a Jew (v. 9) and his answer to the Samaritan woman's question concerning the right place to worship includes this statement: "we [Jews] worship what we know, for salvation is from the Jews" (v. 22). According to Jesus, as presented in John's Gospel, the Jews have a unique knowledge of God; furthermore *only as a Jew* could Jesus contribute to God's saving work (4:22,42). Thus, the fourth Gospel, which contains the clearest statements concerning the incarnation (1:14; 16:28), also contains the clearest statement concerning the whole world's indebtedness to the Jewish nation.

MATTHEW 21:43

In this passage Jesus addresses the Jewish leaders who rejected him with these words: "Therefore I tell you, the kingdom of God will be taken away from you and given to a people producing its fruit." According to Chrysostom, here Jesus is teaching the repudiation of the Jews.[25] In reality the subject of the sentence is not the Jews themselves but rather

---

27, 29, 30; 7:24; 8:16; 12:31 and *schisma*, (division), in 7:43; 9:16; 10:19" (See Dunn, op. cit., 156-157; C.H. Dodd, *The Interpretation of the Fourth Gospel*, Cambridge: Cambridge University Press, 1960, with particular reference to 352-353).

[24] See F. F. Bruce, *The Gospel of John* (Grand Rapids, MI: Eerdmans, 1983), 13.

[25] John Chrysostom, "Homilies on the Gospel of Matthew" *in Patrologia Graeca* (Paris: J. P. Migne, 1856-65), 58:631-634.

the kingdom with which they had enjoyed a special relationship.

According to Scot McKnight, this announcement reflects the thrust of Matthew's Gospel: "the message of the kingdom is for all, and one of the major foundations for this offer is the suspension of national privilege" (21:43).[26] On the other hand, David Hill echoes Chrysostom when he writes: "the Jewish nation, as a corporate entity, had now forfeited its elect status".[27] D. A. Carson understands the announcement to refer to Israel's role as agent in the administration of the kingdom. He writes:

> Strictly speaking, then, v. 43... speaks of the ending of the role the Jewish religious leaders played in mediating God's authority.[28]

The post-resurrection mandate which Jesus entrusted to his Jewish apostles, and subsequent disciples (Matt 28:18-20) spelled out the exact nature of the authority conferred upon them and the role of the Church in the administration of God's rule. Although the Jewish people, as such, do not

---

[26] Scot McKnight, "A Loyal Critic: Matthew's Polemic With Judaism in Theological Perspective" in Craig A. Evans and Donald A. Hagner, eds. *Antisemitism and Early Christianity* (Minneapolis, MN: Fortress Press, 1993), 77. McKnight observes: "It is a fact that the traditions of Israel consistently explain destructions of cities in Israel and deportations as God's judgment" (ibid., 75). He concludes: "Matthew... is no more anti-Semitic than Amos or Jeremiah" (ibid., 77).

[27] David Hill, *The Gospel of Matthew,* The New Century Bible commentary, Matthew Black, NT ed. (Grand Rapids, MI: Eerdmans, 1972), 301.

[28] D. A. Carson, *Matthew,* The Expositor's Bible Commentary, Frank E. Gaebelein, Gen. ed. (Grand Rapids, MI: Zondervan, 1984), 8: 454.

RONALD E. DIPROSE

feature in this mandate, the Apostles were Jews, as were the overwhelming majority of the first generation of Christ's witnesses. Moreover, the book of Acts teaches that the Church's role in the present administration of the kingdom precedes the eschatological kingdom which includes the restoration of the kingdom to Israel (Acts 1:6-8, 3:19-31, 14:21-23).

ACTS 15:14-18

The question addressed at the Jerusalem Conference was whether Gentile converts were required to accept circumcision and embrace the Mosaic law, in order to be saved (Acts 15:1-5). Peter's negative answer (vv.7-11) was based on God's way of working in the house of Cornelius, purifying the hearts of Gentiles who had believed the Gospel through a direct work of the Holy Spirit.

The distinctiveness of James' contribution to the discussion (vv. 14-18) lies in his use of the term *laos* and in the fact that he puts the Gentile mission into eschatological perspective. According to Kevin Giles, the fact that James "can transfer the title [laos] to Christians, irrespective of their nationality, shows that a theological transition in his thinking on the status of Christians is well under way".[29] This theological transition refers to the idea that the Church is understood to supplant ethnic Israel.[30]

There is no doubt that James' description of those called from the Gentile nations as *a people for his name* "was for

---

[29] Kevin Giles, *What on earth is the Church?* (Downers Grove: InterVarsity Press, 1992), 88.
[30] Ibid., 32). Giles conceives of the Church as "restored Israel" (ibid., 51) and as the new Israel" (ibid., 132).

148

Jewish ears an astounding and even revolutionary saying".[31] This is due to the unprecedented juxtaposition of the terms *ethnōn* ("Gentiles") and *laos*, which in Jewish thinking had been mutually exclusive (Exod 19:5; 23:22; Deut 14:2; 28:9-10; Amos 3:1; Isa 43:1). However this need not imply that the Church supplants Israel. According to Strathmann:

> The circle of the word λαος is given a new centre. Only faith in the Gospel decides. The title is not herewith taken from Israel. But another λαος now takes its place along with Israel on a new basis.[32]

The conviction that the use of *laos* to describe Gentile believers does not imply disinheriting Israel of the title, finds support in the fact that the definite article is not used with *laos* in Acts 15:14. Furthermore we know from other passages in Acts and the New Testament Epistles that the new people that God is calling to himself is composed of Jewish *as well as* Gentile converts.[33]

James' statement in v. 15, "And with this the words of the prophets agree" is clearly a generalisation. The fact that God is calling from the Gentiles a people for his name, should not come as a surprise to readers of the Old Testament. After all, the Abrahamic covenant and the Hebrew prophets had envisaged Israel being a means of blessing to all peoples. As an example of the agreement between "the words of the prophets" and God's work of "to take from them a people of

---

[31] Hermann Strathmann, in G. Kittel and G. Friedrich, eds. *Theological Dictionary of the New Testament*, trans. and ed. G.W. Bromiley (Grand Rapids: Eerdmans, 1964-76), 4:54.

[32] Ibid.

[33] Cf. my discussion (below) on Eph 2:11-3:6.

his own name", James quotes part of a prophecy relating to the re-establishment of the Davidic dynasty (vv. 16-18, cf. Amos 9:11-12). There is an interesting modification in the Amos prophecy from: "so that they may possess the remnant of Edom" to: "that the remnant of mankind may seek the Lord" (v. 17a), suggesting that Israel's involvement in history, whatever form it may take, is in view of the furthering of God's salvation purpose (cf. Gen 12:3 [Gal 3:8]; Isa 49:5-6).[34] The identification of Jesus as "the son of David" and Israel's promised messianic king, in Matthew 1:1-2:6; 21:9; 27:37, fully justifies James' conviction that "David's tent" was being rebuilt by the victorious conclusion of Messiah's first advent. The continuation of the prophecy in the book of Amos (9:13-15) and such New Testament passages as Matthew 23:39 and Acts 1:6-7; 3:19-21, suggest that the rebuilding of David's tent will also have positive significance for Israel as a nation at the time of Messiah's second advent. James understands that in the benevolent plan of God there is room for the Gentile nations *as well as* for the people of Israel.

GALATIANS 3:26-29

The reason why Paul wrote Galatians was to refute the error of Jewish Christians who attributed a similar importance to "the works of the law" for salvation as the apostle attributed

---

[34] J.A. de Waard has shown that the rendering of Amos 9:11-12 in Acts 15:16-17 agrees, both in meaning and form, with the Hebrew of the Qumran scroll, 4QFlor 1:12 [J.A. de Waard, *Comparative Study of the Old Testament Text in the Dead Sea Scrolls and the New Testament,* Leiden: E.J. Brill, 1965, 24-26, 47, 78-79]. The basis of James' application is his conviction that *God has already acted* (not that he was *about* to act) in a way that is eschatologically significant.

to justification by grace through faith in Christ. Paul met this challenge first by an appeal to his personal history and the experience of the Galatians themselves (1:11–3:5), then by considering some key elements of salvation history (3:6-18). The passage which interests us concludes with these important statements:

> There is neither Jew nor Greek, there is neither slave nor free, there is no male and female, for you are all one in Christ Jesus. And if you are Christ's, then you are Abraham's offspring, heirs according to promise. (3:28-29)

According to H.D. Betz the thrust of Paul's argument is that non-Christian Jews are excluded from the Abrahamic promises. In other words, the Church has taken the place of Israel.[35] Is this so?

A straightforward reading of Galatians would suggest otherwise. The question being discussed is not the status of Israel, as such, but whether justification can be attained by "the works of the law". The idea that when Paul insists that "God's grace" (manifested in the death of Christ) and "righteousness of the law" are mutually exclusive, and that by this he also proclaims the demise of Israel, as an elect people; this is based on too narrow an understanding of first century Judaism. Dieter Georgi has discovered parallels, within first-century Judaism, to Paul's teaching on grace in Galatians[36] and to his polemic with Torah centered Judaism.[37]

---

[35] H.D. Betz, *Galatians* (Philadelphia, PA: Fortress Press, 1979), 116, 142, 146, 250-251.

[36] Dieter Georgi, "The Early Church: Internal Jewish Migration or New Religion?" in *Harvard Theological Review* 88/1 (1995), 62, calls attention

RONALD E. DIPROSE

Dunn concurs that Paul's argument and appeal in Galatians "reflect the concerns and language of intra-Jewish polemic".[38]

Coming now to Paul's argument in 3:26-29, it is important to first understand the meaning of the term translated "seed" in v.16. F.F. Bruce writes:

There is no need to make heavy weather of Paul's insistence that the biblical text has σπερματι (singular) and not σπερμασιν (plural). The essence of his argument can be expressed quite acceptably if it is pointed out that the biblical text uses a collective singular ("offspring") which could refer either to a single descendant or to many descendants.[39]

That "seed" can have a plural connotation, as well as referring to a single individual, is evident from the following passages in Genesis: 12:7; 13:15; 17:7; 24:7 (cf. Isa chaps. 42–53). Thus the word "seed" in Galatians 3:16 can be understood as referring to a single descendant, Christ, without excluding reference to the people to which he belonged (cf. Gal 4:4; John 4:22). Through Jesus the Jew the promised blessing comes to all the Gentiles (Gal 3:8-14). The second use of the term, in v. 29, refers to all who receive this blessing, that is, to all who belong to Christ and are thereby included in Abraham's

---

to Psalms such as 103, 106 and 108 and cites a thanksgiving hymn recorded in 1QH 4,35-37 (cf. 1QH 11,11-14).

[37] The writer of IV Ezra, an apocalyptic work, contests the restoration program of the pharisaic rabbis following the A.D. 66-70 Jewish war (Georgi, op. cit., 53).

[38] Dunn, op. cit., 476.

[39] F.F. Bruce, *The Epistle to the Galatians*, The New International Greek New Testament Commentary (Grand Rapids, MI: Eerdmans, 1982), 172.

spiritual offspring. Thus Paul can write: "For in Christ Jesus you are all sons of God, through faith. For as many of you as were baptized into Christ have put on Christ" (vv. 26-27). Being "clothed with Christ" is the secret of Gentiles becoming heirs of the promise made to Abraham.

It is at this point that Paul writes: "There is neither Jew nor Greek, there is neither slave nor free, there is no male and female, for you are all one in Christ Jesus" (v. 28). *In Christ* believers feature neither as Jews (people whose standing depends on privileges, such as those mentioned in Romans 9:1-5), nor as Greeks (people without any standing before God, Ephesians 2:11-12) but rather as Abraham's seed and, as such, heirs of the promise. Thus the attempt of Paul's opponents to put the Gentile converts of Galatia under law was ill-conceived.

It is instructive to consider the other distinctions — slave/free and male/female — which are eclipsed by the relationship of believers in Christ (v. 28). The interesting thing is that both of these distinctions still subsisted, even though the social distinctions thus indicated did not carry over to the relationship of these various categories of people *in Christ*. It follows from a comparison of these three pairs: Jew/Greek, slave/free, male/female, that Paul is not insinuating the demise of Israel, as a nation. What is new is that such distinctions do not carry over to the standing in grace of believers in Christ.

We conclude that this passage does not allude to the Church substituting Israel. Rather Paul's purpose here, as elsewhere in Galatians, is to demonstrate to his Jewish-Christian opponents, as well as to those Galatians who had been influenced by their teaching, that Gentiles, *as well as* Jews, become "heirs according to the promise" by placing their faith in Jesus the Messiah (cf. Acts 15:10-11).

EPHESIANS 2:11-22

This section of Ephesians treats the change in status of Gentiles who have become part of the Church. Our question is: Does this mean any significant change in status for the Jewish nation? Commenting on v. 19, a century ago T.K. Abbott wrote:

> The clear reference to the *politeia* of Israel shows decisively that the *hagioi* are those who constitute the people of God. Such formerly had been the Jews, but now are all Christians. These are now the Israel of God... The *hagioi*, then, are not the Jews, nor specially the patriarchs or Old Testament saints...[40]

Markus Barth, commenting on the same passage three quarters of a century later, has a very different perspective on the matter. He writes:

> First the Gentiles are reminded that they are received into the house of God, the community of Israel.[41]

Abbott's comment reflects the majority view of the Church before the *Shoah* and the birth of the modern State of Israel: that the Church has entirely replaced Israel. Barth's comment, on the other hand, reflects the renewed attention given to "the place of Israel and the Jew in God's purpose for the salvation of the world, and... the relationship of Israel to the Christian

---

[40] T.K. Abbott, *The Epistles to the Ephesians and to the Colossians,* ICC, S.R. Driver, A. Plummer, C.A. Briggs, eds. (Edinburgh: T. & T. Clark, 1897, 5th reprint 1956), 69.
[41] Markus Barth, *Ephesians 1-3,* The Anchor Bible (New York: Doubleday & Co, 1974), 314.

Church" which followed these events.[42] But is this all there is to it? Which of the two comments reflects more closely the meaning and flow of the Greek text?

Abbott's dogmatic statement only apparently follows the text. The word *politeia* does not occur in v.19, where the status of Gentile Christians is defined, but rather in v. 12, where it is affirmed that, in former times, the Gentiles "were... excluded from citizenship [politeia] in Israel and strangers to the covenants of promise". The word in v. 19 is *sum*-poli tai, meaning "fellow-citizens". The whole phrase, *sumpolitai ton agion* means: "fellow-citizens of the saints", or as the New International Version puts it: "fellow citizens with God's people". In other words, Gentile Christians were accepted into the community of saints which was already in existence. In this way they also become "members of God's household", which is "the household of faith" (Gal 6:10).

In v. 17 Israel is characterised as being "near" (egguv) while the pagan nations are characterised as being "far away" (makran). But being near did not mean that all Israelites were "saints". Both before and after the advent of Christ and the subsequent birth of the spiritual temple, the Church (John 4:21-24; Matt 16:18b), only believing, obedient Israelites are counted among the saints (Eph 2:18; cf. Heb 3:7-19; 11:1-38; Rom 11:5-7; Mal 3:16). What is new is the realisation of God's eternal purpose of uniting Jews and Gentiles in the Church (3:1-12) the foundation of which, besides being Christ himself, consists of twelve Jewish apostles, together with prophets. So it is incorrect to speak of a Gentile church. This

---

[42] Howard Taylor, "The Continuity of the People of God in Old and New Testaments" in *The Scottish Bulletin of Evangelical Theology* 3/2 (1985):13.

"mystery" had only been partially revealed in former times in the last clause of the Abrahamic covenant (Gen 12:3; cf. Isa 49:5-6). Now it is fully revealed. In Christ, believing Gentiles share in the honor of being God's household, while all in this household have greater privileges than in former times (Heb 11:39-40), having become the temple of the Holy Spirit (Eph 2:21-22).

HEBREWS 8:1-13

If this letter is understood to have been written to the Hebrews,[43] it cannot be accused of fomenting replacement theology. However not everyone reads the letter as written "to the Hebrews". For example Clark Williamson writes:

> Whatever its purpose, Hebrews put forth a supersessionist argument against Judaism, claiming that the covenant between God and the Israel of God had been abolished.[44]

In reality the writer to the Hebrews describes the *fulfillment* of Old Testament prophecy (Jer 31:31-34) and nowhere suggests that God's covenant with Abraham has been annulled. His concern is that his readers grasp the nature of the new, better, covenant of which Christ is the great high priest (7:22–10:18). While he shows great respect for all that has preceded the new covenant, he insists that the new is better, as indeed does Jeremiah. The purpose of his "hortatory discourse" (13:22) was to warn his own generation against making a similar

---

[43] See F. F. Bruce (*The Epistle to the Hebrews,* The New International commentary on the New Testament, F.F. Bruce, ed. (Grand Rapids, MI: Eerdmans, 1964, reprint 1981), xxiii-xxx.

[44] Clark M. Williamson, *A Guest in the House of Israel* (Louisville, KY: Westminster/John Knox Press, 1993), 109-110.

mistake to that made by the generation of Israelites which Moses led out of Egypt (see 2:1-4; 3:7-19; 6:4-6; 10:26-29).

While Williamson takes particular issue with the statement that the levitical covenant has been made obsolete, a position he calls "supersessionist",[45] Bruce observes:

> The very words "a new covenant" antiquate the previous one. In saying this our author does not go beyond Jeremiah, who explicitly contrasts the new covenant of the future with the covenant made at the time of Exodus...[46]

This is not a case of the Church presuming to supersede the Israel of God, but rather of one Jewish writer exhorting his fellow Jews to keep in step with developments in salvation history. The place of pagan converts in this plan is not so much as mentioned in this book, but certainly not excluded.

1 PETER 2:4-10

In common with James' speech in Acts 15:14-18, this passage attributes the dignity of "people of God" (*laos*) to converts to the Christian faith (v. 10). Can this be considered evidence for replacement theology? Wayne Grudem believes so:

> What more could be needed in order to say with assurance that the church has now become the true Israel of God?[47]

---

[45] Ibid., 108.
[46] Bruce, op. cit., 177.
[47] Wayne Grudem, *1 Peter*, Tyndale New Testament Commentaries (Downers Grove, MI: InterVarsity Press,1988, reprint 1992), 113.

RONALD E. DIPROSE

Peter Davids goes even further:

> now these Christians know they are elect—not just a people of God, but *the* people of God.[48]

In considering Peter's transposition to the Church of titles of honor used by Hosea (Hos 2:23; 1:6, 9-10), it must be remembered that for Messianic Jews among those to whom the letter was written (1 Pet 1:1-2; cf. Gal 2:8-9) these words would have had much the same meaning as they had for the Israelites of Hosea's own time. The name *Lo-Ammi* (Hos 1:9), meaning "not my people", stood for a severing of the covenant relationship between God and Israel through Israel's acting like an unfaithful wife. However God's faithfulness toward unfaithful Israel meant that there was a future for the nation. Thus Hosea prophesied:

> Yet the number of the children of Israel shall be like the sand of the sea, which cannot be measured or numbered. And in the place where it was said to them, "You are not my people," it shall be said to them, "Children of the living God." (Hos 1:10)

To understand how Peter could legitimately apply this prophecy to Jews who had come to faith in Christ, it is helpful to bear in mind the theme of repentance and forgiveness in Hosea (14:1-4) and these promises contained in Jeremiah's prophecy concerning the new covenant:

---

[48] Peter H. Davids, *The First Epistle of Peter,* The New International Commentary on the New Testament, F.F. Bruce, ed. (Grand Rapids, MI: Eerdmans, 1990), 93.

I will be their God,
and they shall be my people…
For I will forgive their iniquity
and will remember their sin no more (Jer 31:33-34)

John the Baptist (Luke 3:1-18) and Jesus (Mark 1:14-15) stressed the need for repentance. Moreover, Jesus' earthly ministry concluded with the stipulation of the new covenant prophesied by Jeremiah (Luke 22:14-20) and after his resurrection, he entrusted the Good News to his apostles (Mark 16:15-16; Acts 1:6-8). To those Jews who believed the gospel, God became their God in a new, more intimate way and they became his people in a new way, just as Hosea and Jeremiah had predicted (Acts 2:38-47; 3:19-26; 4:23-31).

We may presume that there were also Gentile Christians among the first readers of Peter's letter. Peter knew that Gentile Christians had been admitted into the new covenant (Acts 10:1–11:18; 15:7-11). By applying the Hosea prophecy to the whole Church Peter gave further demonstration of having accepted this fact.

We need to bear in mind what Peter says elsewhere about the future fulfillment of God's promises to Israel (Acts 3:19-21). Thus, we may conclude that he uses Old Testament titles of honor analogically, without attributing to these titles, and hence to the Church, the exclusive sense suggested by Davids. This is confirmed by the fact that, like James in Acts 15:14, he avoids using the definite article with "people" in 1 Peter 2:10, a detail overlooked by Davids.

1 THESSALONIANS 2:15-16 AND PHILIPPIANS 3:2-7

Further Pauline passages such as these are thought to express anti-Judaic attitudes.[49] Such strong language was well known to readers of the Hebrew prophets and can actually be seen as confirmation of the special love of God for unfaithful Israel (Amos 3:1-2). Romans 11:28-29 sums it up well: "As regards the gospel, they [the majority of ethnic Israel who have not yet recognised Jesus as Messiah] are enemies of God for your sake. But as regards election, they are beloved for the sake of their forefathers. For the gifts and the calling of God are irrevocable."

CONCLUSION

Our investigation has shown that the claim that *replacement theology* has roots in the New Testament is unfounded. A Jewish reader who shares the conviction that Jesus is the Messiah would be surprised if he found no evidence in these writings of the gospel being taken to the Gentiles (see Gen 12:3; Isa 49:5-6; cf. Acts 13:46-47; Gal 3:8).

Regarding apparent anti-Judaic attitudes, what we actually find is a lively debate within I century Judaism. The followers of Jesus did not present his claims simply as a new option within Judaism but rather as the *only* option for those desiring to remain faithful to the God of Israel. This claim provoked a strong response on the part of those Jews who were not prepared to recognise Jesus as the promised Messiah. Jesus and the Apostles also used strong language to

---

[49] See Ernst Käsemann, "Paul and Israel" in Ernst Käsemann and W.J. Montague, *New Testament Questions of Today* (Philadelphia, PA: Fortress Press, 1969), 183-187.

define those Jews who refused to believe the *great salvation* which they announced (cf. Heb 2:1-4). That this language did not have anti-Judaic intent is evident from the use of similar language to describe Gentiles who refused to believe the gospel (1 John 3:10).

CHAPTER 7

Biblical Theology, Israel and the Alien

Calvin L. Smith

Biblical theology is not easily defined. This is because the term has had quite diverse meanings and methods at different stages in the recent history of biblical studies.[1] For the purposes of this paper I define biblical theology as that discipline which combines biblical studies and theology to establish and explore the Bible's unifying central story (or "metanarrative", that is, the Bible's overarching narrative), together with a focus on tracing and analysing major themes across both Testaments. Thus, this approach to biblical theology moves away from a post-Enlightenment focus upon distinct and separate Old and New Testament theologies, as if both parts of the Bible were somehow unrelated, to emphasise the divine authorship and unity of the whole of Scripture.

The result is a discipline (biblical theology) which contributes to hermeneutics by drawing on the Bible's "big picture" to interpret its individual components and texts in

---

[1] For a useful academic treatment of biblical theology see Craig Bartholomew, Mary Healy, Karl Moller and Robin Parry, eds. *Out of Egypt: Biblical Theology and Biblical Interpretation.* Scripture and Hermeneutics Series. Volume 5 (Bletchley: Paternoster, 2004).

light of the whole of the canon. Therefore, biblical theology moves beyond the essential work of Bible background, linguistic and word studies, verse-by-verse exegesis, and detailed book studies (vital components of biblical interpretation), to the next stage of hermeneutics: interpreting individual segments and passages in light of and in constant reference to the contents of the canon of Scripture as a whole, sometimes referred to as canonical interpretation.

It is immediately clear that such a definition of biblical theology moves away from a rather narrow understanding of the term (as favoured by some academics) to something that encompasses both biblical studies and theology, the end product of which is the formulation of a system of doctrine. In other words, biblical theology defined this way is central to systematic theology. Some theologians separate biblical and systematic theology into two distinct theological disciplines, but personally I believe both are co-dependent, relying completely on each other, and therefore cannot be separated in this manner.

Tracing themes across the Bible is a powerful way of allowing the Bible to speak for itself. In this chapter I intend to explore one such biblical theology theme – Israel (or "the house of Israel") – to assess its viability and strength. When the theme of Israel is traced across both Testaments the case against supersessionism becomes particularly strong.

Today's Evangelical supersessionists, of course, focus on several biblical themes too, notably who owns the land. They state that this was an important Old Testament theme but is completely relegated in the New Testament. So, it is maintained, the land is superseded, spiritualised and replaced with a new kingdom of God that spans the whole earth, and therefore those Christians arguing for Israel's right to the land are theologically erroneous. I will not deal with the land theme here as my colleague Stephen Vantassel challenges this view eloquently and persuasively in his chapter. Another biblical theme employed by politically-driven supersessionists is Israel's treatment of the alien within her midst. Given how the themes of Israel and the alien are related in the Bible, after exploring and surveying the theme of Israel I will set out, assess and challenge the political supersessionist understanding and use of the alien theme so often employed in the current debate.

THE BIBLICAL THEME OF ISRAEL

In the Bible Israel represents a key biblical theology theme, not only in size and presence (in my Introduction I highlight briefly how central a theme Israel is across both Testaments), but also in terms of sheer theological weight, in that Israel plays a key role in the Bible's central narrative of redemption and God's unfolding plan of salvation. Biblical Israel is the people of God with whom He makes a covenant, reveals His laws, and ultimately through whom God sends a Saviour, a Jewish Messiah, *Yeshua HaMashiach* (Jesus the Messiah).

In the Old Testament the theme of Israel is so well developed we need hardly dwell on it here. Israel is presented as God's chosen people, first through the calling of and covenant with Abraham (Gen 12:1-3) and the Patriarchs, and later re-stated nationally (Exod 19:5-6, Deut 7:7-8). She was to be a kingdom of priests and a holy nation (Exod 19:6). Israel was separated from other peoples by God Himself to be His own holy people (Lev 20:26). On various occasions in the Old Testament Israel is referred to as God's own people, His inheritance, servant and son. Meanwhile, the love God expresses for His people and the nation of Israel throughout the pages of Scripture is striking. Even when Israel sinned

165

and was exiled God retained a plan and purpose for His people (Jer 29:10-14), while Israel's calling and covenant with God was repeated after the exile and emphasised continually by the prophets. Furthermore, national Israel is described in congregational terms: the "congregation of Israel" (Exod 12:6, 1 Kgs 8:5). Thus she was unique in history because of her relationship with God (Deut 4:34, 2 Sam 7:23). It has been noted how her history is central to the Israelite religious experience.[2]

History, of course, is a vital feature of any nation's self-identity. In Israel's case, however, history and religious self-consciousness were inextricably intertwined and indivisible, a symbiosis which formed a central defining feature of Israel's national identity. This, in turn, shaped and drove Israel's cultural identity, another important marker of nationhood. Moreover, God's covenant with Israel included entrusting her with a land to reside in and serve Him. Though not essential to nationhood (Israel existed as a nation even when exiled from the land), land represents an important dimension of her national identity as described in the Bible.

Aside from these religious, historical, cultural and geographical elements, there was also an ethnic dimension to Israelite nationhood. Israel was to be a distinctly *Jewish* nation. That is not to say this precluded outsiders from joining the house of Israel. As Matthew's genealogy notes, non-Jews such as Tamar, Rahab, and Ruth became not only full participant members of the congregation of Israel, but they are also recognised as direct ancestors of the Jewish

---

[2] Pierre Grelot, *The Language of Symbolism: Biblical Theology, Semantics, and Exegesis* (Peabody, MA: Hendrickson, 2006), 103ff.

Messiah. I explore the issue of ethnicity further in my section on the biblical theme of the alien, below.

Thus, Old Testament Israel had a unique relationship with God that shaped its very history, culture and self-identity. This sense of Israelite nationhood survives into the New Testament. The Jews still regarded themselves as a nation,[3] as did the apostle Paul.[4] The religious dimension was strongly evident, as was Israel's Jewish ethnicity (Acts 7:19). Today, too, these markers of biblical Israelite nationhood survive. Despite being a secular country, Mosaic and Rabbinic Judaism underpin much of Israeli society and the tension between the secular and sacred is tangible. Religious political parties such as Shas (a Sephardic party) and United Torah Judaism (Ashkenazi) are often kingmakers in Israel's particularly thorny brand of proportional representation politics. Orthodox Jews have secured special laws (much to the annoyance of secular Jews) to protect their way of life and finance their studies at *yeshiva*.[5] There is no civil marriage in Israel, thus the institution remains under religious control (unlike in Western democracies where, recently, marriage has undergone considerable redefinition). Meanwhile, Jerusalem especially is deeply conservative and religious (unlike hedonist Tel Aviv). In the Haredi *Meah Sharim* neighbourhood anyone driving a car on the Sabbath or baring their arms do so at their peril. Much of the settler activity is driven by Ultra-Orthodox theology. Even the bulk of everyday, more secularised Jews follow dietary laws, celebrate the Sabbath, and draw strongly on their religious heritage and biblical history. Despite its cosmopolitan nature,

---

[3] For example, Luke 7:5, 23:2, John 11:48, 50, Acts 10:22.
[4] Acts 24:2, 17, 26:4, 28:19.
[5] Religious schools for the study of the Torah and Talmud.

Israel projects a strongly Jewish identity. Proselytisation and evangelism are therefore frowned upon, regarded as detrimental to Jewish identity. Thus, despite Israeli secularism, atheism and behaviour from some quarters that flouts the Mosaic law, nonetheless much of modern Israel exhibits the same zeal for the religion, history, traditions and God of Israel evident in biblical Israel. What is all the more astounding is how this national self-identity has survived for two thousand years of exile and forced wandering. Yet at the time of writing, the Church of Scotland is preparing to debate whether the Jewish people have any right at all to the land, this despite them having exhibited the markers of nationhood for several thousand years longer than many other nations in existence today.

Very many Evangelicals, regardless of their view on whether or not God continues to have a purpose and plan for Israel today, would not dispute how Old Testament Israel served, at one time, as a revelatory vehicle for God's plan of redemption.[1] However, where supersessionists and non-supersessionists disagree is whether God *continues* to recognise and have a plan for Israel now that His salvific plan through Jesus Christ has been revealed. The debate hinges on the extent to which one side recognises what the New Testament has to say about Israel.

In his excellent book *The God of Israel and Christian Theology* R. Kendall Soulen identifies three forms of supersessionism: punitive, economic and structural. I will comment briefly on the first two when concluding this chapter. The third – structural supersessionism – approaches Scripture in such a manner as to relegate Israel in the purposes of God. Soulen explains how some leading early Church theologians, for a number of reasons, downplayed certain aspects of the Bible's metanarrative (he prefers the term "canonical narrative") while elevating, or placing in the foreground, others.

The Bible's central, or overarching, narrative can be traced across four key events: 1) creation, 2) the Fall, 3) Christ's work at the cross, and 4) the end, or consummation, of the age. Upon reflection it is evident that all the Bible's disparate components ultimately fit in with and are subordinate to these four events, which together present the basic story of redemption history. However, Soulen notes how, in response to early challenges faced by the Church, the focus by some influential theologians almost wholly upon the Fall and God's response (Calvary), resulted in the other two events – creation and consummation – being downplayed. By focusing on the New Testament story of Calvary as the zenith of God's eternal plan, the Old Testament is relegated in importance, and of course with it the role of Israel. Furthermore, a downgrading of the consummation of the age similarly writes Israel out of Christian consciousness. This is because Israel features so very strongly in the many eschatological Scriptures. Indeed, eschatology and Israel are, in the pages of the Bible, often inextricably intertwined, which is why those churches that relegate eschatology also tend to relegate a focus upon Israel (and vice versa).

Thus, much of today's supersessionism is based on a structural distortion of how the canonical narrative is perceived, where the Old Testament is cast aside (and with it much of what the Bible has to say about Israel). Thus antinomianism is often emphasised in today's churches, while many Evangelical Christians (and shamefully some church leaders) openly state they have little knowledge of – or need for – the Old Testament. From a supersessionist perspective one frequently hears that, because the land is not a central theme of the New Testament, it has no relevance

CALVIN L. SMITH

today and Israel's covenant and promises in this regard have been annulled.

Yet the New Testament *does* have a great deal to say about Israel. Indeed, throughout Jesus' ministry reported in the Gospels, God's love and continued purposes for His people Israel are strongly evident, and the people and nation of Israel feature prominently. Consider, for example, how when Jesus is presented in the Temple Simeon prophesies over the child and glorifies God for bringing both revelation to the Gentiles and glory for God's people Israel (Luke 2:32). Mary's Magnificat, in response to receiving confirmation of the news originally given to her by the angel Gabriel that she would bear a Saviour, praises God for helping Israel and remembering the descendants of Abraham (Luke 1:54-55). Later, when Jesus commenced His ministry it was the synagogues that He visited and in which He taught at (Matt 4:23). Jesus expressed great compassion for the Israelite crowds (Matt 4:23, 9:35-37), the people He came to minister to, saying to the Syro-Phoenician woman that He was only sent to the lost sheep of the house of Israel (Matt 15:24). He also instructed His disciples to do likewise (Matt 10:5-6), as well as explaining to the Samaritan woman at the well that salvation was from the Jews (John 4:22). Furthermore, Jesus' ministry amazed the people of Israel (Matt 7:28) and His miracles caused them to glorify the God of Israel (e.g. Matt 15:31, John 12:13). He also expressed great love and tenderness towards Jerusalem (Matt 23:37, Luke 13:34).

The point here is that while some espousing supersessionism tend to divide the Bible into two books on the issue of Israel, actually a substantial part of the New Testament – the Gospels – describes unambiguously God's continued love for the Jewish people and the focus of Jesus' ministry upon Israel as God's people. These passages cannot

170

be summarily and cavalierly dismissed as insignificant; the biblical theme of Israel as the people of God is also strongly evident in the New Testament. Given this ministry to and love for Israel it is a hermeneutical stretch always to spiritualise or allegorise the term "Israel",[6] as well as theologically problematic to dismiss the house of Israel as somehow no longer important to God after many centuries of loving and caring for her prior to New Testament times. Yet some do precisely this, arguing that with the commencement of the New Testament era Israel's divinely-ordained role is complete (or else taken from here), that the Church supersedes Israel as the people of God, so that Israel no longer has any theological significance, covenant, calling or divine purpose.

Others argue that with Christ's death and resurrection Israel's role is terminated. Actually, though, there is plenty of post-resurrection biblical evidence to demonstrate that God has not finished with Israel, that He retains a plan and purpose for His people. When the apostles asked the resurrected Jesus if he was about to restore the kingdom to Israel (Acts 1:6), he did not correct them to the effect there would be no such restoration, simply that it was not for them to know the times and epochs. One wonders, if the supersession of Israel by the Church was to be such a central doctrine of Christianity changing everything forever, Jesus did not immediately correct those He was entrusting with

---

[6] Arguably, the word "Israel" in the New Testament [with the oft cited exception of the reference to Israel in Rom 9:6, and "the Israel of God" in Gal 6:16 (cf the false Judaisers) but see Andy Cheung's comprehensive discussion in an earlier chapter] always denotes an ethnic entity. Surely, then, the onus is on those who believe to demonstrate how the New Testament use of the word "Israel" has shifted from an ethnic to an allegorised definition, rather than the other way around.

His Church. Moreover, that there were apostles to both Jew and Gentile in the book of Acts suggests Israel was not dispossessed of her heritage.[7] The nature and circumstances of several sermons in the book of Acts, too, highlight God's on-going dealings with Israel.

It is the apostle Paul who has most to say about Israel in the later New Testament era, devoting nearly a fifth of that seminal epistle so central to Christian doctrine – the book of Romans – to the issue of Israel and God's continued love and purpose for the Jewish people. Early in the epistle the apostle states that the Gospel is to be taken to the Jew first (Rom 1:16). Paul, of course, made it a practice of visiting the synagogue first in any new town or city visited during his missionary trips. But it is in Romans 9-11 especially where Paul focuses on Israel and delivers his treatise on the issue.[8]

Immediately before this section, Paul wraps up chapter 8 with the declaration of the triumph the believer in Christ enjoys. He concludes this "hymn" by declaring how nothing, nothing at all, can separate us from the love of God. But this, of course, begs the inevitable question: If nothing can separate us from God, what about His people Israel? If salvation comes through faith in Christ, which means we have the security of not being separated from God, what about the Jewish people who, on the whole, rejected Jesus as their Messiah? Thus, the Apostle Paul launches his three-chapter discussion concerning Israel.

---

[7] Pierre Grelot makes a similar point in *Language of Symbolism*, op.cit., 142.

[8] Rom 9:1–5 clearly indicates Paul is referring to ethnic, rather than a spiritualised Israel here, and even Colin Chapman accepts that most of this passage relates to the Jewish people, *Whose Promised Land?* (Oxford: Lion, 1983, 2002), 245.

Paul develops his argument in stages across the three chapters, and it is essential to follow and understand the entire thread if the apostle is to be understood. He begins by expressing anguish over his countrymen because of their rejection of Messiah, even wishing it were possible for himself to be cut off from Christ for the sake of his Jewish kinsmen (Rom 9:1-5). (Incidentally, in these first five verses Paul appeals to the very religious, historical, cultural, geographical and ethnic markers of Israelite nationhood discussed above.) But Paul wants his readers to understand that this rejection does not mean God's promises to Israel have failed (9:6). Quite the contrary. Another people (believing Gentiles) join a remnant of Israel, despite the wider nation of Israel rejecting Messiah, and partake of those promises. Thus, God's word has not failed, the OT promises are fulfilled in this *remnant + Gentile* community. And if Paul had stopped here, there might indeed be a case for some kind of "fulfilment theology" claiming the Old Testament promises are fulfilled in this new people of God, of which believing Israelites join. However, Paul does *not* stop there. Indeed, he is only a third of the way through his argument.

Having discussed a remnant of Israel in chapter 9, Paul now shifts to a discussion of the wider nation. The Israelites are zealous for God, he says, but not according to knowledge (of the Messiah). Echoing back to the first eight chapters of Romans, Paul makes it clear that salvation is through faith in the Messiah alone, not through the law (there is no place for dual covenantalism in Paul's theology). Unfortunately, wider Israel has rejected this gospel of faith. Thus, chapter 10 culminates with the observation that while the nation rejects the gospel, God calls a people who are not a nation (the Gentiles). The purpose? To make the nation of Israel jealous (10:19).

It is in chapter 11 that Paul now reaches the climax of his argument. In summary so far: No, the promises of the Old Testament have not failed because a remnant of Israel, together with believing Gentiles, bring about their partial (or initial) fulfilment (chapter 9). Meanwhile, the rest of the nation has rejected Christ (chapter 10). But the story does not end there: Paul goes on to argue in chapter 11, where he shifts his discussion from a remnant being saved at the present time to the whole nation being saved at a future time. Paul's juxtaposition of a remnant versus the whole nation is unequivocal:

remnant (v. 12)		full number (v. 12)
root (v. 16)	versus	branches (v. 12)
first fruits (v. 12)		whole batch (v. 16)
partial Israel (implied)		all Israel (v. 25).

Therefore, Paul makes the startling statement, "If their trespass means riches for the world, and if their failure means riches for the Gentiles, how much more will their full inclusion mean!" (v. 12. Emphasis added)

All this leads Paul to present the analogy of the cultivated olive tree and the wild olive, which he specifically directs towards his Gentile Roman readers. In AD 49 Claudius had the Jews expelled from Rome. Two such Jews later became Paul's colleagues (Aquila and Priscilla, Acts 16:1-2). The edict was repealed in AD 54 and Jews were permitted to return (thus Aquila and Priscilla are back in Rome when Paul wrote his epistle, Rom 16:3). Several commentators have dwelt on this absence of Jewish believers and its effects upon the church in Rome. One can quite easily imagine how, during their absence, Gentile believers who remained in the imperial city interpreted their Jewish co-believers' exile from Rome as evidence of God's judgment upon the Jews as a whole. After all, did not the Old Testament Scriptures indicate exile as a form of judgement upon the nation of Israel? Whatever went through their minds one thing is clear: The Gentile church in Rome had no Jewish believers within its midst for around five years. Eventually, Jewish believers returned to Rome and their churches. But it seemed in their absence some Roman Christians now viewed their Jewish counterparts differently, no longer as God's elect nation but rather as a people subsumed by and indistinct from the Church, which had become the *new* people of God. In short these Roman Christians had become the first supersessionists, leading Paul to challenge their arrogance. Thus, the apostle directly addresses the Gentile Christians in Rome (11:13), setting out his analogy of the wild olive and warning the Gentiles not to become arrogant towards the Jews, because it is *they* (Gentile Christians) who join Israel and not vice versa. This, of course, is completely at odds with replacementism's view that somehow Israel has been (almost begrudgingly) attached to a Gentile Church, almost as an afterthought. This is a far cry from Paul's declaration that it was Gentiles who were separated from the commonwealth of Israel and afar from God (Eph 2:12-13). So whereas replacement theology claims the Church *replaces* Israel, the Church in fact is *joined* to Israel (specifically believing Israel).

Going back to the climax of Paul's argument in Romans 11, how is the vindication of Israel and the ultimate fulfilment of the Old Testament promises to be manifest? In the very shift in emphasis he sets out in that chapter: from salvation of a remnant to salvation of the wider nation, the first fruits (a remnant at the present time, 11:5) to the salvation of the whole batch – "all Israel" – at a future, eschatological date (11:25-6, cf Zech 12:10, 13:1, also eschatological in context).

Why this amazing vindication, this future salvation of the entire nation of Israel? Because, Paul explains, they are loved and the gifts and callings of God are irrevocable (11:28-9).

This juxtaposition of the salvation of a Jewish remnant at the present time with the climactic salvation of the nation as a whole in the eschatological future, at the end of time, is the zenith of Paul's argument in Romans 9-11. In the same way that the kingdom of God is inaugurated but not yet established in its fullness, extended and widened to all the world but not yet having seen in its fullness when Christ returns in person and Israel receives her King, so too there is a present and partial salvation of Israel, together with an eschatological salvation of all Israel. It is no wonder, after 40 days of being taught by the Risen Lord about the kingdom of God (Acts 1:3), that the apostles asked Jesus if He was about to restore the kingdom to Israel (Acts 1:6). They had not misunderstood at all. Far from correcting them Jesus tells them it is not for them to know the times set by God. But for now their task was to preach the kingdom to all nations, until – as Paul makes clear – the time of the Gentiles is fulfilled (11:25).

This eschatological dimension represents another essential aspect to understanding the biblical theme of Israel. Israel is not only present in the first part of God's unfolding revelation of *Heilsgechichte* (salvation history) in the Old and New Testament eras, but she is also present at the culmination of this canonical, or divine narrative. I am not speaking here about the popular and often sensationalist brand of eschatology that seeks to marry prophecy with present world events. Such an approach is often speculative, aimed perhaps more at selling books than anything else. But in reacting against such extremes, some Evangelicals go too far the other way, throwing out the eschatological baby with the pop-eschatology bathwater. After all, salvation history covers the *whole* of human existence, from Creation to the consummation of the age, and if the Church has no eschatological hope to draw upon, what is the point? The eschatological culmination of the age, including its personal and cosmic ramifications, and the promise of spending eternity with Christ are absolutely vital and central aspects of the Bible's metanarrative. Eschatology represents the conclusive outworking of salvation history, marking the stage when history ends and eternity begins. Thus the Gospels present the Kingdom of God as realised *and* eschatological, inaugurated but *not yet* fulfilled.[9] Even the famous liberal theologian Albert Schweitzer pointed out how Jesus' message was ultimately and thoroughly eschatological (even if Schweitzer himself believed Jesus was wrong).

So where does Israel fit in to the Bible's eschatological scheme of things? We have already noted how in Romans 11:25-6 Paul declares all Israel shall be saved at some point in the future. That this event occurs "after the fullness of the Gentiles has come in" indicates he has an eschatological event in mind. This juxtaposition of Israel's eschatological salvation, their washing and cleansing (of sin), and the giving of God's spirit to His chosen people is a theme taken up in Zechariah's eschatological discourse (12:10, 13:1 cf Ezek 18:31, 36:26-27, see also Isa 44:1-3, John 3:5).[10] Zechariah 12, a clearly

---

[9] The debate among biblical scholars concerning the timing of the kingdom is well known. Passages which clearly portray the eschatological aspect of the Kingdom of God include Matt 13:47-50, 25:1 (during Jesus' eschatological discourse), Luke 22:16-18, Rev 11:15, 12:10.

[10] The "heart of stone" detailed in Ezekiel is likely an allusion to the tablets of stone that contained the Law, symbols of the old covenant replaced with a new covenant with the house of Israel (cf Jer 31:31-37) at

eschatological passage, speaks of armies congregating upon Jerusalem and Israel, echoing the final battle described in Revelation. The prophet Joel, too, describes such a battle and the very close linguistic similarities between Joel and Revelation 9 is not lost on Bible scholars. So either the author of Revelation merely copies Joel and reports a past prophecy *ex eventu*,[11] or else both are referring to a future event, a catastrophe to befall Israel. In fact, Joel takes a contemporary catastrophe (the plague of locusts which destroys the land) and uses it as a device to speak about the eschatological future, detailing not only an invading army's invasion of Israel, but how through God's intervention Israel shall be saved physically and spiritually (thus bringing us full circle back to Romans 11:25-6). The central theme in Joel is the "day of the Lord", a well known apocalyptic phrase cited five times in this short book. Yet again this event juxtaposes Israel's eschatological salvation, her cleansing from sin, and the pouring out of God's spirit upon her.

Granted, Peter draws on Joel 2 to explain the outpouring of God's spirit in Acts 2. But the apocalyptic scenario set out by Joel (wonders in the sky, blood, fire, smoke, darkness, moon likened to blood) is not present at Pentecost in the manner described in Revelation. As both books are eschatological, the outpouring is likely two-fold, or takes place in two stages: Pentecost *and* an end-times washing of Israel's sin and regeneration through God's Spirit. Immediately before his reference to the outpouring of God's

---

the time of her eschatological salvation. Another passage worth considering here, apparently in an eschatological context, is Zech 8:23.
[11] Literally, "after the event", whereby a writer describes a prophetic event *after* it has taken place but maintaining it is *yet to come*. Those arguing for this device often do so because they deny the concept of predictive prophecy.

Spirit, Joel likens spiritual blessing to the Holy Land's two rainy seasons (the former and latter rain). If Pentecost is the first (an event, incidentally, where all participants and observers were Jews and proselytes to Judaism), God's eschatological salvation of Israel ("when they shall look upon him who they have pierced", and God pours out His Spirit upon them, Zech 12:10) is to be the second.

Isaiah presents two visions of the Messiah: Suffering Servant and Conquering King. Jesus inaugurated the Kingdom in microcosm, but various Messianic passages in Isaiah indicate a literal kingdom established on earth. One of Jesus' titles is the King of Israel[12] (it was nailed to the cross at Calvary). That He will establish a literal, earthly kingdom is somewhat more inspiring than Him simply being king of our hearts. If we take Isaiah's Conquering King motif seriously, then Jesus' teaching of the eschatological inauguration of His Kingdom must surely have a literal, eschatological outworking, so that the Son of David takes His throne over the house of Israel and the world. It certainly explains better those eschatological passages concerning His reign from Jerusalem and the mountain of the Lord (eg Mic 4:1-4). It also demonstrates that while the land may not necessarily be an issue now, eschatologically-speaking it returns to centre stage in the divine plan.[13]

---

[12] Matt 2:2, 27:11, John 1:49, 12:13.

[13] Bearing in mind Paul's reference to the "full number of the Gentiles", Luke 21:24 echoes a similar phrase in an eschatological context, at which time the land again takes centre stage and comes back under Jewish control. The question is, are we are in those last days now? If so, then the establishment of modern day Israel indeed looks very much part of the divine plan. But if the end times are not yet upon us, it is equally possible to hold to the view of the Jews as God's chosen people and their eschatological restoration, without having to state dogmatically the

Lest one is uncomfortable with the notion of partial, two-fold, or multiple fulfilments of prophecy, the Bible is full of this phenomenon, whether the sign of a maiden with child (Isa 7:14 cf Matt 1:23), God calling His son out of Egypt (Hos 11:1 cf Matt 2:15), or the abomination that makes desolate. This latter example again has an eschatological fulfilment. In intertestamental times Antiochus IV Epiphanes slaughtered a pig to Zeus in the Temple, leading to the Maccabean revolt. Later, Pompey and Titus also defiled the Temple. Yet Jesus also refers to it in an eschatological context.[14] Moreover, if one really desired to be controversial it might be claimed the Dome on the Rock is such an abomination. After all, on the very hill where Abraham prepared to sacrifice his son Isaac (and all the theology that goes with that), and where Jesus' ancestor David bought the Temple Mount from Ornan the Jebusite, stands a Dome within which is permanently inscribed, "The Sonship of Jesus and the Trinity are false", and "It is not fitting that God should beget or father a child".[15] (Such statements put the Danish cartoon protests some years ago in a new context, yet of course the Christian way is to turn the other cheek, even when human nature demands retraction of language against our Saviour which we find deeply offensive.)

---

establishment of modern Israel is divinely ordained (though many non-supersessionists instinctively assume so).

[14] In fact, much like Joel, Jesus' great eschatological discourse in Matthew 24-5 takes a (near) contemporary event (the fall of Jerusalem in AD 70) and projects it into the eschatological future to describe a catastrophe to befall the Jewish people (Matt 24:16-20). It is immediately after these events that Jesus describes the glorious return of the Son of Man (24:29-31).

[15] Moshe Sharon, "Islam on the Temple Mount" in *Biblical Archaeological Review* 32.4 (July-August 2006), 42, 45.

Clearly, from a soteriological perspective Jesus supersedes the old covenant, the New Testament shifts its focus away from the land (for now) to a worldwide community of Christian believers, while for the time being the Kingdom has been inaugurated in our hearts. *But this is not at the negation of Israel!* Neither does the salvation story end at Calvary; there is more to come in the eschatological future. This eschatological culmination of the age is a biblical theology theme that is *widely* represented throughout both Testaments. And it is one that is also closely connected to the theme of Israel throughout the pages of the Bible.

THE ALIEN

Somewhat related to the biblical theology theme of Israel is the Old Testament theme of the alien. Several of today's supersessionists focusing on Israel's responsibilities towards and treatment of the alien consider this a key argument in their anti-Israel polemic.[16] Yet given its selective treatment of Scripture one might be forgiven for concluding that this viewpoint is primarily about providing a theological basis for which to criticise (some might argue demonise) the modern State of Israel.

In summary, the argument goes, the Old Testament sets out various passages concerning biblical Israel's obligations towards the alien living in her midst. Yet in today's Israel, it is argued, the Palestinian people are mistreated, denied justice and treated as second-class citizens. Thus, because of

---

[16] See Gary Burge, *Whose Land? Whose Promise? What Christians Are Not Being Told About Israel and the Palestinians* (Cleveland, Ohio: Pilgrim Press, 2003), 88-93, and Colin Chapman, *Whose Promised Land?* Op. cit., 204ff.

modern Israel's mistreatment of the Palestinians the nation is in fact disobeying the Mosaic law's commandments concerning alien inclusion, and as such the State of Israel is no longer in covenant with God, while the Christian Zionists who stand by Israel are ignoring her failure to observe the covenant as set out in the Torah.

It is indeed true that the Mosaic law has a great deal to say concerning the just and fair treatment of the alien. We read that God loved and welcomed the alien into the house of Israel (Deut 10:18-19). The alien was permitted to join the congregation of Israel was granted various rights and privileges accorded the Israelites, while strict instructions were laid down concerning their fair treatment. For example, aliens could expect justice (Deut 24:17, 27:19). They were also accorded care: when the Israelites were commanded not to reap their field all the way to the edge, this was to provide food not only for the poor but also for the alien resident (Deut 24:19-21). The alien within Israel's midst was also a benefactor of almsgiving commanded by God from the Israelites (Deut 26:12-13). Furthermore, the alien was included in the commandment concerning the establishment of cities of refuge (Num 35:15). The Israelites were even instructed to love the alien within their midst (Deut 10:19). Indeed, in God's eyes there was to be no difference between the alien and Israelite (Lev 24:22, Num 15:14-16), and those Israelites exploiting the alien were condemned by the prophets (Jer 7:6, Ezek 22:7).

Thus it is argued by several of Israel's Evangelical detractors that modern Israel is breaking the Mosaic law, extending no such treatment and rights to the Palestinians, and therefore is in open rebellion towards God rather than in covenant with Him.

Leaving aside how the Palestinians' own leaders and the wider Arab world must shoulder considerable responsibility for the current situation of Palestinian people, or how such arguments by Christian anti-Zionists unwittingly suggests the Palestinian are the alien in a land they claim as their own, the argument of alien inclusion fails the biblical theology test by virtue of its selectiveness of texts. As the Scriptures outlined above make clear, God indeed loved deeply and cared greatly for the alien within biblical Israel. Crucially, however, this alien inclusion into the house of Israel was a *reciprocal, covenantal arrangement*, dependent upon various requirements and religious observances from the alien. In other words it was not a one-way relationship. If the alien was to receive the treatment, rights and care set out in Scripture, it was conditional upon the alien reciprocating in kind. For example, the alien was expected to observe certain religious and other laws (e.g. Ex 12:19, Lev 16:29, 17:12, 17:15, 18:26, 24:16, Num 19:10, Deut 26:11, 31:12, Ezek 47:23). Moreover, if he was to become a member of the congregation and participate in the Passover feast (a key aspect of being an Israelite), the alien was to be circumcised (Ex 12:48-49, Num 9:14). Meanwhile, certain religious observances were expected not just from the alien, but even the sojourner (Ex 12:45, 20:10, Deut 5:1). The Old Testament is clear that any member of the house of Israel, whether the alien or Jew, not abiding by the covenant was to be excommunicated (Num 15:30).

In short, the alien who joined the congregation of Israel was to leave his or her people, nation, and religion and become, to all intents and purposes, an Israelite, as so eloquently expressed in those words of Ruth the Moabitess to her mother-in-law Naomi: "Your people shall be my people, and your God, my God" (Ruth 1:16). Therefore, we see here

183

an Old Testament type, or allusion, of the Gentile being grafted in to Israel, as discussed by Paul in Romans 11:13-24. Just as in the case of the alien, Gentiles were separated from the commonwealth of Israel (Eph 2:11-14). However, as in Old Testament days, the non-Jew who agreed to come into covenant with the God and people of Israel joined the congregation of Israel and became, to all intents and purposes, a Jew. So too Gentile believers are grafted in to believing Israel as illustrated in Paul's olive tree analogy and are adopted sons. Unfortunately I have never, in the context of its usage in order to condemn Israel, heard the biblical theme of the alien presented in its entirety to reflect the reciprocal nature of the alien-Israelite relationship.

Aside from this selective use of texts, the alien argument fails for another reason. Many Palestinians (not all), and certainly their leaders, are *not* in a reciprocal covenant – whether religious or political – with Israel today. It is hard to reconcile, by any stretch of the imagination, firing thousands of rockets on a daily basis, organising and condoning suicide bombings, constantly broadcasting the vilification and demonisation of Israelis on the basis of their Jewish ethnicity and religion, with the expected standard of behaviour from the alien as laid down in the Torah.

Moreover, the alien argument completely ignores how modern Israel's relations with West Bank and Gaza Arabs differ considerably from those with its 1.6 million or so Israeli Arabs (i.e. Arabs with full Israeli citizenship living within Israel's nationally recognised borders, as opposed to Palestinian Arabs in what the U.N. regards as occupied territory). By formally accepting Israeli citizenship it might perhaps be argued more consistently that these Israeli Arabs most closely resemble the alien described in the Bible, having come into a covenant of sorts with the State of Israel.

Reciprocity is therefore expressed in the form of Israeli Arabs being permitted to vote, form political parties, sit in the Knesset, lobby parliament, take their grievances to the Israeli courts, like the Haredim (Ultra-Orthodox Jews) be exempt from compulsory military service, and so on. To be sure, Israel's relations with its Arab citizens are far from perfect, neither do all Israeli Arabs support the State of Israel (some clearly do not). Nonetheless, there *is* a covenant and reciprocity of sorts between Israeli Arabs and the state in a democratic Israel that extends far more rights to its Arab citizens than many autocratic Arab states do to theirs (as the recent protests defining the so-called Arab Spring, now sadly becoming an Arab Winter, demonstrate).

Related to the issue of the alien is the issue of ethnicity of the Israelite in the Bible. In my television debate with the well-known Christian anti-Zionist author and activist Stephen Sizer,[17] he argued for an Old Testament people of God that was not based on ethnicity at all, citing passages highlighting the inclusion of the alien within the promises of Israel. This position is known as covenant theology, which understands the term "Israel" to mean the people of God and not the Jewish nation. Hence, the Old Testament people of God were Jews and foreigners combined, while the New Testament people of God is the Church. Thus, it is claimed that the Old Testament people of God were not chosen on the basis of their ethnicity, that chosenness had no connection whatsoever with Jewishness. This is an important point for Sizer who claims Christian Zionist support for Israel is racist. If Old Testament Israel is chosen, partly at least, on the basis of Jewishness, it is far more difficult to argue against the view

---

[17] The television debate is available in full online on my website at www.calvinsmith.org.

that the Jews remain God's chosen people. But if it can be argued that Old Testament Israelites were not, after all, chosen on the basis of their Jewishness but rather something else, this permits the Christian anti-Zionist claim that any concept of chosenness involving ethnicity is inherently racist. Sizer, of course, has stated on several occasions that Zionism (and thus Christian Zionism) is a racist ideology.

One wonders how someone of a Reformed persuasion, and who therefore presumably has little problem with the concept of election and chosenness as set out in Calvinist soteriology (the end product of which leads to something – eternal torment in hell – far graver than who owns a chunk of land) struggles with the election of a nation to fulfil God's plan. Neither does chosenness have to denote ethnic superiority. Quite the opposite, in fact. When God explains to the Israelites why He chose them, He leaves them in doubt that it was not because they were a numerically great or special people, but rather because of His oath made to their fathers (Deut 7:6-8). With the biblical concept of "chosenness" comes great responsibility and adversity (as the Jewish people can testify over thousands of years). The biblical concept of chosenness is a far cry from today's understanding of the term denoting exclusivity and superiority, which a postmodern, pluralist *Zeitgeist* (spirit of the age) is bound to eschew.

But leaving all that aside (together with how Scripture makes abundantly clear how God is free to choose whom He wills, Rom 9:14-15), attempts to deny the Jewishness of Old Testament Israel are, of course, completely absurd. Yes, the alien was permitted to come into covenant with the congregation and God of Israel, but they joined a nation that was defined, partly at least, by its inherent Jewishness. If it is not the case that the Old Testament people of God were not identified by their Jewishness, one wonders why Jesus tells the Samaritan woman, "You worship what you do not know; we worship what we know, for salvation is from the Jews" (John 4:22). Or why Paul says that the Gospel should be taken to the Jew first (Rom 1:16 cf 2:9). Or why the apostle twice highlights this ethnic and physical dimension of Israel's self-identity in his opening treatise on Israel (Rom 9:3, 5). Or why Stephen refers to "our race" when speaking about the Israelites held in captivity in Egypt. Or even why Zechariah prophesies, "Thus says the Lord of hosts: In those days ten men from the nations of every tongue shall take hold of the robe of a Jew, saying, 'Let us go with you, for we have heard that God is with you'" (8:23).

Israelite nationhood, then, included a distinct Jewish element (though Jewishness is more than ethnicity alone). Biblical Israel also incorporated individuals from various ethnic backgrounds who were *assimilated* into the prevailing national (and religious) culture, similar in some respects to how non-Europeans have settled and fully assimilated into the United Kingdom. It is important to understand this assimilationist model practiced in biblical Israel because it highlights how although the nation was predominantly Jewish, nonetheless it also allowed non-Jews to join the congregation of Israel and come into covenant with the God of Israel. Yet retaining a distinct Jewishness ensured biblical Israel retained its unique identity.[18] Consider, for example,

---

[18] Several supersessionists argue that a Jewish state is by its very nature racist, thus rendering modern Israel theologically in error. Yet today (much like in Old Testament times) Israel's Law of Return permits Jewish proselytes (i.e. *not* ethnically Jewish) to make *aliyah* (emigrate to Israel). Moreover, citizenship is automatically extended to *non*-Jewish spouses, children, and grandchildren, while the inclusion of Ethiopian and Yemenite Jews demonstrates that Jewishness moves beyond ethnicity and

when in the Bible Israel mingled *en masse* with outsiders, they are condemned because such activity diluted Israel's religious identity and enticed the nation to serve foreign gods (for example, Ezra 9:2).

Finally, Christian anti-Zionist attempts to compare how the alien was given land inheritances in biblical Israel with the current Israeli-Palestinian conflict and the issue of land ownership simply do not stand up to scrutiny. The alien in biblical times was never given a land inheritance in order to establish himself as a rival religio-political entity within the borders of Israel, in enmity with the Israelite people. The fair treatment of the alien was conditional on being in covenant with the congregation and God of Israel.

CONCLUSION

This chapter has focused on exploring the theme of Israel across both Testaments, as well as Israel's place in the eschatological aspect of the canonical narrative. As such, its aims has been to challenge a distorted hermeneutical approach to the Bible's central narrative which Soulen refers to as structural supersessionism. We have seen how Israel remains an important biblical theme into the New Testament, whether in the Gospels, in epistles such as Romans and Ephesians, and also in the many eschatological passages of the Bible, including Paul's declaration in Romans 11:25-27 that one day in the future all Israel shall be saved. It is not insignificant that in that passage Paul quotes from Isaiah

---

Israel is *far* from racist. For details of the Law of Return see the document posted on the Jewish Agency for Israel website at www.jewishagency.org/JewishAgency/English/Aliyah/Aliyah+Info/The+Law+of+Return/The+Law+of++Return.htm (accessed 16 July 2007).

59:20, a text where in the very next verse the prophet points out the perpetual nature of God's covenant with Israel (v. 21). The concept of a perpetual covenant is also unambiguous in Jeremiah 31, following the verses setting out the New Covenant, where in verses 35-37 God declares that Israel will not cease to be a nation before Him.

Aside from structural supersession there are, of course, other expressions of supersessionism. The view that Old Testament Israel's theological purpose has been superseded is sometimes known as "soft supersessionism". Soulen has labelled this view of Israel having been superseded in the economy of salvation as "economic supersessionism".[1] Soft, or economic supersessionism focuses on the notion of Israel having completed her God-given task now that Christ has come. However, it begs the inevitable question, who next will God ditch once they have completed their divinely-ordained task?

But perhaps the most objectionable and harsh expression of supersessionism, which is strongly triumphalist in nature, is so-called "hard supersessionism, which Soulen refers to in his book as "punitive supersessionism". This view states that because of her disobedience and wickedness the divine promises given to biblical Israel have been taken away and given instead to the Church (as I noted in my Introduction, those espousing this view rarely emphasise the accompanying curses, only the blessings). In an earlier chapter Colin Barne poignantly explains where this can lead, highlighting its ultimate expression, or denouement, in the triumphalist form of supersessionism evident among the European churches which helped make the Holocaust possible. Strikingly, Christians who harshly declare God has punished the Jewish people, taking everything away from them, and finishing with them forever (such language is not a

189

straw man; I've encountered it within a Christian context three times in the past week alone) in some ways echo the language of the Islamist. What the Islamist seeks vis-à-vis Israel and the Jewish people is little different from some of the views in Holocaust Europe Barnes cites. An Islamic understanding of God's unfolding revelation creates an environment in which triumphalist supersessionism can thrive. Islam believes Allah first revealed himself and entrusted this revelation to the Jews but latter took it away and gave it to the Christian. Their distortion of the revelation resulted in Allah entrusting "the final revelation", the Koran, to Mohammed and Islam. Yet historically Islam has, arguably (in some countries at least), been more tolerant of the Jews. To be sure, today's Islamic extremists seek Israel's destruction and display a breath-taking form of anti-Semitism, while Jews' *dhimmi* (permitted but inferior) status in Muslim lands has been well-documented. Yet in some Muslim lands over the centuries Jews have arguably been treated far better than in some Christian lands. Thus, Christianity's punitive supersessionist history and excesses, including some Christian anti-Zionists and Arab Christians who express a particularly punitive or triumphalist form of anti-Judaic supersessionism in their claims to be the *new* Israel, is closer in tone to more extreme versions of Islam than in the greater historical sweep of that religion. Such demonisation of the Jewish people by some Christians certainly does not bode well for ministries involved in Jewish evangelism, Messianic relations with both the Church and the wider Jewish world, and good Jewish-Christian relations.

CHAPTER 8

Apostolic Jewish-Christian Hermeneutics and Supersessionism[1]

Jacob Prasch

Many people looking at the issue of replacement theology tend to do so from an historical, theological or ethnic perspective. Fewer explore the issue from a hermeneutical angle. Thus my aim is to explore how, throughout its history, the Church has often failed to employ the methods of biblical interpretation practised by the Apostles and a Jewish first century Church. This survey offers two observations relating to the wider issue of supersessionism, one directly, the other indirectly. First, how a shift away from the first century Church's interpretation of the Scriptures has given rise to a form of allegorical (symbolic) interpretation of the Bible which has contributed to the rise of supersessionism. Meanwhile, this supersessionism has resulted in much of the Church ditching a Jewish interpretation of Scripture,

---

[1] This chapter was constructed from a conference paper and several lectures delivered by Jacob Prasch at Midlands Bible College, UK. The material has been organised, edited and adapted for this volume by the editor with approval of the final manuscript from the speaker.

resulting in it missing out considerably in its interpretation and application of the Bible.

TWO HERMENEUTICAL SCHOOLS

During the Patristic period (the 2nd to 8th centuries) two separate schools of hermeneutics emerged, one associated with the city of Antioch, the other with Alexandria, in what is now Egypt. Both schools would eventually come to dominate how the Church, at different times during much of its history, interpreted the Bible.

The Antiochene school, generally followed by the Eastern Church Fathers, emphasised a literal approach to the interpretation of the Bible. The Alexandrian school, on the other hand, took a more symbolic approach in how it interpreted Scripture. This allegorical hermeneutic (a mystical approach which moved beyond the plain, literal meaning to seek a hidden, deeper meaning and base doctrines on it) already existed within Judaism, as expressed by Philo, a Jew who lived in Alexandria. While neither school offered a hermeneutical methodology fully faithful to that practised by the Apostles and the New Testament Church, nonetheless the Antiochene school strayed away less from Scripture (and its interpretation) than its Alexandrian counterpart because, being more literal in its interpretation of the Bible, it was less prone to error.

Eventually, the Alexandrian school became the dominant approach to the Bible during the medieval Church period. This was because after the Emperor Constantine pseudo-Christianised the Roman Empire in the fourth century, the theologian Augustine of Hippo (AD 354-430) redefined Christianity by drawing on the thought of the Greek philosopher Plato. Platonic thought, which was the dominant worldview at the time, fitted in nicely with the Alexandrian school's emphasis on the allegorical interpretation of the Bible so favoured by the likes of Philo, Clement and Origen. It is important to note that, to this day, replacement theology draws upon this Alexandrian approach, allegorising and spiritualising passages in the Bible relating to Israel so that instead they are appropriated as promises for the Church.

The Alexandrian allegorical approach suited the purposes of medieval Roman Catholicism, especially the papal office, very well. Its emphasis on a mystical, subjective interpretation of Scripture and a *sensus plenior* (deeper, hidden meaning) went hand in hand with the view that biblical interpretation was the privy domain of a pope who claimed to be the direct heir of the Apostle Peter (who Catholics regard as the very first pope). It allowed the pope to speak as if from the chair of Peter himself (this is known as *ex cathedra*). In other words, when the pope makes a theological declaration it is regarded as infallible. Actually, I can show you plenty of popes who contradicted other popes, but of course they do not like to discuss that too much.

Thus, for hundreds of years, stretching from the end of the Patristic era to the Reformation, the dominant intellectual and hermeneutical approach to the Bible was based on medieval scholasticism and heavily influenced by the Alexandrian school. It resulted in a form of hermeneutics which drew heavily on symbolism, and indeed made symbolism and type the basis for *new* doctrine, rather than the correct approach, which is to utilise symbolism and typology to illustrate *existing* doctrines. The result was a form of medieval Gnosticism[2] whereby a medieval Church taught

---

[2] Editor's note: Gnosticism was originally an early Church heresy claiming salvation came through secret knowledge imparted to a chosen few. The

doctrines on the basis of secret knowledge, or allegorical interpretation, which was the private realm of the pope and Catholic elites. I have seen this same hermeneutic, which emphasises special, secret insight by the leadership, among hyper-Pentecostals and my fellow Charismatics, most notably the Kansas City Prophets, who do something very similar. They take a passage out of context, spiritualising and imbuing it with a subjective, mystical meaning to suit their own purposes, thus creating a pretext.

In the sixteenth century the Reformers rejected this approach to the Bible, ditching allegorical interpretation and instead taking a strongly literalist line, much like John Calvin's commentary of a piece of secular literature, Seneca's *De Clementia*. Thus, with the Reformation we see an important historical shift within the Church, from an Alexandrian to a more Antiochene approach, focusing on the plain, literal meaning of Scripture. This Western Protestant focus on the plain meaning, history and language of the Bible text is known as grammatico-historical interpretation.

Western grammatico-historical interpretation is all well and good, but from the perspective of first century Jewish Christianity I contend it is right in what it confirms yet wrong in what it omits. It allows people to see the basic truth and as such pointed people back to the Gospel. The grammatico-historical approach focused on many important things, such as the literal meaning of the text, context, induction over deduction, exegesis (interpretation of a biblical text) over *eisegesis* (reading something into a biblical text not there), and so on, and the essentials of this approach are correct. But it

---

nature of this esoteric knowledge, or *gnosis*, which adherents claimed Jesus came to impart, was that those who received it were divine beings.

did not travel far enough down the road towards restoring a first century Jewish-Christian hermeneutic.

Let me put it this way: if you work in a corner shop, you only need arithmetic; but if you want to be a rocket scientist, you need calculus. Both arithmetic and calculus are mathematics, but the latter takes the discipline of mathematics much further. Likewise, if you want to understand, say, properly apocalyptic literature in the Bible, you cannot limit a study of it to the grammatico-historical approach. Quite simply, you will never fully understand Jewish apocalyptic literature if you only interpret it with the linguistic and historical tools of grammatico-historical interpretation. Something more is needed, which some people began to realise some time after the Reformation.

RENEWED INTEREST IN JEWISH HERMENEUTICS

There have been efforts stretching back for some four hundred years to restore a Jewish understanding of biblical interpretation. One of the first major figures to attempt this was an Englishman, a Puritan by the name of John Lightfoot, who wrote a midrashic commentary during the time of Cromwell. Another Puritan, John Robinson, a chaplain to the Puritan Fathers who sailed on the *Mayflower* to the North America, was of the opinion that "there is more light in God's Word than we presently see". He understood there were things the Apostles knew concerning the Scriptures which the Church had lost sight of. Such Puritans believed the Reformation's emphasis on *sola scriptura*[3] was important, that

---

[3] Literally "Scripture only", a Reformation emphasis upon the Bible as the final authority on all issues of Christian belief and practice, rather than other authorities (e.g. the church, papal decree).

it had helped put the Church back on the right track to appropriating correct biblical interpretation. But what was needed was to continue travelling *further* down that track. The Puritans and several others recognised, for the most part, this had not happened in any significant way.

It was not until the nineteenth century, with the emergence of the early dispensationalists and the Plymouth Brethren, that a New Testament Jewish-Christian hermeneutic took a closer step. These people began to take a perspective of Scripture that closely resembles what I would call *midrash*, which was how I believe the New Testament Church viewed Scripture and handled typology. (The term and concept of midrash is introduced to us in 2 Chronicles 13:22, where it is translated "treatise". Although Kings and Chronicles are largely synoptic in their structural delimitation of narratives, the Books of Kings emphasise the account of a royal reign from a *biographical* perspective, while the Books of Chronicles places more emphasis on the *historical* perspective. In the parallel biographical account of Abijah in Kings we are synoptically informed of the historical deeds of Abijah in Chronicles, yet Chronicles informs us the deeds are further recorded midrashically by an obscure figure known to us as Iddo.) This was probably the closest the Gentile church has come to interpreting correctly the Scriptures as a Jewish book, like the Apostles did. Sadly, the Plymouth Brethren, once a dynamic movement, largely disintegrated over time, which is a tragedy for a variety of reasons, not least their many virtues.

Aside from these Church efforts, there were also several scholarly (particularly German) attempts to engage in a Jewish interpretation of the New Testament. Yet such efforts soon became bogged down in academic debate.

More recently, however, the Jewish scholar Jacob
Neusner has argued that the New Testament represents an
important, even pivotal, body of Second Temple period
Jewish literature located between the intertestamental Jewish
writings and the post-New Testament rabbinic writings.
Many rabbis dismiss the New Testament as a Gentile
distortion of the Jewish Scriptures, but when major academic
figures such as Neusner and others argue that the New
Testament is thoroughly Jewish in its literary forms and
genre, this is a powerful apologetic in Jewish evangelism.
Importantly, it should be noted such scholars do not believe
in Jesus, they simply seek to explore the New Testament from
the perspective of Jewish scholarship. Nonetheless, they
reach the conclusion that the New Testament is, to all intents
and purposes, thoroughly Jewish. Not only does this directly
contradict Protestant liberal views that the New Testament
narratives (particularly in the gospels) are fabrications by a
later Gentile church, but more importantly, it highlights how
major Jewish scholars increasingly recognise the thoroughly
Jewish nature of the New Testament. In short, the New
Testament Church is a Jewish Church, which in turn has led
to increasing academic interest in the Jewish roots of
Christianity. Significantly, some of these studies also identify
a New Testament hermeneutic reflecting the culture of first
century Palestinian Judaism, but which much of the Church
today has lost.

EARLY RABBINIC HERMENEUTICS AND THE
NEW TESTAMENT

In recent years, with the discovery and study of the Dead Sea
Scrolls at Qumran, scholars have noted the manner in which
the New Testament handles and interprets the Old

Testament, which parallels how the Dead Sea Scrolls handle the Old Testament. When we consider this New Testament use of the Old, it is noticeably quite different to how much of the Western Church traditionally interprets the Bible. (Incidentally, I believe one of the gravest threats to the Church today is how many leaders do not follow an apostolic model of ecclesiology, increasingly drawing on a medieval Church model and emphasising things such as contemplative prayer, regarded as the means to restore the Christian ideal. Instead of going back to the book of Acts and the New Testament, they draw on the monasticism and mysticism of the Dark Ages.)

Liberal Protestant scholars, particularly people like Rudolf Bultmann in the early twentieth century, focused on what we call the *Sitz im Leben*, or life setting and context, of the Bible text. But their approach (known as form criticism) assumed most of the narratives in the gospels were the invention (or embellishment) of a *later*, less Jewish Church. For the form critics, then, a focus on Sitz im Leben was an attempt to get back to the life setting of what they assumed was a New Testament text written by a late first and early second century, predominantly Gentile Church, rather than the Sitz im Leben of the early apostolic (and thus Jewish) Church described in the Bible.

But recent studies of the Dead Sea Scrolls demonstrate how the New Testament is *not* an invention of a later Gentile Church. Rather, its literary style, together with the manner in which the New Testament authors handled the Old Testament is *thoroughly* Jewish. Thus, a *peshat-pesher* approach (which we will look at shortly) eventually forced J.A.T. Robinson, the noted liberal scholar, to reverse his position on the dating of the Gospels, acknowledging they had to be the product of a much earlier Jewish church, rather than a fabrication or embellishment by a later Gentile church.

So it is essential we take into account the Sitz im Leben of the text and when it was written – not the setting postulated by the form critics, but the thoroughly Jewish milieu in which the New Testament was written, as demonstrated by the Dead Sea Scrolls. So when we focus on the Sitz im Leben of the New Testament writings, we are focusing on how they are culturally, literally and theologically the product of early first century Jewish society. Also, and very importantly, we must not focus just on the cultural setting of the text, but also how the authors' historical, cultural and theological backgrounds led them to interpret Scripture. Consider how, for example, Paul was a disciple of Rabbi Gamaliel, the grandson of Hillel. There were two major Pharisee schools and Hillel represented one of them, and this theological and hermeneutical background inevitably had a bearing on how Paul handled Scripture. Therefore, you simply cannot divorce biblical interpretation from the Jewish Sitz im Leben in which the New Testament was written.

So how did rabbis in the first century Church interpret Scripture? The essential principles of midrashic hermeneutics which helped to frame the hermeneutics of the Apostolic Church are the Seven Middoth of Rabbi Hillel, from the rabbinic academy where Rabbi Shaul of Tarsus (Paul The Apostle) was schooled by Gamaliel. The two most important of these are *Qal wahomer* (light to heavy; general truths become amplified in importance in weighty situations) and *Binyan 'ab mishene kethubim* (building a doctrinal argument from two texts; where cognate circumstances, idioms and metaphors occur the texts referentially relate and the same exegetical considerations must apply to both). Rabbis also employed what we refer to as the *mashal-nimshal* format. A mashal is a description of something from everyday life (for example, something from nature), while nimshal is its spiritual interpretation or application. Let me illustrate it thus:

> Like a gold ring in a pig's snout [mashal]
> is a beautiful woman without discretion. [nimshal]
> (Prov 11:22 ESV)

> A word fitly spoken [nimshal]
> is like apples of gold in a setting of silver. [mashal]
> (Prov 25:11 ESV)

We can employ this approach in our interpretation of the parables. Western hermeneutics has sought to understand parables in terms of correspondence: high correspondence - low correspondence. But a first century Jew would not have approached parable the way a Western post-Enlightenment scholar would. Instead, they would have explored parable from the point of view of mashal-nimshal. Indeed, the parables are simply elongated mashals. A mashal *is* a proverb – in fact, in Hebrew the book of Proverbs is called *Mishle (Shlomoh)*, the Proverbs (of Solomon), or the book of mashals. To the Jewish mind in biblical days, a parable would simply have been regarded as an elongated mashal, expressed in the form of a story. This was central to their understanding and interpretation.

This would have been particularly relevant to Jesus' listenership when He spoke the parables. In first century Jewish society, although people were literate, the *Am ha'Aretz* (common people, literally "the people of the land") would learn things by rote, that is, through stories. So by teaching in parables Jesus was appealing to the Am ha'Aretz. He would take theological concepts and make them comprehensible and practical for ordinary people. Other rabbis also used parables, but unlike Jesus they would not explain or interpret this to people.

Consider Jesus' interpretation of the parable of the vineyard, in which the owner's servants and son were killed by the workers. The Pharisees knew He spoke it about them (Matt 21:45), in other words, they were able to interpret the parable, but they kept silent. Interpretation, or knowledge, was for the initiated only, and so they refused to teach it to the everyday folk. You see, knowledge is power, but the Pharisees kept their knowledge to themselves to help retain their position as not only a theological, but also a social, economic and political elite. In Luke 11:52 we read how the scribes sought to retain the keys of knowledge. So when Jesus came preaching and teaching, He was, in effect, taking away from the Jewish religious teachers the hermeneutical keys and giving them to the Apostles, the poor people He preached to, and even (eventually) the Gentiles. Imagine how this upset the applecart!

Another feature of rabbinic interpretation is *peshat* and *pesher*. Peshat is the simple, straightforward meaning, while pesher is what it actually means theologically or spiritually. A Western interpretation of John's gospel would differ considerably from that of a first century Jew. Consider, for example, the similarities between the Creation account in Genesis (peshat) and the book of John, which the evangelist[4] presents as a new creation (pesher). At Creation God walks the earth and Adam hears Him walking in the garden, while in John's gospel God walks the earth in the new creation. In Genesis, God separates the light from dark, while in John

---

[4] The technical term for an author of one of the four gospels.

201

God likewise comes to separate light from darkness. In the Creation narrative you have the small light and the great light, while in John's new creation you have Jesus (the greater light) and John the Baptist (the lesser light). In Genesis the Spirit moves on the water and brings forth the creation, while in John 3:5, when Jesus talks of being born of the water and spirit, the Spirit moves on the water and brings forth a new creation. In the Creation narrative, on the third day, God does a miracle with water; and so in the new creation narrative in John, on the third day of the wedding of Canaan, God does a miracle with water.

God begins his first plan for mankind with a nuptial, a wedding, between Adam and Eve. In John, God begins His second plan for mankind with a nuptial, when Jesus launches His ministry at the wedding at Canaan. In Genesis there is the tree of life. Ancient sources inform us that in Judaism the fig tree represents the Tree of Life. Now when Jesus tells Nathanael, "I saw you under the fig tree" (John 1:48), what did He mean? A strictly literal interpretation would not see anything significant about this event, but there is more to this narrative than the literal meaning. Jesus indeed saw Nathanael under a literal fig tree, but what He was saying to Nathanael in Hebrew metaphor was this: "I saw you from the Garden, the creation, from the foundation of the World. I saw you under the fig tree, the Tree of Life, right at the beginning."

Now all this makes perfect sense to a Jewish Christian in the first century, or to a Messianic Jew, but it has lost this sense to much of the Western Church. Instead of taking a hermeneutical approach from the Apostles, they draw on an approach from the sixteenth century.

Another example can be found in Hosea 11:1 which states, "When Israel was a child, I loved him, and out of

Egypt I called my son." Note how Hosea makes a retroactive reference back to the Exodus under Moses. Yet Matthew (2:15) takes the same quote from Hosea and, in the context of Jesus' nativity, he says this is about *Jesus* coming out of Egypt. According to liberal Western exegesis and its focus on history, Matthew takes the text completely out of context in an unscientific way. But actually, within a first century Jewish understanding this is a classic case of the peshat-pesher approach. The Exodus (peshat) points to Jesus (pesher). Jewish hermeneutics would have followed a motif, in this case the Exodus event. But this motif begins, not with Jesus or the Exodus itself, but rather with Abraham. During a famine Abraham goes to Egypt, God judges Pharaoh, and Abraham *comes out* of Egypt. Abraham's biological descendants, the children of Israel, also go to Egypt during a famine. Likewise, they *come out* under Moses, and again God judges a wicked king, Pharaoh. It happens to Abraham, the father of all who believe, and so it also happens to the nation of Israel, his descendants. Likewise, Jesus fits the same pattern: God judges Herod, another wicked king, and the Messiah comes out of Egypt. Moreover, in his discussion in 1 Corinthians 10, when we are saved, Paul says, metaphorically *we also* come out of Egypt (Egypt being a picture of the world, while Pharaoh is a picture of Satan, the god of the world).

Thus the Exodus motif continues. As Moses made covenant with blood, sprinkled it and took the people of Israel out of Egypt through the water into the Promised Land, so Jesus covers us with the blood of the Paschal Lamb and takes us through baptism into heaven. At salvation we – the Church – are also called out of Egypt. Also, in the Passion narratives we see a typological recycling of Paschal themes using a peshet–pesher format, the Exodus providing the peshat and the execution of the Messiah furnishing the pesher.

But it does not end there; there is also a future exodus. In a Passover seder there is the commemoration of the judgments of Egypt to this day: darkness, blood, frogs, the cup of God's wrath filling up. And these same judgements on Egypt are replayed eschatologically in the book of Revelation. Moreover, the manner in which Pharaoh's magicians counterfeited the miracles of Moses and Aaron is a picture, a type, of the way the Antichrist and false prophets will counterfeit the miracles of Jesus and His witnesses (Matt 24:24). Also, why did they bring Joseph's bones out of Egypt? The dead in Christ rise first. It is a picture of the *parousia* (the second coming), in other words, it is a motif (the same motif, that of Exodus). So as we have noted, the Exodus motif can be applied to Abraham or Israel, but it equally applies to Jesus. Paul also takes the same Exodus motif and applies it to the Church in 1 Corinthians 10, while Revelation takes the same motif, the Exodus story, and applies it to the rapture and resurrection. This is quite different from the way some in the Western Church relying solely on sixteenth century hermeneutics might understand Hosea 11:1 and Matthew's use of this text.

Having mentioned the end times, it is worth at this stage dwelling a little further on a Jewish understanding of eschatology. The intertestamental period saw the development of a preoccupation with the end times (*eschaton*) and the messianic age, which much of the Church today has lost. Moreover, Western theologians tend to insist on the need to hold to one of four main approaches to the study of the end times. Consider how a typical Western college or seminary will detail four main approaches to end-time prophesy: preterism, historicism, idealism (symbolism) and futurism. Preterism says it has already happened (in grammar, the preterite denotes a verb in the past tense). So it is argued the events described in Revelation occurred in the first century at the time of the Fall of Jerusalem in AD 70. Thus, there is no Antichrist, no falling away, or Great Tribulation. All this happened in the first century, it is maintained. Historicism, on the other hand, is the view the Reformers favoured, which focuses on an *ongoing* historical dynamic featuring the pope and Roman Catholicism. Thus, historicists regard the Antichrist as an institution, rather than a person. Meanwhile, idealists (symbolists) see Revelation as holding symbolic truths and ideals, rather than a description of actual historical events, whether in the past or present. Revelation, then, is regarded more or less as poetry, designed to encourage us in times of persecution and hardship and to assure us during these periods that the Lord is coming. Then there is futurism, associated with the popular end times fiction series by Tim LeHaye. This is the view that everything (or nearly everything) described in Revelation is yet to happen.

So a Western mindset expects you to choose one of these eschatological positions. However, the Jewish approach says it is not a case of choosing *any one*, but rather *all four*. Consider how in Matthew 24 Jesus spoke eschatologically of the abomination of desolation spoken of by Daniel, something that had already happened. So the abomination of desolation is presented by Jesus as both in the past *and* the future, preterist and futurist. Meanwhile, we see various examples or types of the abomination of desolation throughout history, whether that prophesied by Daniel (fulfilled under Antiochus IV Epiphanes), Pompey's desecration of the Temple before Jesus was born, Titus's destruction of Jerusalem in AD 70, Julian the Apostate's attempt to rebuild the temple, or what Jesus prophesied about in the eschatological future in Matthew 24. Meanwhile, at this time on the Temple Mount is the Dome of the Rock, which has an inscription stating God has no son. However, 1 John 2:22 states he who denies the Father-Son relationship is Antichrist. So from a Christian perspective the inscription in the Dome is an affront, an abomination to the very central revelation of Christianity, that Jesus is the Son of God.

Thus in all these cases, just as in historicism, we see an historical, repeated expression of the Antichrist. Meanwhile, the events described in Revelation also draw on catastrophic events which occurred in the first century, at a time when the Church desperately needed encouragement. And so we see an idealist, symbolic comfort for suffering Christians. So in the Western mind, you tend to hold to any one of these four eschatological positions. But actually, the truth is to be found in all four, and the Jewish approach is not to be forced into making an artificial choice like this.

Akin to apocalyptic, midrash relates both to the hermeneutical method and literary genre (type of literature) bearing the name. Just as we have apocalyptic material defined from a literary perspective, requiring hermeneutical considerations appropriate to symbolic entities, numbers, typologies, and metaphors for conflict with anti-heroes and protagonists in portions of Ezekiel, Isaiah, Joel, Daniel and Zechariah, so in the New Testament we have a book composed in the genre bearing the name – the Book of Revelation – which is a treatise drawing on Old Testament apocalyptic themes. Likewise, the epistle of Jude is a midrashic treatise. It employs pesher interpretations of Old Testament motifs, applying them to the circumstances being addressed in the early Church.

Midrashic pesher is nowhere more indispensible than in eschatology. New Testament eschatology essentially borrows the themes of the final days of pre-Exilic Samaria in 721 BC and the final days of pre-exilic Judah in 586 BC from the books of Isaiah, Joel, Micah, Daniel, Jeremiah, and Ezekiel, as well as the events of 70 AD, and applies them all with midrashic pesher to the eschatological Church. These themes include "Fallen is Babylon", the destruction of the temple, and the pandemonium and confusion generated by a proliferation of false prophets among backslidden Israelites.

New Testament eschatology, then, applies a pesher interpretation to future prophetic events, reinterpreting them as a future repetition of past events which are recorded in biblical history. Hence, efforts to explain New Testament eschatology by solely conventional grammatical-historical interpretation are implausible and have led to a reduction of a three-dimensional portrait of prophetic events to a two-dimensional portrait among those conservative Evangelicals favouring a sixteenth century exegetical approach, and to a one-dimensional reduction by the liberal proponents of higher critical presupposition. Yet when observed midrashically, New Testament eschatology fits the hermeneutics of Qumran eschatology like a glove. Thus, hermeneutics should not be extricated from Sitz im Leben.

CONCLUDING THOUGHTS

Within biblical hermeneutics we have noted two errors. There are those who base their doctrine on a symbolic or spiritual interpretation, and as such follow the Alexandrian school of interpretation. This is, hermeneutically at least, where supersessionism originates and finds sustenance, by allegorising promises for Israel in the Bible and spiritualising them for the Church.

Yet in the Jewish hermeneutics of the first century, the hermeneutics used by Jesus and Paul, you *never* base a doctrine on a type or a shadow. Instead, you use a type or a shadow to illustrate doctrine or to illuminate it. For instance, we could set a Passover *seder* table and, comparing it with the last supper, illustrate the doctrine of atonement and substitutionary propitiation through the typology and the symbolism of the meal. But we do not base the doctrine on the symbolism, rather we use the symbolism to illuminate the doctrine. In Gnosticism it is the complete opposite: you base the doctrine on some kind of a symbolic meaning; you essentially negate the literal meaning in favour of a spiritual one. However, in *midrash* you *amplify* the literal meaning in light of the spiritual meaning. You *never* negate the literal, which is how the Jewish approach differs from allegorical interpretation.

Neither do you ever base a doctrine on a type, or allegory, or hyperbole. This is deadly and it is dangerous. You use them to illustrate a doctrine. So pesher must not be confused, then, with Gnosticism. Ironically, at about the same time Christian hermeneutics deviated from a New Testament hermeneutical approach in the Patristic period, so too Rabbinic Judaism deviated away from this path, resulting in a much more allegorical approach.

Then there are those who follow rigidly a strict grammatico-historical interpretation, focusing solely on the literal meaning. They state, "When the plain sense of Scripture makes sense, seek no further sense", or "There are many applications of a Scripture, but only one interpretation". But who says it has to be this way? Rabbis said there are multiple interpretations. With whom did Jesus agree? Consider, Jesus said "No sign will be given to this generation accept the sign of the prophet Jonah". Yet consider this statement synoptically. In one place the sign of the prophet Jonah is three days and three nights, in another place, it is Nineveh, where the Gentiles repented, contrasted with the Jews who refused to do so when Jesus preached. Thus, Jesus gives two entirely different interpretations for the sign of Jonah. In short, they are not mutually exclusive, they are simultaneously true. If I were to take a literal, Western approach, there would be only one interpretation. But Jesus Christ happens to disagree. He taught the way the rabbis did. By ditching Israel, we ditch the Jewish root of the Church. As a negative bi-product of ditching the root, we miss out considerably on how a first century Jewish hermeneutic enhances our understanding of the Scriptures.

Further Reading

For an understanding of the Sitz im Leben of Judaism in the first century, consider E.P. Sanders' *Paul and Palestinian Judaism,* and also *Jesus and Judaism.* Alfred Edersheim's *Life and Times of Jesus the Messiah* is a nineteenth century work but nonetheless provides useful insight into the cultural and religious world of first century Jews. Notable also is James H. Charlesworth, an Evangelical within the Ivy League, who notes a strong Jewish element within New Testament interpretation. Walter Kaiser's *Uses of the Old Testament in the New* offers a detailed treatment of the subject. For a very useful book exploring the Jewish nature of New Testament interpretation, see Richard Longenecker's *Biblical Exegesis in the Apostolic Period.* Finally, two books exploring the Jewish roots of the Church are Marvin Wilson's *Our Father Abraham: Jewish Roots of the Christian Faith,* and Daniel Grubers' *The Church and the Jews: The Biblical Relationship.*

CHAPTER 9

A Calvinist Considers Israel's Right to the Land

Stephen M. Vantassel

To those familiar with Calvinist theology, it may seem unusual to be reading a defense of Israel's right to the land from that theological tradition. Historically Calvinism, and its umbrella view known as Covenant[1] or Reformed theology[2], has been allied with amillennial[3] and postmillennial views of eschatology. Reformed theology contends that Israel, as a distinct covenantal community, has been subsumed in and superseded by the Church. Since the Church, which lacks

---

[1] Paul Enns, *The Moody Handbook of Theology* (Chicago: Moody Press, 1989), 503, 510

[2] For the purposes of this paper I am treating, Covenantalists, and Reformed theologians as synonymous.

[3] Amillennialism believes we are presently in the millennium. The thousand years is a figurative number. At the end of the Millennium there will be an outbreak of evil and an anti-Christ which will be followed by Christ's return to establish his final and perfect rule. Postmillennialism, of which amillennialism is a subset, believes that the Church will grow in influence until it establishes Christ's rule over the world. It is an optimistic eschatology. At the end, Armageddon will occur followed by Christ's return and establishment of the New Heavens and New Earth. The Reformed Reader website has a chart of the different positions at http://www.reformedreader.org/mchart.htm (last accessed 23 April 2013).

both ethnic and territorial claims, has replaced Israel (Gal 6:16), Israel has lost any continued right to the land.

So how can someone from a Calvinist perspective defend Israel's right to the land given that such a position has been traditionally the domain of premillennialists and dispensationalists? Perhaps the answer lies in my relative newness to Calvinism. I was raised in an Arminian, dispensational and premillennial espousing household. I adopted Calvinism after having become convinced that the preponderance of Scriptural evidence teaches that Christ chose me before I chose Him. Rest assured, my transition was neither sudden nor flippant. I actually fought the shift for years because of Calvinism's support of infant sprinkling. I figured if Calvinists could not accurately determine the meaning of a simple a word like "baptism"[4] then how could one trust their perspective on ideas as complicated as predestination and free-will? Nevertheless, an error in one element of a theological system does not necessarily falsify the entire theology. Just to be clear, readers should understand that my support of Calvinism does not extend to include Reformed[5] or Presbyterian theology *in toto*. It simply centers on the doctrines of Grace as defined by The Calvinist Tulip, Total Depravity, Unconditional Election, Limited Atonement, Irresistible Grace, and Perseverance of the Saints. [6] So to prevent tarnishing Reformed theology with an anti-

---

[4] The religious movement known as Presbyterianism traces its heritage to Calvin which expresses baptism by sprinkling. In contrast, Greek Orthodox Christians understand the meaning of baptism as demonstrated by their immersing their infants in the waters of baptism.

[5] Reformed theologians are also known as covenantal theologians.

[6] I am pleased to learn that premillennial views of eschatology, while not common, are concordant with Covenantal views. Barry E. Horner, *Future Israel: Why Christian Anti-Judaism Must Be Challenged* (Nashville:

land view, I will use the term "replacement theology" to designate the view that rejects the continued validity of the Jews right to the land that was promised to Abraham (Gen 12: 15).

Before delving into the controversy concerning Israel's right to the Promised Land, a word of caution should be heard. I think it is essential that readers recognise that the debate over Israel's right to the land is essentially a hermeneutical conflict.[7] In other words, advocates on both sides of the debate, though sharing similar views of Scripture, disagree with how that Scripture should be interpreted. On one side, replacement theologians adopt a typological reading of scripture and therefore tend to read Old Testament eschatological prophecies concerning Israel as ultimately being fulfilled in and through the Church. The people of God in the Old Testament are called Israel, but in the New Testament they are called the Church. On the other, non-replacement theologians take a more direct reading of Scripture and therefore tend to keep Israel and the Church as separate covenantal entities. The upshot of this is the importance in recognising that one's hermeneutical preference will significantly determine whether one adopts a replacement or non-replacement view of Israel. Acknowledgement of interpretation's role does not mean that the answer is pre-determined. It just means that there are

---

Broadman and Holmann, 2007), 88. See also Willem A. Van Gemeren, "Israel as the Hermeneutical Crux in the Interpretation of Prophecy (Ii)" in *Westminster Theological Journal* 46 no. 2 (1984), 254-5, who states that Calvin did not have a clear theology on Israel's place in eschatology and observes that some Reformed theologians in the 17th century looked for Israel's restoration to the land, 257.

[7] Norman L. Geisler, Church, *Last Things*, 4 vols., Systematic Theology, vol. 4 (Minneapolis, MN: Bethany House, 2005), 413-458. Geisler provides an excellent introduction to the issue.

differences between the two positions that are so foundational to one's understanding of Scripture that to change positions requires one to fundamentally reorient his/her approach to Scripture. It also means that the answers are not as clear or obvious as dogmatists on both sides of the controversy would like us to believe because our preferred hermeneutical model biases our perception of the scriptural data. It is similar to two people, one wearing red glasses and the other blue, each trying to convince the other that the flower before them is red or blue respectively. As heated as our opinion regarding Israel's right to the land may become, we must remember that this is a fight between fellow Christians. I do not believe that one's salvation is determined by one's convictions in this area. In other words, Christians can (and do) disagree over the status of Israel's right to the land without losing their status as faithful followers of Christ.

As noted above, replacement theologians argue that the Old Testament promises to Israel are transferred to the church. All Old Testament prophecies regarding the Israel's right to the land, and other elements of her national life should be interpreted in figurative or typological terms awaiting their fulfillment in the New Covenant. Replacement theologians contend that the predictions concerning Israel were ultimately fulfilled in the person of Christ. Christ, in effect, became Israel and since the Church is the body of Christ, the Church is the new Israel. So when replacement theologians read Genesis 12:1-3 and 15:13-21, they believe that those promises were universalised into the Church. They base their understanding on three inter-related points.[8]

---

[8] I am relying heavily on the paper presented by Robert L. Reymond, "Who Are the Real Heirs to the Land Promises of Holy Scripture?" in *Advancing Reformation Truth and Spirituality* (Fort Lauderdale, FL: Coral

First, they contend that the Church has replaced Israel because her disobedience voided the old covenant requiring God to make a new one (Jer 31:31-32). Any chance Israel had to restore her position in the old covenant and retain its promise of land was demolished when she rejected her Messiah (Matt 21:37-45; Mark 12:1-12; Luke 20:9-19).[9] In fact, some replacement theologians contend that Paul actually acknowledges that God has rejected Israel for all eternity (1 Thess 2:14-16).[10]

Second, Israel's special status before God is no longer in effect because Christ eliminated ethnic distinctions in the New Covenant. They cite Paul, who said that in Christ there is neither Jew nor Greek (Gal 3:28), circumcision or uncircumcision (Gal 6:15). Gentiles are no longer to be excluded from the Commonwealth of Israel (Eph 2:12). God, they claim, is no longer interested in your heritage; He is only concerned with your relationship to His son, Jesus Christ. Furthermore, replacement theologians maintain that continued emphasis on ethnic distinctions between Jew and Gentile undermines our unity created in Christ. For additional support, replacement theologians point out that the New Testament writers identify the Church as the new Israel by their re-appropriating Old Testament terminology

---

Ridge Presbyterian Church, 2006). Although written from an Adventist position, see also Hans K. LaRondelle, *The Israel of God in Prophecy: Principles of Prophetic Interpretation*, Andrews University Monographs, Studies in Religion, vol. XIII (Berrien Springs, MI: Andrews University Press, 1983).

[9] In the parable, the landowner represents God, the vineyard, Israel (Isa 5:7), and the farmers, the leaders. Reymond claims that the language in Matt 21:37 and Mark 12:6 suggests that God was giving Israel one final chance to obey His commands.

[10] Reymond, 9. See also Horner, 37-38 who finds this interpretation in *The Seed of Abraham* (c. 1950) by A. Pieters.

to the Church as Peter did in 1 Peter 2:9.[11] The logic is flawless. If Israel no longer retains its identity as the people of God then in like manner, she forfeits any right to land.

Finally, replacement theologians ask that if the issue of Israel's right to the land was so important, why were the Apostles so silent on the subject? Why does the New Testament only speak of land in a global and not localised manner as would be expected if Israel had a continued right to the land? In Romans 4:13, Paul converts the promise of Abraham's right to Canaan to his inheritance of the whole world.[12] Replacement theologians conclude that since Old Testament Israel becomes the Church in the New, notions of Israel's right to the land become irrelevant. For how can a nation that has been absorbed, or perhaps universalised, into the Church have the right to a particular plot of land when the Church will inherit the entire world?[13]

EVALUATION

At first glance, the replacement argument is quite compelling. Replacement theologians are correct to believe that Israel is under judgment and that Gentiles are saved through the work of Jesus Christ. Additionally, Christ is the center of the New Testament and the fulfillment of O.T. prophecy (Luke 18:31ff; 24:27; John 1:45; Acts 3:18). Despite these

---

[11] Isa 61:6; Exod 19:6. See also the parallel between Isa 65:17 and 2 Pet 3:12-13 New Heavens and Earth.

[12] LaRondelle, 141.

[13] To make the matter more complicated Moshe Weinfield, *The Promise of the Land: The Inheritance of the Land of Canaan by the Israelites*, The Taubman Lectures in Jewish Studies (Berkeley: University of California Press, 1993), 214-215, finds Josephus and Philo transferring the idea of Israel's right to Palestine to Israel's right to the whole world (Ant 1:282: 4:114-116; Book of Jubilees 32:18-19).

commendable positions, replacement theology suffers from problems that fall into two broad categories.

The first category centres on the overall approach taken by the replacement theologians. Academics are frequently accused of turning simple ideas into complicated ones. While undeniable, it is also true that academics love theories that explain everything in a simple way.[14] What could be simpler than replacement theology's view that says all eschatological prophecies pertaining to Israel in the Old Testament actually apply to the Church? I am not arguing that simplicity makes replacement theology wrong. Rather, I am suggesting that it is rare for a simple theory to account for all of the Biblical data. It is analogous to a police detective who is more concerned with wrapping up a case rather than making sure that his theory of the crime accounts for all the available evidence while discounting alternative theories. In other words, good theology must consider alternative theories of the evidence as well as carefully consider the possibility that it may have ignored the significance of some data simply because it did not fit the established theory.[15] Proper theological method must avoid tunnel vision. We do need to have exhaustive knowledge; I doubt we will ever have enough information to come to a definitive conclusion (at least on this side of eternity). But we can strive for and obtain knowledge of sufficient weight and value to arrive at a

---

[14] Gardner speaks of how the coherence of a theory (or its beauty) can convince people to adopt it, Howard Gardner, *Changing Minds: The Art and Science of Changing Our Own and Other People's Minds* (Cambridge, MA: Harvard Business School Publications, 2006). See also Thomas Kuhn, *The Structure of Scientific Revolutions,* Third ed. (Chicago, IL: University of Chicago Press, 1996), and Horner, 292.
[15] Cf. Paul Feyerabend, *Against Method,* Revised ed. (New York: Verso, 1988).

responsible conclusion based upon the preponderance of all the evidence.

The other global difficulty with replacement theology lies in its rejection of direct (commonly referred to as literal) fulfillment of Old Testament prophecies related to Israel. I have already noted how replacement theologians interpret many Old Testament prophecies as typological. The problem with this perspective is that it raises questions about what the original audience understood when those prophecies took place. Consider the Abrahamic covenant (Gen 12:1-3 and 15:13-21). God promised Abraham that he would: receive an heir, obtain a reputation, be a blessing, and receive land. All Christians agree that the first three promises were literally fulfilled. Jesus was a Jew, a physical descendent of Abraham (Matt 1:1). Jesus would be a blessing to many nations, and Jesus would give Abraham a great reputation because Abraham became known as the father of the faith (Rom 4:16).

But why do the replacement theologians deny that the Jews would receive the land of Canaan? Is it not possible that Jesus could be a Davidic King over the physical land of Israel, while simultaneously ruling the nations with a rod of iron as prophesied in Psalm 2? Furthermore, do we really think that David (2 Sam 7), and Micah (Mic 4:1-5:2) and other prophets (Isa 65:17-25; Amos 9:11-15; Ezek 37; Zeph 3:14-20; Zech 14:8-24)[16] conceived a future Davidic kingdom and Jerusalem in only a spiritualised or globalised sense? In other words, did they really believe that God's promise to give Abraham's physical descendents particular land boundaries was an

---

[16] I have added these passages to correct my lack of attention to the prophetical books in my earlier version of this chapter, published in the first edition of this book. Many thanks to Dr. Walter Kaiser for pointing out this oversight.

optional promise?[17] I suggest they did not and if the promises were simply spiritualised or universalised then David and the prophets either completely misunderstood God's revelation[18] or they failed to communicate that revelation in an appropriate way that made the typological or universal claim clear to their respective hearers. I contend that adopting either of the aforementioned options has serious and negative consequences for the interpretation of scripture.

Let us turn to the second category of problems for replacement theologians, namely the inadequacies of their three arguments. They assert that Jeremiah 31:31-32 states that the Old Covenant containing Israel's right to the land has ended. The problem with this interpretation is that Jeremiah was proclaiming the demise of the Mosaic covenant[19] not the Abrahamic covenant, which contained God's promise of Land. Observe that in 31:35-37, God declares that His promise to Israel will end when the sun and stars stop shining, in other words, never. Lest one think that Israel will be a landless nation, Jeremiah 31:38 says that God will restore Jerusalem and that it will be established as His holy city, which will be immune from conquest. 1 Thessalonians 2:14-

---

[17] For a defense of a literal fulfillment of the land promise to Israel see Walter C Kaiser, Jr., "The Promised Land: A Biblical-Historical View" in *Bibliotheca Sacra* 138 no. 552 (1981); Jeffrey L. Townsend, "Fulfillment of the Land of Promise in the Old Testament" in *Bibliotheca Sacra* 142 no. 568 (1985), 324-329. Both also discuss problems and possible solutions with the precise boundaries of the promise.

[18] Hebrews 11:13 says the faithful Old Testament people saw the promises of God from a distance. While they did not understand the promises of God in their entirety, they certainly understood accurately the portions they perceived. Furthermore, the heavenly land or city does not refer to an otherworldly place, but rather to a location where God is visibly and actively ruling (cf. Heb 11:10, 16; 12:22).

[19] LaRondelle,143. Even LaRondelle recognises that it was the Mosaic covenant being superseded.

16 does not help the replacement theologians either. As the context shows, Paul is not condemning Jews in general but only those Jews who are actively opposing the Gospel of Christ.[20] To suggest that Paul was condemning Jews comprehensively flies in the face of not only the 1 Thessalonian testimony but also that of Acts 17:2-5, which explicitly tells us that some Thessalonian Jews accepted Christ.

In their second argument, replacement theologians claim that ethnic identity carries no standing in the New Covenant (Gal 3:28; Eph 2:11-22). Thus if national Israel no longer bears any theological significance then it can no longer have any claim to a geographical heritage. The problem with this interpretation lies in its misunderstanding the force of the Apostle's testimony. Jews in the first century believed that Gentiles had to become Jews (i.e. children of Abraham) in order to gain salvation. To be saved required one to become ethnically Jewish, with all the requirements of circumcision and Mosaic Law keeping entailed in that notion. The problem, as already mentioned, was that by the New Testament period Israel had made salvation (righteousness before God) a combination of ethnicity and obedience to the Law. That is why the New Testament records Christ telling Jews that their lineage to Abraham is not as significant as they think it is. Christ asserts that God could cause stones to be the children of Abraham (Matt 3:9 and parallels). God intended Israel to be the vehicle of salvation not the destination of salvation. Consider how Christ told the

---

[20] Abraham J. Malherbe, *The Letters to the Thessalonians: A New Translation with Introduction and Commentary,* ed. William Foxwell Albright and David Noel Freedman, *The Anchor Bible,* vol. 32B (New York: Doubleday, 2000), 174-9. Malherbe also states that Paul was involved in an intra-Jewish polemic.

Samaritan woman salvation is of the Jews (John 4:22) and how He described the future state of glory in terms of the patriarchs and the Kingdom of Heaven (Matt 8:11). The New Testament separates salvation from race and the Law of Moses. But because the notion of race and law was so tied together with salvation and God's blessing, New Testament writers go to great lengths to show that Gentiles and Jews constitute the People of God (apart from the Law) when they follow Christ. Christ is the barrier breaker. In Christ, we are a chosen people, a holy nation.[21] That is why it says, the Gentiles have been adopted, we have become children of Abraham by faith, not genetics or obedience to the law. Paul declares that Abraham is the father of all who believe (Rom 4:11-12). Galatians 3:29 says that all who belong to Christ are the seed of Abraham. Abraham could rejoice when he saw Christ (John 8:56) because he knew that Christ would be the means through whom all promises to him (described in Gen 12 and 15) would be fulfilled. Certainly, the Gentiles had to repent of their immoral behaviour. They needed to love the true God with all their hearts and their neighbours as themselves. But they did not have to become circumcised and adopt Jewish customs. The Apostles had to correct their compatriots that their Abrahamic lineage and obedience to the Law of Moses did not grant them an automatic pass to salvation nor did Gentiles have to become Jews (through circumcision) in order to become children of Abraham.

The first century Jews were wrong in this view for two reasons. First, faith, not works, justified one before God (Gen 15:6; Hab 2:4). The Old Testament did not require Gentiles to

---

[21] While appreciating Horner's argument that 1 Peter was written primarily to benefit Christian Jews, I contend that 1 Peter was written to converted Gentiles also in order to emphasise the unity and equality of Jews and Gentiles in Christ, Horner 285-290.

become Jews by adopting the laws of Moses as demonstrated by the conversion of Naaman, the Syrian general (2 Kgs 5:1-14), and Nineveh, during Jonah's revival. Gentiles only had to forsake idolatry and the immorality that accompanied it and worship the true God of Israel. God's purpose for Israel was that she would be a light to the Gentiles (Isa 42:6f). Remember, many of the laws of Moses could only be fulfilled if one lived in the land of Palestine. If you lived elsewhere then there was no way to obey them. Those laws were in a sense geographically, and I would argue even temporally limited, in their scope.[22] Once we understand what the Apostles had to confront, we can immediately recognise that many of the passages that appear to downplay the Law and Jewish cultural practices were simply the Apostles' attempt to clarify that faith, not genetics or behavior, was the proper basis for salvation.[23]

Nevertheless, while ethnicity has no value in salvation, it is not irrelevant. Just as gender distinctions remain important after Christ[24], so also ethnicity remains important. For although Gentiles are adopted as children of Abraham, the New Testament still speaks of Jews as ethnically identifiable as demonstrated by the circumcision of Timothy (Acts 16:3) and Paul's Nazirite vow (Acts 18:18). Even the compromise at the Jerusalem Council (Acts 15) reaffirmed ethnic distinctions as it provided a way for Jewish and Gentile believers to maintain positive relations through cultural sensitivity. Put another way, I as an American, share a faith in Christ with

---

[22] I remember reading this point in an article in the Westminster Theological Journal but regret not being able to find it.
[23] For detailed reviews of relative passages consult Arnold G. Fruchtenbaum, *Israelology: The Missing Link in Systematic Theology* (Tustin, CA: Ariel Ministries, 1994, 2001).
[24] Horner, 242.

believers in England. But there are cultural elements that are important to being British that I just do not share, such as black pudding. In Christ, this distinction in cultural dietary tradition is irrelevant. But I would think that to be British, one's attitude toward black pudding would be strikingly different than that held by most Americans. So it is with Jewish/Gentile believers. Paul had to demonstrate that the Law of Moses did not save anyone, Jew or otherwise. But just as culture is not important for salvation nor is it something that necessarily must be condemned. Thus in Christ, Jews and Gentiles are one. But that oneness does not negate God's promise of land to the physical descendants of Abraham. Jews still had a role in Eschatology.

To support this consider the following. First, note Christ's response to the disciples' question recorded in Acts 1:6. The setting is just prior to Christ's ascension into heaven. The disciples finally accept that Christ had risen from the dead and were wondering whether Christ would now establish the Davidic Kingdom. Christ responds: "It is not for you to know times or seasons that the Father has fixed by his own authority." (Acts 1:7 ESV). The question is, "Why didn't Christ rebuke the disciples and tell them that the promise of a Jewish kingdom has been voided?" I contend that Christ's failure to take up this opportunity to correct His disciples stemmed from His desire to fulfill His promise that they would sit on the thrones of Israel (Matt 19:28). In other words, the establishment of the kingdom was still to come otherwise, there would be no Israel for the disciples to rule. Those who assert that Christ's comments were metaphorically referring to the Church are guilty of special pleading. For one would have to wonder what words would Jesus have had to use to make the point clearer, namely that the state of Israel would exist one day.

Of course, one would be remiss to neglect Paul's conversation in Romans 11, which detail Israel's failure to follow Christ. Nevertheless, Paul says, God hasn't rejected his people. From the replacement perspective, it begs the question, "How can God even consider rejecting or not rejecting his people if they can no longer be identified after Christ's death and resurrection?" The problem for replacement theologians is that Paul's comments assume that physical descendants of Abraham can be identified and that they matter to God in a way that ordinary Gentiles do not.[25]

It seems to me that this notion of becoming part of the people of God is what God had in mind by offering salvation to the Gentiles. The Gentiles are being blessed with fellowship with God through the Holy Spirit to make the Jews jealous by making them recall their own special relationship with God. The distinction is that I as a Gentile am grafted in to the tree of Israel by faith. What this means is that I have the opportunity to share in God's blessings and fellowship. But this does not mean that I have the right to the land of Israel. God clearly gives certain ethnic groups their own land. Note Paul's comment in Acts 17:26. When speaking before the philosophers at the Areopagus, Paul says, and I paraphrase, that God made from one person all the nations of the earth and have determined the boundaries of their habitation. Now you could argue that Paul is just arguing from concession. But I think Paul could have proffered this notion because he knew that God would ultimately fulfill the promise of the land to Israel as God promised.

We must ultimately remember a few things:

---

[25] Ibid., 292ff.

1. God owns the land. Lev. 25:23: "The land shall not be sold in perpetuity; for the land is mine; for you are strangers and sojourners with me." (ESV)

2. The land is special to God and Israel's right to it is not linked merely to her obedience to the biblical commandments. The Torah understands the Israelite victory as succeeding in part because the land itself was so holy that it vomited out the inhabitants who defiled it by their abominable practices (Lev 18:28; Deut 9:4–5; Zech 2:14; Ps 78:54).

3. God's promise of Israel's right to the land cannot be broken. Even their failure to obey His commands will not negate the promise (Deut 9:24–29). In every prophetic message the prophecy of judgment and doom is tempered by the prophecy of consolation and restoration. Like the dry bones in Ezekiel's vision (Ezek 37:1–14), the old community of Israel will be restored, and from it the future generations will grow and flourish. The land will be cleansed of its pollution and sin and will welcome home its scattered people and become repopulated. Isaiah announces a second exodus through the wilderness to the Promised Land. God, who had "exiled" Himself along with his people, returns to dwell in Jerusalem (Isa 52:8), the center of the earth. The primary emphasis turned to the restoration of the temple and its cult and the rebuilding of the city of Jerusalem.[26]

---

[26] For details see the article "Temple, Jewish" in Stanley E. Porter and Craig A. Evans, *Dictionary of New Testament Background: A Compendium of Contemporary Biblical Scholarship*, electronic ed. (Downers Grove, IL: InterVarsity Press, 2000).

4. The destruction of Jerusalem in A.D. 70 was God's punishment for Israel's rejection of her messiah. It was a way for God to show Israel that she needed to rethink her understanding of salvation and her relationship to God. That is why Paul continues to say that the Holy Spirit was a down payment of the promise of eternal life (Eph 1:14). The Holy Spirit showed God's relationship with the Gentiles and thus His blessing upon non-Jews. The Spirit's presence, prophesied by Joel 2:28-32 was to encourage jealousy among the Jews and goad them to repent and return to God (Rom 9-11).

What should be said about replacement theology's third point regarding the relative silence about Israel's continued right to the land? Arguments from silence are fraught with difficulties. Although Acts 1:6-7 demonstrate that the New Testament was not silent about Israel's right to the land, I do agree that the subject was not a central one for the New Testament. Nevertheless, the relative silence of the New Testament regarding the land lacks argumentative force. Perhaps the easiest answer is that the Apostles had to be discreet about Israel's right to the land out of concern for how Rome would interpret such a message.[27] Boldly proclaiming Israel's right to the land could have easily resulted in a military reaction along the lines of Hadrian's quelling of the Bar-Kokhba Revolt.[28] More importantly, we must state that the New Testament does not deny Israel's right to the land.

---

[27] Paul ignored the restoration of the Israelite kingdom not because it was irrelevant but because its introduction had to wait for the Lord's return. Contra Weinfield,178-179.
[28] Werner Eck, "Hadrian's Hard-Won Victory: Romans Suffer Severe Losses in Jewish War," *Biblical Archeology Review*, September-October 2007, 44.

There is nothing in the New Testament that tells us that God's promise to Abraham is no longer valid (Gen 15:18). To the Apostles, there was no need to belabor the issue because they knew that God would keep His promise to Abraham. As a Calvinist who emphasises God's decrees, I can think of no surer argument than that. *(cont'd on page 231)*

Excursus: More on the Debate over Genesis 15:18

It reads, "On that day the LORD made a covenant with Abram, saying, "To your offspring I give this land, from the river of Egypt to the great river, the river Euphrates." (ESV). What is noteworthy is the section uses the identical Hebrew word translated as "descendant" (15:13,18) in a way that clearly emphasises the genetic aspect of the meaning of descendant. In other words, God promised the land to Abraham's physical descendants not his spiritual ones. To further emphasise the ethnic particularity of the promise, note how God distinguished Abraham's descendents from the Egyptians. God did not give Israel the right to have the land of Egypt because God gave the Nile region to the Egyptians. By limiting Israel's right to certain land, God's promise of Canaan to Israel is further clarified.

Replacement theologians employ two arguments to dilute the notion of Israel's right to the land. First, they can assert that Hebrews 11:9f says that the territory Abraham was really seeking for was a spiritual one. Reformed theologian Robert Reymond puts the matter this way:

... the author of Hebrews stated that the administration of redemption under the old covenant was "but a

---

227

> shadow of the good things to come" (Heb 10:1), so also he taught that Abraham knew that God's land promises in their fulfillment entailed something far more glorious, namely, a better and heavenly homeland whose designer and builder is God, than the land of Palestine *per se* that served only as the type of their fulfillment.
>
> Reymond then quotes Hebrews 11:8-16 and continues saying:
>
> Quite plainly, Abraham understood that the land promised to him actually had both its *origin* and its antitypical *fulfillment* in the heavenly, eternal reality that lay still in the future. Possession of a particular tract of land in ancient times might have significance from a number of perspectives with respect to God's redemptive working in the world, but clearly the land promise under the Abrahamic covenant served simply as a type anticipating the future reality of the coming of the messianic kingdom with the Messiah himself assuming the throne of David in heaven[29] and ruling the universe after his resurrection/ascension and reigning until all his enemies have been put under his feet.[30]

---

[29] Because any throne he as the messianic Son of David (Matt 9:27; 20:30-31; 21:9; 22:41-46; Luke 1:31-33) would sit upon would be "the throne of David," Jesus Christ's present session at the right hand of God has invested the throne of God in heaven with a messianic character, that is to say, God's throne is "the throne of David". And *this* Davidic throne is the throne of the only "Jerusalem" that matters today, namely, "the Jerusalem above," the glorified Church of Jesus Christ (see Gal 4:26; Heb 12:22; Rev 21:9-26).

[30] "Who Are the Real Heirs to the Land Promises of Holy Scripture?" Robert L. Reymond, An Address Delivered to "Advancing Reformation

Reymond's point is obvious. Abraham's ultimate goal was the attainment of a spiritual land. We must ask, however, "Did Abraham really have only a spiritual view of land in mind?" I think not.[31] The land in Abraham's eyes would have been worthless if God was not with him. The city was where God would be. Abraham's goal was to be in fellowship with God. But to suggest that the land was irrelevant or was universalised to the entire world, misses the point. A city cannot exist without land. Abraham received the promise of an heir, but he did not see the fulfillment of God's promise of land. Thus he had to look forward to the day when that would occur. It is interesting to note that the New Jerusalem will be coming down from heaven (Rev 21:10). It being a city, is the place of God's indwelling accompaniment with his people. But it is not a New Hong Kong. It is a New Jerusalem, the city where God would put his name (1 Kgs 11:36), and therefore the city ties together the theme of land and fellowship with God together.[32]

Replacement theologians also support their interpretation that the land promise to Abraham was universalised to encompass the entire world by appealing to Romans 4:13. It reads, "For the promise to Abraham and his offspring that he would be heir of the world did not come through the law but through the righteousness of faith." (ESV) Our understanding of "world" lies at the heart of the interpretive

Truth and Spirituality" (ARTS), 6, on April 21 2006. DeVos Chapel, Coral Ridge Presbyterian Church. Fort Lauderdale, Florida.
[31] Carson calls interpretations which rely on a mistaken either/or polarity a "false disjunctive" D.A. Carson, *Exegetical Fallacies* (Grand Rapids, Michigan: Baker Book House, 1984), 94-97.
[32] Horner, 250. He cites various authors noting that heavenly in Hebrews does not mean extra-terrestrial but unpolluted because God is there.

dispute. Reymond interprets it to mean the planet earth. While that is certainly a possibility, the lexicography and context make it unlikely. The Greek word translated world is *kosmos* occurs 9 times in Romans (Rom 1:8, 20; 3:6, 19; 4:13; 5:12, 13; 11:12, 13). Only 1:20 definitely refers to the physical planet. All the remaining occurrences of *kosmos* can be interpreted as referring to human activity and not to geography. For example, in Romans 1:8, Paul says that the faith of the Romans is proclaimed throughout the whole world. Clearly, Paul is referring to the preaching of the Gospel to people and not to physical locations. Even if one says, that Paul intended *kosmos* to refer to people and places, we still must ask if one is primary. Barrett's observation that Paul is probably referring to Genesis 22:18, adds further evidence for my position.[33] Even if we concede that Paul wanted *kosmos* to refer to the planet, the verse still lacks sufficient force to overthrow the view that God promised ethnic Jews the land of Israel. Paul never denies that Israel still has a right to a particular plot of land. Paul only says that Abraham would inherit the entire world. The replacement view fails to consider that a literal bestowal of land to physical descendents of Abraham can be accomplished simultaneously with the spiritual blessings that Christ will grant to Gentiles.[34]

---

[33] C. K. Barrett, *A Commentary on the Epistle to the Romans*, ed. Henry Chadwick, Harper's New Testament Commentaries (NY: Harper & Brothers Publishers, 1957), 94. See also James R. Edwards, Romans, ed. W. Ward Gasque, *New International Biblical Commentary*, vol. 6 (Peabody, MA: Hendrickson Publishers Inc., 1992), 122-3. See Moo for an interpretation more amenable to the replacement theology. Douglas J. Moo, *The Epistle to the Romans,* ed. Ned B. Stonehouse, F. F. Bruce, and Gordon D. Fee, *The New International Commentary on the New Testament* (Grand Rapids, MI: William B. Eerdmans Publishing Co., 1996), 273-4.
[34] Horner, 246.

APPLICATION

If you agree that God has eternally promised to give Canaan to Israel, what political policies should Christians support? The question is pertinent given that the modern State of Israel is not only a secular institution but also one that has restricted Christian evangelism and denied citizenship to Messianic Jews.

First, we must clearly maintain that salvation comes only through Jesus Christ. Peter when preaching in Jerusalem said that there is no other name under heaven by which we can be saved (Acts 4:10ff). Paul in Rom 9-11 acknowledged that his fellow citizens were lost without Christ. So Jews who have not accepted Christ, though remaining in covenantal relationship with God, remain under condemnation for their refusal to accept their Messiah (John 3:18). God has not rejected His promise to restore them to the land once the time of the Gentiles is complete.[35] Regrettably, many Jews think that following Christ means forsaking their cultural heritage. We must affirm that Jews can retain their cultural identity. Jews must only give up those elements of Judaism that contradict the teachings of Jesus Christ. Our only desire is to reaffirm Christ's words that He, and He alone is the way to the Father (John 14:6). Therefore Christians must press the Israeli government to allow true religious freedom in the country.

Second, Christians can choose to support the Israeli government. However, support of the Israeli government's right to exist does not mean that Christian backing constitutes a blank check. Just as Christians must reject the idolatrous patriotism that says, "My country right or wrong",

---

[35] Ibid., chapter 11.

we must similarly reject the idea that Israeli policy is always right.

Third, pro-Israel supporters must be sensitive to those Christians, who believe that God has promised Jews the land, but have moral objections to Israel's policies.[36]

Fourth, I think care must be taken to properly distinguish Christian support for Jews as an ethnic people from support for the nation of Israel as a political entity. The ideas are not necessarily coterminous. While believing that God has a plan for the modern nation of Israel, the mere fact that she exists should not blind us to the possibility that the actual workings of God's prophetic plan may take a turn that is not possible for us to foresee. Christians must never be so involved in politics that they forget that their first mission is to

---

[36] For the record, I believe that there are a number of practical reasons Christians should support Israel (despite her imperfections). It is naïve to think that governments can only be supported if they are perfect. Fact: Israel offers Christians far more freedom than those had in Muslim countries. If we should condemn the excesses of Israeli nationalism, then we should condemn in even harsher terms the countries surrounding Israel that are held captive by political systems enslaved by a failed religion and political ideology. I once spoke to a Muslim Imam who encouraged me to consider the importance of justice. I responded in agreement and said that I knew of Jewish organisations in Israel that fought for the rights of Palestinians. I noted my ignorance of the Arab world and asked if he was aware of any similar Muslim organisations fighting for the rights of resident Jews in the surrounding Arab countries. He just looked at me. Acknowledging how I must have caught him off guard, gave him my card, and asked him to send the names of the organisations when he found them. I should note that even after several years I never received any list. The point being, that perfection is a high standard to uphold in a fallen world. I think Christians would be better served to work for sufficient justice, a justice that "works" well enough to protect life and liberty and basic rights than to be mired in the intransigence of utopian politics.

evangelise. As a friend put it, "First the Gospel, then Politics."[37]

Finally, Christians should focus on the spiritual struggles affecting these issues. God has commanded us to pray for our leaders and for the good of mankind. In the final analysis, no matter our eschatological views, Christians should be united with a fervent expectation and call of our Lord's return. We must be cautious about our criticism of those who disagree with us. Not that we shy away from conflict within the Church. However, we must be sure that our tone is moderated and our statements endeavor to assume the best of those of which we disagree. For in the end, our goal is to represent the love of Christ to a lost world. Even so, Come Lord Jesus.

---

[37] Rev. John C. Rankin of the Theological Education Institute of Hartford, Connecticut has this slogan as a title for his ministry work, http://www.teii.org/tei-radio/tei-journal/

Part 3

SUPERSESSIONISM AND THE JEWISH
PEOPLE TODAY

CHAPTER 10

Jewish Believers in Jesus and the New Supersessionism

Brian Brewer

It would be a reasonable question to ask why there is a chapter devoted to Jewish believers in Jesus in a book addressing supersessionism. The very nature of the more commonly used, synonymous phrases "Messianic movement" or "Messianic Jews" (MJs) inherently establish a relationship between Israel and Christianity—between Yeshua (Jesus), the Jewish Messiah, and Christianity's basis of existence in Christ Jesus.

There is, however, a vocal segment within Christianity—and not a small group at that—who strongly adhere to the belief that the Church is the "new Israel". Messianic Jewish believers, therefore, are proverbially "caught between a rock and a hard place" because their existence both ethnically and spiritually place them in the middle of a theological battle that has existed since the early days of the Christian era.[1]

---

[1] Jonathan Frankel and Ezra Mendelsohn, ed., *The Protestant-Jewish Conundrum: Studies in Contemporary Jewry an Annual XXIV* (Oxford: Oxford University Press, 2010), 143-44.

What must not be understated or overlooked is that this theological battle also has profound impact on the everyday lives of those who are culturally Jewish yet live as disciples of Messiah Jesus.

The aim for discussing Jewish believers in Jesus and supersessionism is twofold. First, to introduce this unique segment of believers to others in the same family of believers who may be unfamiliar with MJs. Non-Jewish believers typically have a very limited understanding of Jewish believers in Jesus. Regrettably, and all too often, Gentile believers also have a limited view of the Messianic movement and view it as one essentially comprised of Gentiles trying to be Jewish. To the greater disconcertment of cultural Jews, these "Jewish wannabe" merely ends up looking like an "escapee from a road company of Fiddler on the Roof".[2] Conversely, many cultural/ethnic Jews regard Jewish believers in Jesus as traitors to their faith by joining themselves to the very ones who have a history of persecuting the Jewish people.

Secondly, this chapter will explore tangible effects of the new supersessionism upon MJs. Supersessionism not only exacerbates the polarisation that has developed over many centuries between Israel and Christianity, but it also adds substantially to the already existing struggles that Messianic Jews genuinely deal with. The theological battle of supersessionism for the non-Jewish believer is all-to-easily fought in the relative comfort of academia. For MJs, however, it affects their everyday lives and spiritual walk in ways

---

[2] Steven Charles Ger, "How Jewish will the Messianic Jewish Community of the Future Be?" from *Borough Park Symposium* (October 2012), 6.

generally not considered by those outside the Messianic cultural and spiritual environment.

Therefore, this chapter consists of two parts. Part one begins with a definition and brief history of the Messianic movement, followed in part two by a brief survey of the modern Messianic movement and some of the major issues it faces – including identity, Torah observance and relationship to Judaism, Gentile inclusion, and postmodern Jews – and how these are detrimentally affected by supersessionism.

THE MESSIANIC MOVEMENT AND ITS DEVELOPMENT

What is the Messianic Movement?

It is generally common within the development of any social movement to have difficulty in coming to a consensus definition of "What is?" a particular social movement. Variables that exist and give shape to its very reason for existence also create a challenge in defining the name by which it is or will come to be known. This challenge is no less applicable for MJs, and perhaps it is even more difficult because the Messianic movement represents less than one percent of the Jewish community,[3] yet is comprised of numerous congregations who are all generally autonomous. Even that brief description is troublesome, because within these autonomous Messianic congregations their compositions include a considerable number of non-Jewish believers, which means there are cultural and ethnic diversities that only add to the challenge of adequately defining the movement. A tangible representation of the challenge in defining the Messianic movement is available by

---

[3] Chaim Urbach, "A Retrospective Look At Our Movement" from *Borough Park Symposium* (Oct 2012), 4.

reading through the *Borough Park Symposium* papers (readily available on the Internet).[4] Within this excellent resource of working papers is the clear reality that there is great diversity of opinion amongst those within the Messianic movement.

Michael Schiffman's work is one example of an earlier attempt to define terms and establish a framework by which one can progressively build an understanding of MJs. Space here permits only the briefest discussion of what would seem to be the most necessary aspects for a context of discussing the Messianic movement. Thus, I appreciate and will adopt Schiffman's description that the Messianic movement "is a movement of restoration"[5] because the term "restoration" sums up the essence of the Messianic movement and implicitly embraces the many intricate, complex details associated with it.

The Messianic movement is indeed returning something to its former place and condition, and this "something" is of profound importance for all believers in Jesus/Yeshua. It implies that Jewish and non-Jewish believers are being called to return to the origin of their common spiritual heritage. It challenges those who have "ears to hear" to re-examine—or possibly for many to examine for the first time—their stance towards Israel, the Jewish people, the Bible, and an important missional concept "to the Jew first" (Rom 1:16). Not that the apostle Paul implied a strict chronology of how we are to present the Gospel, but it emphasises that the Gospel should be pro-actively taken to this group of people to whom the Gospel is most directly connected.[6] This is particularly

---

[4] http://www.boroughparksymposium.com/
[5] Michael Schiffman, *Return of the Remnant: The Rebirth of Messianic Judaism* (Baltimore, MD: Lederer Publications, 1989), v
[6] Baruch Maoz, *Judaism Is Not Jewish* (Ross-shire, UK: Christian Focus Publications Ltd., 2003), 77.

relevant for MJs because there are increasing numbers of those who have been raised in traditional Christian backgrounds only to discover in their adult life that they are actually of Jewish descent—commonly only one-to-two generations removed.[7]

An important caveat at this point is to stress that the Messianic movement is not and never has been a call for everyone "to become Jewish". The New Testament is clear in its presentation that Jewish and Gentile believers maintain ethnic distinctions. The Jerusalem Council of Acts 15 took deliberate steps to free Gentile believers from any suggestion that they were obligated to keep Jewish religious laws and customs. Paul's address in his letter to the Galatians is also a clear argument against those who were essentially demanding that non-Jewish believers should observe aspects of the Law of Moses. Therefore, when one hears commonly used phrases among MJs such as "Yeshua", "Messiah", "Messianic", "Congregation" (rather than "Church"), and "Tree" (rather than "cross"), these are a few examples of the ways the Messianic movement is an attempt towards restoration. Such attempts are generally not legalistic demands[8] or insistence on ritualistic observance, but are for the purpose of "getting back to our roots"—roots that extend back to when Jesus lived and ministered on earth and all within a definite cultural context through which historic Christianity was sired.

---

[7] Cf. Barbara Kessel, *Suddenly Jewish: Jews Raised as Gentiles Discover Their Jewish Roots* (Hanover: University Press of New England, 2000).

[8] "Generally" is used here because there is a minority of MJs who can be quite dogmatic about use of terminology—unhappy with words such as "Jesus", "Christ", "Christian", "baptism", and "Testament".

Antecedents and Contemporary Development

While it should be obvious that Christianity has Israel as its root (Rom 11:18), supersessionism's long history has gradually and stealthily removed Israel out of the picture for a significant percentage of Christians. Most Gentile believers accept that Jesus (as well as the first disciples) was Jewish. But during the very early stages of Christian theological development and expression a pervasive notion entered and resulted in the subtle removal of Jewishness from early Christianity. Therefore, we can read Acts 13:46 where Paul reacts towards antagonistic Jews saying, "we are turning to the Gentiles" and mentally embrace that Paul is subsequently turning his back on Jews—as if God Himself was rejecting them and turning His attention to Gentiles. So pervasive has that thought process been replicated over the centuries that we do not take notice that just a few verses later, Paul entered the synagogue once again to teach, so that "a great number of both Jews and Greeks believed" (Acts 14:1). Granted, it did not take a long time, relatively speaking, for the followers of Jesus/Yeshua to become ethnically/culturally mixed. However, the implied census of Acts 21 reveals that this seminal, formative context found non-Jewish believers far outnumbered by Jewish believers: "how many thousands (lit. "ten thousands") there are among the Jews of those who have believed" (v. 20).

The burgeoning Messianic community in Jerusalem continued to live a Jewish life-style that was apparently never perceived by non-believing Jews as having embraced a different way of life. The only difference was that these early MJs were now simply another sect within the Jewish community who believed that their Messiah had already come. The fact that some Pharisees were among the believers (Acts 15:5) indicates that the community was not distinctly different at that point than it had been before embracing Jesus as Messiah. A survey of the book of Acts should alert all non-Jewish believers to the important characteristic of early MJs that they remained very Jewish. The following are representative examples:

1. The apostles continued to go to the Temple (Acts 2:46; 3:1; 5:20-21)

2. They continued to go to the synagogue (Acts 13:14-15; 14:1; 17:1, 10; 18:4, 19; 19:8); and

3. They continued to observe the feasts and the law (Acts 20:6; 21:24)

In spite of the evidence that early MJs maintained a distinct Jewish lifestyle, there did exist a definite conflict between MJs and the non-believing Pharisees; but then again "there was rivalry between all the Jewish sects at that time".[9] While Jewish suspicion and antagonism towards MJs was clearly present in the early days of the "The Way" (e.g., Acts 9:1-2; 19:9; 24:5), it was the destruction of the Temple (AD 70) and disastrous results of the Bar Kochba revolt (AD 135) that resulted in the eventual disappearance of Jewish sects and the ability to express varying ways of being Jewish. The Pharisaic party became the only legitimate sect, with Rabbinic Judaism becoming the only recognised form of being Jewish. The result was that the Jewish community increasingly viewed MJs as foreigners. While the Messianic population continued in Jerusalem after the Temple's destruction, it progressively declined, yet survived until the

[9] Schiffman, 11.

fourth and fifth centuries. Conversely, the gradual development of the Gentile-dominated Church resulted in a drive for uniformity that led to the eventual Nicean period (fourth century) and view of MJs as heretical.[10]

Hugh J. Schonfield (*The History of Jewish Christianity*) provides a very helpful chronology of the early separation between Jewish and Gentile believers—accompanied by the seminal development of supersessionism that was engendered by Christian anti-Semitism (a notable contradiction of terms). Thus, among the early Church Fathers (e.g., Justin Martyr, Irenaeus, Origen, Augustine) to the Ecclesiastical Councils (e.g., Nicaea, Chalcedon, 3rd and 4th Lateran, Oxford) up to the present time (through the new supersessionism) there is a sorry history of Christianity that has continuously attempted surreptitious removal of Israel and Jewish culture from Christianity's perceived heritage. The history of intolerance against Jews that led to virtual inability to meet as believers has resulted in little formal MJ history. Consequently, Arnold Fruchtenbaum is quoted as summarising MJ history from AD 135 to 1800 as "one brief history".[11]

However, this regrettable fact of Christianity's historical development must not overshadow a positive aspect of its maturation. By the eighteenth century an awakening occurred in the hearts of certain Christians—that God's desire for all to be saved included Jewish people. A clarion call was sounded by Callenburg in 1732 for a renewed concept of Christian duty that became a catalyst which would eventually see the end of the nineteenth century with nearly one hundred agencies devoted to working among the Jews

---

[10] Ibid, 11-15.
[11] Ibid, 25.

around the world. Throughout and by the end of the nineteenth century at least a quarter of a million Jews were won for Christ.[12] There was a new era of Jewish Christianity that was blossoming, and it is at this time that the distinct restoration of Messianic Jewish identity begins to occur.

The first exclusively Hebrew Christian Association was formed in London in 1813 and was named *Beni Avraham* (Children of Abraham). This was followed by the first united stand of Jewish Christians in 1866, accompanied by the formation of a Hebrew-Christian Union and the first Jewish Christian periodical, *The Scattered Nation*.[13] These first Jewish Christian associations, however, were all within the bounds of the established churches. It was not until 1882 that the first Jewish Christian association in modern times was founded by Joseph Rabinowitz and belonged to no definite Christian denomination.[14] What Rabinowitz initiated was the first of many steps that would progressively accomplish what Schiffman was noted earlier to describe: restoration of Jewish Christianity by Jews from within its own ranks. Schonfield states that Rabinowitz was not an isolated case for he had contemporaries and immediate successors who represented a new generation of Jewish Christians that resembled the pattern of the original Nazarenes.[15]

Sadly, this positive development was also accompanied by a negative reaction on the part of Christian denominations, but what Rabinowitz and others started could not be stopped. As the number of associations grew during the late nineteenth century and into the twentieth

---

[12] Hugh J. Schonfield, *The History of Jewish Christianity: From the First to the Twentieth Century* (London: Duckworth, 2009, c. 1936), 154.
[13] Ibid, 160-61.
[14] Ibid, 163.
[15] Ibid, 167.

century, Christian denominations began to officially acknowledge that the Messianic movement required recognition. The reestablishment of Israel as a nation (1947) and the outcome of the Six Day War (1967) served as markers for two significant developments. First, within Christian denominations a series of official Resolutions resulted calling for increased dialogue regarding Israel and Christian relations.[16] Secondly, the aftermath of the Six Day War restored Jerusalem to the Jewish people, fulfilling the prayer of the Jewish people—*Next Year in Jerusalem*—that had gone unfulfilled for almost two thousand years. Since that time a large number of Jewish people have not only come to faith in Yeshua as Messiah, but it is also from this point that many new Messianic Jewish congregations have been formed.[17] As with any natural birth accompanied with a new name, the birth of the modern Messianic Jewish Movement was similarly accompanied by a new name. The contemporary representation of the late nineteenth century Messianic movement is made distinct by a shift away from being known as "Hebrew Christians" to the now commonly recognised names "Messianic Judaism" or the "Messianic Jewish Movement".

There is so much more detail that could be added, but it is hoped that this brief overview will provide sufficient background for grasping the present reality of internal issues facing the Messianic movement as it stands between historic Christianity and Orthodox Judaism.

---

[16] Helga Croner (compiler). *Stepping Stones to Further Jewish-Christian Relations* (New York: Stimulus Books, 1977).
[17] Schiffman, 32.

KEY ISSUES FACING TODAY'S MESSIANIC MOVEMENT

At the beginning of the previous section the challenge was highlighted regarding how the Messianic movement is to be defined and understood. However, what are often never considered from those outside this movement are individual and/or corporate challenges faced by those within the Messianic community. MJs are currently facing a number of internal conflicts and issues, several of which are especially made all the more difficult and exacerbated by the recent and more militant expression of supersessionism currently circulating. Space limitations do not permit a survey of all of them, thus this chapter will address four issues directly impacted by supersessionism: Identity, Torah observance and Orthodox Judaism, Gentiles within the Messianic movement, and postmodern Jews. Addressing these four topics will hopefully become a catalyst for greater reflection leading to definite pro-activity on the reader's part—whether towards further study and awareness or, for example, if a Messianic congregation is located nearby, to initiate some active dialogue and partnership.

Identity

Defining what it means to be Jewish is a task that realistically may never achieve a consensus agreement. Notice, I did not yet specify "Jewish believer, but more generally Jewish identity because defining that is challenging enough. David Stern acknowledges that the question, "Who is a Jew?" arises continuously in the religio-political life of the State of Israel. *"Halakhah"* (Jewish religious law) defines a Jew as anyone "born of a Jewish mother or who has converted to Judaism. ... Meanwhile, it is commonly accepted that the Bible traces

247

Jewishness through the father".[18] It becomes quickly apparent that being a Jewish believer in Jesus adds significantly to the complexity of Jewish identity.[19] Oded Shashani summarises succinctly the dilemma: Messianic Jewish identity "is made up of two parts: Jewish identity and Messianic identity. The two parts have some common and some conflicting values".[20]

Jewish identity is both ethnic and religious—a common ancestry from Abraham coupled with a common belief in the monotheistic God revealed in the Old Testament scriptures. As a result, Jewishness is connected to a physical land as well as inherent separation from the nations of the world. The Messianic characteristic, conversely, calls for a more universal perspective that sees no difference between people and their ethnicity with regards to salvation in God. So then, are Messianic Jews "Jewish"? Here is where numerous pages could be filled attempting to address multiple nuances that are concomitant with this challenge of identity. With only limited space available, perhaps this identity conundrum is explained better through the opposing viewpoints of two Messianic Jews. Baruch Maoz proffers:

---

[18] David Stern, *Messianic Judaism: A Movement With an Ancient Past* (Clarksville, MD: Messianic Jewish Publishers, 2007), 16. Stern later expounds *halakhah*: "In Jewish discourse, when one speaks of 'the Halakhah,' one is bringing to mind the whole framework of Jewish life as seen from a particular viewpoint"—including not only Jewish law (what is permitted or forbidden) but also customs (p. 136, fn #9).

[19] Several papers from the 2012 *Borough Park Symposium* highlight this challenge of MJ identity: E.g., Mara Frisch, *How Jewish will the Messianic Jewish Community of the Future Be?* and Steven Ger, *How Jewish will the Messianic Jewish Community of the Future Be?* [*sic*]. Additionally, works by Baruch Maoz and Mark S. Kinzer are excellent examples of the difference of opinion that exists in attempting to explicate what it means to be Jewish.

[20] Oded Shashani, "What Is Our Relationship With The Wider Jewish Community" from *Borough Park Symposium* (Oct 2012), 4.

There are no biblical grounds to require or encourage Jews to reject their national identity in order to serve God. ... But, please note, we are speaking here of Jewishness as a *national* identity. When we speak of a *religious* identity, we must admit that we are Christians because Judaism is not biblical while the true message of Christianity is.[21]

In opposition Mark S. Kinzer asserts:

It is time to challenge the notion that Christianity and Judaism are two separate religions. We should heed the advice offered by Karl Barth a half-century ago: "The Church must live with the Synagogue, not, as fools say in their hearts, as with another religion or confession, but as the root from which it has sprung.[22]

Clearly, Jewish believers are struggling with their identity as being both Jews and Christians. This dilemma is only intensified by supersessionism, which causes MJs to feel even less inclined to associate themselves with a Christian Gentile church that is so anti-Israel. With an air of shock or surprise, one may question, "In what way is the Gentile church so anti-Israel?" It is not an overt anti-Israel stance, but a "soft" form of supersessionism. The Christian church affirms the eternal destiny of individual Jews who trust in Messiah. The deceptive dichotomy, however, is that the Church has

[21] Maoz, 2003, 75.
[22] E.g., Mark S. Kinzer, *Post-Missionary Messianic Judaism: Redefining Christian Engagement With the Jewish People* (Grand Rapids, MI: Brazos Press, 2005), 21.

traditionally *not* affirmed the future of ethnic, political, national Israel:

> [T]he subject of practically the entire Bible, the special object of God's favor and grace, and the recipient of God's covenanted promises of blessing.[23]

How can Messianic Jews feel comfortable about belonging to a body that is so anti-Israel, even anti-Jewish? Does it not strengthen the argument that their unbelieving Jewish compatriots are right—that they have sided with the enemy and are traitors? It is obvious from the above examples that within the Messianic community itself, there is not a consensus on just this one aspect regarding Messianic Jewish identity. Maoz and Kinzer both identify as being Jewish in ethnicity, yet they are polar opposites when it comes to a foundational characteristic regarding what it means to be a Jewish believer and his/her relationship with Judaism. Their opposing viewpoints are no insignificant matter, for if there is notable disagreement regarding this issue of Judaism it naturally begs the question, "How do Messianic Jews then view Torah?"

Messianic Judaism and Torah Observance

It should already be coming to light that it is impossible in this brief chapter to solve the question of identity let alone the three remaining topics listed. The goal is to jumpstart a process of reflection regarding challenges facing MJs and, ultimately, how supersessionism exacerbates those

---

[23] Craig A. Blaising, "The Future of Israel as a Theological Question" in *To the Jew First*, Darrell Bock and Mitch Glaser, ed. (Kregel Publications: Grand Rapids, MI, 2008), 102-03.

challenges. The question of Torah observance seems naturally to follow identity questions, if not actually be a part of it. As would be generally acknowledged among MJ writers, kippas (skull caps), prayer shawls, lox[24] and bagels, and other stereotypical Jewish elements are not sufficient to sustain Jewish identity over many centuries. This requires something much more substantial, and it leads to the Torah, which, next to the physical land of Israel, is perhaps one of the single, most unifying elements of Jewish religious identity.

Seth Klayman addresses the question of Torah observance from the position of a Messianic "practitioner" rather than a theologian. As the leader of a Messianic Jewish community, his position more tangibly highlights the difficulties encountered trying to come to a consensus about the relationship of MJs to the Torah. Klayman's position is that what informs their Torah observance is both "our faith in Yeshua" *and* "Jewish tradition". Even so, he issues an important disclaimer that this does *not* mean his Messianic congregation never deviates from strict halakhic[25] application of Torah, and he provides various examples proving that point.[26] Why this is important is that it illustrates how Torah observance can vary from one Messianic Jewish believer to another or from one Messianic community to another.

"Torah", however, carries with it more than what may be expected by the non-Jewish believer. Joshua Brumbach illustrates this point well:

---

[24] Typically smoked salmon.

[25] See *halakhah* in the previous section above on 'Identity' as well as footnote 19.

[26] Seth N. Klayman, "Reflections on the Role of Torah and Jewish Tradition at Congregation Sha'arei Shalom" from *Borough Park Symposium* (Oct 2012), 11-12.

> If we think of the Torah as the Constitution, then the body of interpretative case law would be the *halachic* codes and responsa. Just as a body of courts were established to interpret and apply the Constitution, so too Jewish courts and *halachic* authorities were established to interpret and apply Torah. As such, just as the United States cannot operate in accordance with the Constitution without the interpretative guidance of the judiciary, so too we as a movement cannot operate in accordance with the Torah without the interpretive guidance of our tradition.[27]

Speaking alongside Brumbach, however, Baruch Maoz offers an opposing viewpoint of Torah:

> Let it not be thought that we can better impact our people if we put on a show of keeping the Law and the traditions. Remember Josephus' testimony that James, the brother of our Lord, was put to death "as an offender of the law" in spite of his strict observance of the Torah simply because he believed in Jesus. Our protagonists understand clearly what we are sometimes loath to recognize, namely that reliance on Jesus for justification and for sanctification is exactly contrary to what Judaism teaches on the role of the Torah. We must, therefore, choose between Judaism and Jewishness, as well as between Judaism and Israel's Messiah.[28]

---

[27] Joshua Brumbach, "Helpful Points to Consider: The Role of Torah and Jewish Tradition In the Messianic Jewish Community" from *Borough Park Symposium* (Oct 2012), 11.
[28] Baruch Moaz, "The Role of Torah and of Jewish Tradition in the Messianic Jewish Community" from *Borough Park Symposium* (Oct 2012), 12.

Again, two Jewish believers in Jesus sharply contrast one another and further highlight the potential challenges resulting from great diversity of opinion within the Messianic community. It is important to clarify here that MJs are not speaking of Torah observance in any soteriological (salvific) sense, as if the Old Covenant is superior to the New and must be observed in order to "earn salvation". Rather, Torah observance is from the perspective of covenant and love for God. Just as Jesus specifically linked "love" with "obedience" (John 14:15, 21, 23), this is a similar sense motivating MJs when they speak of "Torah observance". Rather than re-erecting a wall—as is a common concern of or even accusation against the Messianic movement by Gentile believers—MJs are emphasising an inherent equality between the Old and New covenants.

Ironically, it is here that supersessionism is guilty of re-erecting a wall through establishing an "us" (Christians) and "them" (Jews) mentality based on a rejection of the Old Testament covenant. Therefore, the new supersessionism's militant "us" and "them" attitude makes Torah observant Messianic Jews feel even less comfortable with being in the Church. Instead of welcoming MJs, the new supersessionism demands their inclusion on supersessionist terms alone. Thus, the implicit demand upon MJs by the new supersessionism is complete assimilation. Because both historic replacement theology was and the new supersessionism is Gentile dominated, it should not be difficult to conceive of probable challenges that would arise when Gentile believers desire to attach themselves to a Messianic community. This leads to the next critical issue.

BRIAN BREWER

Gentiles and Messianic Judaism

There is a trend that is acknowledged in both Orthodox and Messianic Judaism—the dramatic rise in intermarriage between Jews and non-Jews that has substantially blurred cultural and religious boundaries. With this factor alone the rise in non-Jewish believers assimilating into Messianic Jewish congregations has created another challenging issue— non-Jews attempting somehow to take on a Jewish persona. In addition to the 2012 *Borough Park Symposium* specifically addressing this issue, others have acknowledged the Gentile and MJ dynamic such as David Stern's *Messianic Judaism: A Movement With an Ancient Past.*

Stern echoes other Messianic writers who voice reserved acceptance of non-Jewish believers—not from an attitude of class distinction or rebuilding a wall of separation,[29] but from an evangelistic perspective. What does that mean? If, we return to the earlier comment by Baruch Maoz that "to the Jew first" carries an implicit priority to go to those to whom the Gospel would be most relevant, Messianic Jewish reservation towards Gentile inclusion is how a congregation of non-Jewish believers might negatively impact reaching out to non-believing Jews—to those who still believe in a separation from the nations as part of their identity rather than the Gospel's universal embrace of all nations. There is a greater nuanced discussion that could take place, but the call to take the Gospel to the Jew first is possibly the single most important reason why Gentiles in the Messianic community create a unique challenge. Long-standing Christian anti-Semitism has progressively developed great antagonism towards the Gospel among non-believing Jews. The new supersessionism's perceived Gentile superiority and demand

---

[29] Stern, 175 and 249.

254

for assimilation implicitly demeans Jewish ethnicity as inferior and recreates an "air" of Gentile domination.

Once again, how can Messianic Jews feel comfortable about belonging to a body that is so anti-Israel, even anti-Jewish? The covertly common notion among major Protestant churches and Evangelical scholars is that "Christianity and the new covenant remain the highest fulfillment of the old covenant"[30]—that Jewish conversion to Christianity is something that is still needed or wanted. Should there be any wonder why MJs desire an environment that allows both freedom from this stigma as well as the heightened potential for reaching out to non-Jewish believers? Therefore, the presence of Gentile believers, particularly in leadership positions, within Messianic Jewish congregations is not an inconsequential side note. Ultimately, it can become a very real hindrance for evangelistic outreach to non-Jews.

Of course, the potential problem of Gentile inclusion in Messianic communities implies non-Messianic Jews are indeed coming into a Messianic Jewish congregation. While this does take place, the overall statistics indicate that this is less likely to occur today not because of Gentile presence, but due to a socio-religious phenomenon that has progressively witnessed fewer and fewer Jews having any interest at all in religious matters. This brings us to the final problematic area for MJs—the postmodern Jew.

---

[30] Robert W. Jenson and Eugene B. Korn, ed. *Covenant and Hope: Christian and Jewish Reflections* (Grand Rapids, MI: Wm B. Eerdmans Publishing Co., 2012), 165. Jenson *et al* immediately follow by describing another version of soft-supersessionism: "*eschatological* supersessionism", which similarly views Christianity as the highest fulfillment of God's word to all the earth, but that the full return of Jews to the Church is hardly possible ("perhaps not even desirable") and is a matter for God at the end of time.

Messianic Movement and Postmodern Jews

Although being Jewish previously included both an ethnic and religious characteristic, that is changing today. How do MJs communicate the truth of the Gospel to growing numbers of younger Jews who no longer believe in or are suspicious of propositional/absolute truth; i.e., postmodern Jews? The advent of modern transportation and communication have engendered a strong global outlook in those who are Jewish by birth. They have a commitment to local and global social issues that produces a pseudo-spirituality that is different from being religious. "Religion" is opposed and religious opinion is generally considered valid as long as it remains personal and does not enter into the public arena.[31] Though it seems a contradiction in terms, the postmodern Jewish situation is illustrated well by S. Daniel Breslauer's *Creating a Judaism Without Religion: A Postmodern Jewish Possibility* (Lanham: University Press of America, 2001).

Jhan Maskowitz proffers that the Jewish community has at least three ideas that most, if not all, Jewish people have been socialised into: (1) The Holocaust – to deny the Holocaust is to remove oneself from the Jewish people; (2) The State of Israel – its right to exist and some allegiance to it; and (3) The rejection of Jesus.[32] The fact that postmodern Jews typically see themselves as spiritual as opposed to religious, hints at the reality that they are searching for some divine spark within; and, as Maskowitz put it, "the Awe of the transcendent (What they are looking for is exactly what we are offering them in the Incarnation.)".[33]

---

[31] Jhan Moskowitz, "How to Effectively Communicate the Deity of Messiah to a Jewish Post-Modern Community" from *Borough Park Symposium* (April 2010), np.

[32] Ibid.

[33] Ibid.

The new supersessionism militates against that message of incarnation being easily received. Postmodern Jews already have a stereotyped idea of Gentile Christians who, along with their propositional "gospel truth", gave assistance to the destruction of Jews via the Holocaust. The new supersessionism aggravates the great challenge MJs already have in reaching out to younger, contemporary Jews in two notable ways. Firstly, supersessionism espouses as propositional truth that which is errant, yet perceived by postmodern Jews as "biblical" and "Christian". Secondly, supersessionism's implicit demand for assimilation becomes one group seeking to take authority over another; and, because MJs are rejected by Judaism and the Jewish community as having "gone to the other side", postmodern Jews consider them part of that same dominating "Christian" culture—resulting in outright rejection of MJs and further complicating Messianic efforts to evangelise non-Messianic Jews.

The new supersessionsim is not just one flagrant doctrine and movement espoused by an isolated group of adherents. It occurs much more broadly as the result of stealth-like characteristics that permeate Christianity and are astutely highlighted within R. Kendall Soulen's work *The God of Israel and Christian Theology*.[34] Soulen's efforts notably highlight the result of how God's identity as "the God of Israel" has been systematically expunged from the Christian concept of God. The new supersessionism's impact on MJs has been addressed in the context of the above four topics, all of which

---

[34] R. Kendall Soulen, *The God of Israel and Christian Theology* (Minneapolis, MN: Augsburg Fortress Publishers, 1996), 29-30; where he introduces *economic, punitive,* and *structural* supersessionism.

represent only a very brief introduction to a complex series of issues.

CONCLUSION

In conclusion let us bring together and summarise ways in which an aggressive expression of supersessionism impacts the Messianic movement, its relationship with the Church and the wider Jewish world:

- Supersessionism removes the Church's focus and attention from the Jewish people, resulting in a lack of appreciation for Christianity's historic roots and preventing accurate interpretation of Scripture (e.g, misunderstanding Gal 3:28: "There is neither Jew nor Greek").

- Supersessionism implicitly calls for Jews to assimilate into non-Jewish ways and denies the right to express Jewish ethnicity.

- Supersessionism, therefore, creates a hindrance towards ministering to Jews who have accepted Jesus as Messiah by not respecting their ethnicity. Churches increasingly allow for Spanish, Korean, and other ethnic uniqueness in worship, and there is no reason why the same should not be embraced for Messianic Jews.

- Supersessionism causes Messianic Jews to feel even less inclined to associate themselves with a Christian Gentile church that is so anti-Israel. This destroys a particular witness to the world through prevention of the healing effect the gospel is meant to have on Jewish-Christian relations.

- Supersessionism hinders MJs from creating an environment that is useful in evangelising non-Messianic Jews.

- Supersessionism stirs up unnecessary conflict with Gentile believers. E.g., aggravating the argument that the Messianic movement is rebuilding a wall of separation or considers Gentile Christians as second-class citizens in the Kingdom of God.

Paul refers to the diverse human body as the backdrop for his rhetorical argument asking whether all are apostles, prophets, and so on (1 Cor 12:20-30). The same type of rhetorical argument could be made about the body of Christ: Are all Jews? Are all Lithuanians? Are all Africans? Are all Asians? The impact of the new supersessionism is that it implicitly calls for the Messianic movement to conform to a uniformity rather than unity—an imposition not placed on other ethnic groups. One can openly express abhorrence at the history of Christian anti-Semitism and supersessionism. One can even profess to believe that Israel remains God's chosen people. However, when the theological curtains are pulled back concealed forms of supersessionism lurk in the darkness of many churches or in the recesses of people's hearts that ultimately cause increased trouble for Messianic Jewish believers as they seek to follow their Messiah in the context of their cultural heritage. We do not begrudge Koreans having Korean churches ... Nigerians having African-oriented fellowships ... or Hispanics having Spanish-speaking congregations. The impact of supersessionism, however, is that it contributes to a distinct suspicion of Jewish people who simply want to worship Messiah Jesus in a way that honors their ethnicity and culture, and which recognises their distinct heritage and history as Jews who, as believers in Jesus, are in direct continuity with biblical Israel. In its wake, supersessionism creates unnecessary turbulence and challenges not only for Jewish believers but also for non-Jews and how they relate to this unique expression of Christ's body on earth.

CHAPTER 11

Supersessionism, Messianic Jews and the Jewish Community: A Messianic Leader's Perspective

Richard Gibson

Messianic Jews are born of Jewish parents and come at some point in their lives to the discovery that Yeshua (Jesus) is the Messiah promised by their prophets in the Hebrew Scriptures. Just as a man remains a man after professing faith in Jesus, and a woman remains a woman after professing faith in Jesus, so too do the Irish remain Irish, the Arabs remain Arabs, the Chinese remain Chinese and Jews remain Jewish. One cannot deny one's birth heritage. Faith in Jesus is not about cultural realignment, rather the triumph of the Cross of Jesus over sin that separates the sinner from the Saviour.

For Jewish people in Messianic fellowships and in local churches outside of Israel, supersessionism provides the subliminal soundtrack that can profoundly affect how they are viewed and treated. A Messianic Jew recently shared her frustration at Christian responses to her, feeling she was either hated too much or loved too much for being a Jew.

"Why can't they just accept me as a human-being?" was her exasperated question. In trying to treat Messianic Jews like everyone else in the church, supersessionists often end up treating them less charitably, while in turn philo-Semites can react to the dark and shameful history of Church persecution of the Jewish people by over-compensating.

Supersessionism is so deeply ingrained in the Church that it affects even those who are pro-Jewish, pro-Messianic, and pro-Israel, in that it causes an exaggerated reaction to theological antipathy to *any* expression of Jewish identity, anti-Semitism or anti-Zionism. This albeit well-intentioned over-reaction to supersessionism can often leave Messianic Jews bemused in the face of oozing expressions of love "for the Jewish people", many feel like curiosities in some anthropological museum. More worryingly it leaves the question, is it such an effort to love me that you have needed some special revelation from God? I am reminded of a joint meeting the Messianic Fellowship I lead had with the local Farsi speaking fellowship where an ex-Afghani Mujahedeen shared his testimony. He addressed the Jewish people there, both Messianic and not: "I used to hate you and want to kill you but now because of Jesus I love you." This was exhilarating and deeply disturbing in equal measure. It was disturbing to know there was an ideology that elicited such a level of hate towards Jewish people that it needed such a dramatic spiritual revelation to change it.

Supersessionism is so pervasive in Christian thinking that it has affected how all sectors of the Church thinks about Jewish people. This has even influenced many positive responses to Messianic Jews. Typically these responses easily become off-balanced. Therefore supersessionism is so etched into the Christian psyche that even the Christians who want to be positive to Jewish people can easily over-compensate.

Either extreme of this spectrum of too much love or two much hate from Christians will leave Jewish people feeling suspicious and disturbed.

Supersessionism declares that while Jewish people were once special, now that Jesus has brought salvation to the whole world, Jews are no longer special and are like everyone else. However what has really happened is that Jewish people are not treated like everyone else. Instead, they are treated as if they were *less* special than everyone else in their "post-special" status. Consider a politician with all the privilege that person may have, then think of them becoming embroiled in a scandal and losing their special status. Such a politician would not return to the status of being like everyone else. Instead, he would be considered *less* than everyone else, having been shamed in public. This is the dynamic at work when Christians think about Jewish people. In real life experience Messianic Jews are faced with people in churches who feel compelled to tell them, often at their first meeting with them, that Jews are not special anymore. Many Messianic Jews have sadly experienced a supersessionist-influenced Christian attempting to put them in their place.

The Jewish people can too easily become intellectual abstracts for many Christians, viewing them as mere theological concepts that can be disagreed with and then dismissed. If Jewish people have become the battleground upon which the adherents of different theological viewpoints within Christendom fight one-another, how much more so are Messianic Jews de-humanised as they become "proofs" for the faithfulness of God or evidence of a certain eschatology? The alienation that Messianic Jews can feel from their fellow disciples of Jesus, who are not Jewish, is palpable, frustrating and painful.

This chapter offers a three-fold examination into how supersessionism has had, in reality, a negative effect firstly upon ministry, secondly upon Messianic Jews and Messianic fellowships, and thirdly upon the wider Jewish community. The evidence offered will be mostly anecdotal with personal observations and analyses reflecting eighteen years of leading a Messianic fellowship in Britain and twenty years in ministry where I have witnessed the grassroots effects that the new militant supersessionism has had, as an idea that subverts Christian reactions to Messianic Jews, and perverts what should be the biblical attitude to the Jewish people.

SUPERSESSIONISM AND MESSIANIC MINISTRY

In ministry, one of the most immediately noticeable things is the automatic suspicion that is often evoked when Messianic Jews and Jewish people are mentioned. More often than, not Christians from most traditions influenced by supersessionism will feel threatened in some way by any sort of expression of Jewish identity, whether that comes in the shape of traditional Jewish life, secular Israelis or Messianic Jewish life. The most emotional reaction will come in response to a Messianic Jew professing his or her Messianic Jewish identity. S/he will typically face accusations of the Galatian error, Judaising and rebuilding the wall of separation (I will respond to these charges later on in this chapter). This is not to say that there are not some peculiarities and problems in the Messianic movement. Such issues do exist, but they are often magnified and distorted by those seeking to justify pre-existent hostility toward Messianic Jewish identity and practice.

Just recently a letter was published in a British Christian newspaper where Messianic Jews who celebrate the Passover were accused of denying Christ's death by so doing. The author of the letter anachronistically charged that "the Passover denies that Christ, the Passover Lamb, has even come".[1] Passover celebrates the deliverance of the Children of Israel from Egypt around 1300-1500 years before Jesus had his earthly ministry.[2] Arguably, without the Exodus there would not have been a virgin from King David's line in Bethlehem Ephrata to give birth to a child who would be called Immanuel – "God with us". The Passover was a historical act of divine salvation that Jewish people are commanded in the Old Testament to memorialise as a lasting ordinance (Exod 12:14). Christians are supposed to accept the whole Bible as God's inspired Word, so there is no logic for the prejudice toward something God commands Jewish people to keep to this day. Jesus is not denied, quite the opposite occurs. In many Messianic Passover meals Jesus is highlighted as the Passover Lamb. It seems to me that the powerful negativity towards any functioning Jewish identity expressed by Messianic Jews is rooted in supersessionist assumptions that Jewishness is now redundant and somehow anti-Christian. According to this logic Jesus was the ultimate Israel and fulfilled what Israel was supposed to do, therefore it is claimed that there is now nothing left for the Jews or Jewish history other than cultural submission to the Church triumphant in its non-Jewish form. This is in line with the ancient origins of supersessionism, the Councils of Antioch (c. 341CE) and Laodicea (c. 360CE) declared that participation in Jewish rituals was officially banned by Cannon law.[3]

---

[1] Letter in the British Church Newspaper, 19 April 2013.
[2] Dating of the Exodus is a contentious issue among biblical scholars.
[3] Peter Tomson, *Paul and the Jewish law: Halakha in the Letters of the Apostle to the Gentiles* (Assen: Van Gorcum, 1990), 2-3.

There is an arrogance expressed against Jewish people that impacts Messianic Jewish experience in churches that is far from the Apostle Paul's exhortation not to boast against the natural branches (Romans 11:18). Beyond the overtures of theological correctness, there is an unpleasant sneering sense of superiority that is expressed against Jewishness. I was told by a Chinese friend that members of his Chinese church in Britain were laughing that Jews could not light fire on Saturday and were bound by so many silly rules. My friend told them that they were members of a denomination that had made up so many rules and regulations not found in the Bible that they were in no place to laugh. Rather, they could learn from Orthodox Jews who were so committed to God's commandments that they sought to keep all of them. It is hard not to see this as anything other than a profound antipathy towards Jewish culture, tradition and religious history fed by theological prejudice against Jews and Judaism. At the very worst there is the "a" word – anti-Semitism, anyone daring to use it in order to give a name to this prejudice, will cause people to cry foul at its very mention. To avoid the charge of anti-Semitism, what has been called the Livingstone Formulation[4] is invoked. This rhetorical device is employed as a counter-accusation levelled at the person who expressed concern at anti-Semitism, and they end up being accused of disingenuously playing the anti-Semitism card. The tables are turned and it is increasingly difficult to challenge the deep-seated anti-Semitism that is expressed in European culture and church life without it being victim to the Livingstone Formulation.

---

[4] http://engageonline.wordpress.com/2010/10/05/david-hirsh-the-livingstone-formulation/ [accessed 30/4/13].

A well-known conservative British Christian preacher once preached that Jews are not Jews.[5] The same preacher urged Christian students at a Christian Union meeting in a Welsh University to stand across the street from Orthodox Jewish tourists to the town and shout at them that they are not real Jews, but rather the Christians are the "real Jews".[6] Another British evangelical scholar claims that all the Palestinians are descendants of first century Jews[7] presumably to prove Palestinians have more historical right to Israel than the Jews, and asserts that Christian Zionists are wrong because Joan Peters' claim in her book *From Time Immemorial,* that Ottoman records revealed that most Palestinians are descendants of immigrants from other Arab nations, was invalid. However Norman Finkelstein's assault on Peters' scholarly integrity has been refuted by Erich and Rael Jean Isaac in "Whose Palestine?" (*Commentary,* July 1986).[8]

Yet another example of the embedded antipathy towards Jewish identity in the Evangelical subconscious comes in the form of the astonishing claim by the highly respected evangelical scholar Alec Motyer that "I still cannot find any 'Jews' in the Old Testament."[9] It is hard to imagine how any of these claims would encourage prayer and support for Messianic Jews, Jewish ministry and outreach – let alone a

---

[5] http://roshpinaproject.com/2011/10/05/british-preacher-stuart-olyott-claims-jews-are-not-jews/ [accessed 30/4/13].

[6] Eyewitness account from Joel Barder. "New Prospects" in The British Messianic Jewish Alliance *Chai* magazine 243 (2011), 4.

[7] http://www.al-bushra.org/latpatra/anthony.htm [accessed 30/4/13].

[8] Quoted in Edward Alexander & Paul Bogdanor, *The Jewish Divide Over Israel* (New Brunswick: Transaction Publishers, 2006), p.155-6.

[9] http://www.e-n.org.uk/4298-Israel-God's-servant.htm [accessed 30/4/13].

RICHARD GIBSON

balanced and appreciative attitude towards Jewish people generally.

Any ministry in a Jewish context therefore has to fight against multiple layers of suspicion and prejudice on top of the challenges that come from the ministry itself. However in recent years it has been the politicised supersessionism of a well-organised, well-funded and highly-motivated international group of Christian ministers and scholars that has pushed supersessionism in order to promote their own political views on the Israeli-Arab Palestinian conflict. Leaders of various missions to the Jewish people have acknowledged that they have lost support for their evangelistic work precisely because of this hybrid of supersessionist theology and anti-Israel political activism. However it must be noted that one high profile Christian anti-Zionist has started to support some Jewish missions, seemingly after criticism that his ideology was having a negative impact upon Christian witness to the Jewish people. Mike Moore, the General Secretary of Christian Witness to Israel had expressed concern that this militant politicised supersessionism would damage the cause of the Gospel amongst the Jewish people.[10]

However, what kind of results would a supersessionist supporter of Jewish evangelism like to see, a de-Judaised converted Jew who is won for Jesus but lost to his own Jewish people? A supersessionist hermeneutic sees no continuing place for national Israel and therefore no place for a Jewish identity for Jewish disciples of Jesus.

---

[10] Mike Moore "Stephen Sizer and Anti-Zionism" in *Mishkan – A Forum on the Gospel and the Jewish People* 55 (2008).

SUPERSESSIONISM AND MESSIANIC JEWS

Supersessionism implies no lasting place for Messianic fellowships or a distinctly Jewish identity for Jewish disciples of Jesus the Messiah and seems to insist upon the cultural obliteration of Jewish expressions of worship and discipleship for Messianic Jews. A lady once approached me after I preached in the church she was attending: "Why can't these Messianic Jews just be like me, why do they have to be different?" she exclaimed, "after all they are Christians like me". One could argue that disciples of Jesus should only be like Him (and he was a Jew!) rather than like each other. Displays of intolerance towards Messianic Jews maintaining their Jewish identity in a variety of ways, whether they only attend a local church, a Messianic fellowship or both, reveal only the insecurity of their accusers, who feel uncomfortable by the unashamed Jewishness of Messianic Jews.

I am not accusing adherents of supersessionism of automatic anti-Semitism, but supersessionism does inevitably make anti-Semitism harder to identify, stop, challenge, and seems to make the deprecation of Jewish culture and identity an acceptable part of public discourse when talking to and about their Jewish brothers and sisters in Jesus.

I was approached by an elderly gentleman in a large Pentecostal church where I had been preaching about God's ongoing covenant faithfulness to Israel, "I've been waiting thirty years to hear that in this church" he told me, "I am Jewish but I've not told anyone here, they wouldn't understand." The conversation moved on as someone else engaged him in conversation and a leader from the church leaned over to me and said, "I knew it, he is a Yid". I was staggered that I would hear such racist sentiment from a church leader. In the same church a new Christian was cautioned by a prayer group leader about another new believer: "Be careful of her, she is a Jew". The impact of supersessionism upon the life of Messianic Jews who make their primary worshipping community a local church can often be one that makes them regret that choice.

These are many things that are said about Messianic fellowships, but why is it that a group of people meeting together for worship of God, mutual support and teaching should cause so much controversy and, at times, consternation? Messianic fellowships are often the one place that Messianic Jews are not made to feel that their Jewish identity is the problem.

A phrase that has gained more popularity and use in the Messianic movement is Messianic Judaism,[11] which is defined by Richard Harvey as "the religion of Jewish people who believe in Jesus (Yeshua) as the promised Messiah. It is a Jewish form of Christianity and a Christian form of Judaism, challenging the boundaries and beliefs of both.[12]

It is precisely the challenge to the boundaries and beliefs of both Christianity and Judaism that has put Messianic Jews individually and, especially communally, firmly in the firing line from both sides and sometimes friendly fire from within.

Distinctly Jewish Messianic Jews do not fit easily into any theology that implies and explicitly claims God has finished with *national* Israel and there is no corporate spiritual future hope, and God has therefore moved exclusively to the Gentiles with the exception of a small elect in each Jewish generation. Neither do Messianic Jews accept the idea of being an ex-Jew, converted Jew or once a Jew but now a

---

[11] http://www.umjc.org/home-mainmenu-1/global-vision-mainmenu-42/13-vision/225-defining-messianic-judaism [Accessed 21/8/12].

[12] Richard Harvey. *Mapping Messianic Jewish Theology, A Constructive Approach* (Milton Keynes: Paternoster, 2009), 1.

Christian, assuming that the latter term obliterates the former. Rather they are Jewish disciples of Jesus, as were his first disciples and followers.

The Galatian Heresy is quoted as evidence of questionable theology, however the Judaisers were so-called because they were insisting that non-Jews observe Torah and be circumcised in order to be real Christians that drew the Apostle Paul's criticism. The word "Judaiser" does not appear in the New Testament, it is a later term. Interestingly there is no direct claim in the New Testament that the Judaisers themselves were Jewish. Paul was positive about his Jewish identity; he was not an ex-Jew, even if he did write about his *former life in Judaism* in Galatians 1:13-14. Young's Literal Translation has a fascinating rendering of this verse which makes the context even more pronounced: "for ye did hear of my behaviour once in Judaism, that exceedingly I was persecuting the assembly of God, and wasting it". It must be remembered that Paul also wrote: "Then what advantage has the Jew? Much in every way" (Rom 3:1-2). Paul continued to identify himself by the appellations of his 'former life in Judaism' claiming "I am a Pharisee" (Acts 23:6). Paul has an expanded version of this in Philippians 3:5 "circumcised on the eighth day, of the people of Israel, of the tribe of Benjamin, a Hebrew of Hebrews; in regard to the law, a Pharisee." For someone who taught that we should abstain from even the appearance of evil (1 Thess 5:22), he obviously saw nothing wrong, evil or 'theologically dodgy' with an active Jewish identity for a Jewish follower of Jesus.

The charge that Messianic Jewish groups are re-building the middle wall of separation is also a mischaracterisation. Firstly *that* wall can never be rebuilt because Jesus Himself destroyed it with his once and for all sacrifice on the cross. Secondly most Messianic groups are sometimes better at providing a home for Jews and Gentiles together in Jesus, than many Gentile-culture-dominant churches. Thirdly there is an unequal measure at work, those who attack Messianic Jewish fellowships and congregations, would seldom, if ever, attack other non-white, non-European origin churches in the same way they would a group of Jewish people meeting together as disciples of Yeshua/Jesus. Why can everyone except Messianic Jews maintain their cultural and ethnic integrity when they come to faith in Jesus the Messiah? There is not one verse in the Bible that explicitly prohibits Messianic Jews from worshipping Yeshua the Messiah communally as Jews. The Early Church in Jerusalem, at least, was a proto-Messianic Jewish congregation and even issued a code of conduct for Gentile believers. It is, therefore, unhelpful to conflate all Jewish practice with the New Testament criticism of "the Judaisers" seeking to circumcise Gentiles.

The early Jewish followers struggled at first, but eventually managed to accommodate all the new Gentile followers of Jesus without demanding they abandon their cultural identities. It should therefore not be hard for the wider Church to reciprocate this generosity to Messianic Jews.

SUPERSESSIONISM AND THE JEWISH PEOPLE

With everyone from the Rastafarians to the Jehovah's Witnesses claiming to be the real Israel, it appears that everyone is Israel apart from the Jewish people! The Jewish community looks at supersessionism where Jesus has replaced Israel and its clumsier manifestation as Replacement Theology where the Church has replaced Israel, as the ultimate proof that the claims of Jesus cannot possibly be for Jews. Author and lawyer Anthony Julius states in his tome about anti-Semitism in the Diaspora, in a section titled *A restated Supersessionism*:

> It is in Christianity that for the first time in the world's history Jew-hatred becomes sanctified. As against the pagan confrontation with the Jews, which was mostly voluntary and occasional, the Christian Church was *compelled* to confront the Jews.[13]

Supersessionism is a view that many genuine Christians hold as a result of the hermeneutic that they accept. Most would be horrified to realise that it is one of the great stumbling blocks for those Jewish people who are interested in the Messianic claims of Jesus. They should be more horrified to know that this is used as an evidence that those who believe that Jews should not even consider Jesus' Messianic claims are correct. However it is the new dimension of utilising supersessionism to serve the cause of Christian anti-Zionism that has caught the attention of Jewish writers like Anthony Julius.

While Christian anti-Zionism is the pursuit of activists, inevitably a minority within their various denominations, it also has a normative theological aspect that speaks to *all* Christians. This aspect is what might be termed a revived, even somewhat politicised, supersessionism. [14]

It may be an uncomfortable truth to some, but it can be argued that the revived and politicised theology of Supersessionism is taking Christian theology back to Medieval times where anti-Judaic theology led to the

---

[13] Anthony Julius, *Trials of the Diaspora, A History of Anti-Semitism in England.* (Oxford: Oxford University Press, 2010), 563.
[14] Ibid., 567.

marginalisation of Jews in Europe and then to persecution. The Chief Rabbi of Great Britain notes that the result of supersessionism is, "to deny legitimacy to Jews because they deny legitimacy to Judaism".[15] The State of Israel has become, by extension, the Jew amongst the nations, and Jews in the Diaspora have become Israel for the majority of anti-Zionist activists. This is seen in list of companies drawn up by the boycott and divestment proponents which typically include Jewish rather than just Israeli firms.

What must be a grave concern for the Jewish community is, alongside the rise of this political supersessionism, the fact that negative thinking about the Jews has always historically been the precursor to negative actions against the Jews.

The Christian "Teaching of Contempt" about Jews and Judaism furnished stereotypes that enabled Nazis to focus on the Jews as scapegoat and create a climate of anti-Semitism in Europe. This climate enabled some Christians to feel they were doing God's duty when they either helped kill Jews or did not stop the killing.[16]

Christian supersessionism is not an ideology that leaves Jewish people with any sense of the humility and love of Jesus Christ. Rather Jewish people see it as one of triumphalistic arrogance that has taught that contempt of the Jews is good Christian theology. Churches of various denominations do not have the influence and power that they used to have; however if priests, pastors and preachers are not cautious and recognise the impact that supersessionism

---

[15] Jonathan Sacks, *Future Tense, A Vision for Jews and Judaism in the Global Culture* (London: Hodder & Stoughton, 2009), 73.

[16] Irving Greenberg, "The Shoah and the Legacy of Anti-Semitism: Judaism, Christianity, and Partnership After the Twentieth Century" in Tikva Frymer-Kensky, et al, eds. *Christianity in Jewish Terms*, (Boulder: Westview Press 2000), 26.

historically has had upon the fate of the Jewish people in Europe, they will be doomed to repeat the mistake of their forebears. Inevitably, supersessionists are unlikely to change their minds as they think that they have the truth of the Early Church Fathers and are being faithful to the New Testament's reading of the Old Testament. However, what we can ask of them is to make more of an effort not to sound so anti-Jewish.

I well remember a conversation with an Israeli friend in which he was sharing with me the impact that a significant book in the Jewish world called *Pirkei Avot* (The Ethics of the Fathers) had upon him during his military service. The book famously starts with the statement that "All Israel has a share in the world to come". When I noted that it reminded me of something in the New Testament, he looked shocked. I quoted the Apostle Paul from Romans 11:26 "and all Israel shall be saved." He was even more shocked. "Is that really in the New Testament? Because my rabbis told me it was a book of hatred against the Jews! How else can you explain why Christians has done what they have done to us Jews? I thought that the New Testament was kind of like Hitler's *Mein Kampf*!"

The historical development of supersessionism has been documented elsewhere such as Diprose's *Israel and The Church*, and is outside of the scope of this chapter, other than to note that it was not found in the earliest years of the Church when the Jewish disciples of Jesus were numerically dominant in this new community of faith.

CONCLUSION

The choices Diaspora Messianic Jews have to face in the light of supersessionism are, to hide or limit their identity in order to fit-in at a local church congregation, find a Messianic

275

Jewish fellowship where they can exist naturally and not feel the need to deny their heritage, stay at home and avoid the conflict or simply stay in the Jewish community. In Israel things are different to some extent as the communal expression of faith in Jesus is predominantly a Jewish one.

Faith in Jesus is not simply an idea that is subscribed to, but also a community that is joined. However, when that community thinks the deprecation of your culture and traditions is somehow good theology, Messianic Jews can feel shunned in the community that claims to welcome believers from all cultures and backgrounds.

The Jewish community is vibrant, caring, and family-orientated with clearly defined boundaries and identity that Messianic Jews often lose or have limited involvement in because their faith in Jesus is seen as a betrayal of their people. The church community could become a far more welcoming place if it were willing to expunge the effects of supersessionist negativity about Jewish people, culture, tradition and Judaism. Messianic fellowships could be viewed as something to support rather than treated with suspicion. There have been many former Messianic Jews for whom the relentless supersessionist inspired negativity from pulpit and pew towards their existence as Jews was just too much for them to continue.

We must note however that the Jewish community sees Christian mission to the Jews as part of the outworking of a Judeophobic supersessionism that needs to see Jews *become Christians* in a cultural as well as spiritual sense, to fulfil theological and eschatological expectations. Even if Messianic Jews retain and celebrate their Jewish heritage and culture, they are often viewed by the Jewish community as stealth missionaries. Supersessionism and the history of Church persecution of Jewish people have made it very difficult for Messianic Jews both in the Church and Jewish community.

As Mike Moore wryly noted: "like it or not, the Messianic movement exists – warts and all – and Gentile believers must choose whether to help their Jewish brothers and sisters to grow in the faith or whether to stand on the sidelines and carp."[17]

For the person sat in the pew hearing week after week how terrible the Jews were, the church is now the new Israel because the old Israel was so bad; any nuance that supersessionist theologians may seek to introduce is lost. The fact is supersessionists believe that Jews need to hear the Gospel like the rest of humanity, even if they don't believe there will be much of a response. However this does not ameliorate the undeniable bias caused by supersessionism that creates an automatic treating of all Jews as enemies for the sake if the Gospel without the counterbalance of loved for the sake of the patriarchs as Paul so carefully explains in Romans 11:28.

Graham Keith concludes his survey of anti-Semitism with this statement:

> Clearly it is as difficult today as at any time for the gentile churches to hold in balance the two elements of Paul's perspective in Rom, 11:28. Yet, they must strive to do so. If they forget that the Jewish people are beloved of God and their elective is irrevocable,

---

[17] Mike Moore, "Blessed and a Blessing – The Messianic Movement Today and Tomorrow" in *Mishkan – A Forum on the Gospel and the Jewish People* 59 (2009).

inevitably they will slip into anti-Semitic attitudes and practices.[18]

Many Messianic Jews feel distrusted, which sometimes takes the form of latent and blatant hostility from those who are their brothers and sisters in Jesus, all thanks to the lack of this biblical balancing of ideas.

---

[18] Graham Keith, *Hated Without a Cause? A Survey of Anti-Semitism* (Carlisle: Paternoster Press. 1997), 283.

CHAPTER 12

Is the Gospel Relevant to the Jewish People?

Tony Pearce

For I am not ashamed of the gospel, for it is the power of God for salvation to everyone who believes, to the Jew first and also to the Greek. For in it the righteousness of God is revealed from faith for faith, as it is written, "The righteous shall live by faith." (Rom 1:16-17)

In Romans 9-11 Paul deals with the issues relating to the above question. In 9:4-5 he reminds us of what Israel has from the past:

> They are Israelites, and to them belong the adoption, the glory, the covenants, the giving of the law, the worship, and the promises. To them belong the patriarchs, and from their race, according to the flesh, is the Christ who is God over all, blessed forever.

In chapter 10:1-4 he speaks of God's present will for Israel:

> Brothers, my heart's desire and prayer to God for them is that they may be saved. For I bear them witness that they have a zeal for God, but not according to knowledge. For, being ignorant of the righteousness of God, and seeking to establish their own, they did not submit to God's righteousness. For Christ is the end of the law for righteousness to everyone who believes.

It is clear Paul understood that salvation comes to Israel through the Gospel and that the means of them coming to this faith was to be the preaching of the Gospel:

> How then will they call on him in whom they have not believed? And how are they to believe in him of whom they have never heard? And how are they to hear without someone preaching? And how are they to preach unless they are sent? As it is written, "How beautiful are the feet of those who preach the good news!"... So faith comes from hearing, and hearing through the word of Christ. (Rom 10:14-15, 17).

In 11:25-27 he sees the future for Israel:

> Lest you be wise in your own sight, I do not want you to be unaware of this mystery, brothers: a partial hardening has come upon Israel, until the fullness of the Gentiles has come in. And in this way all Israel will be saved, as it is written, "The Deliverer will come from Zion, he will banish ungodliness from Jacob"; "and this will be my covenant with them when I take away their sins."

The quotation is a composite quote from both Isaiah 59:20-21 and Jeremiah 31:31-34. For this future hope for Israel to be fulfilled, it is necessary for her to remain a people, with a covenant relationship with God, until the end of days and the return of the Messiah Jesus.

Some have commented on the fact that the future for Israel as given by Paul makes no mention of the land:

> The prophecy of Romans 11 is a prophecy that many Jews will return to Christ, but the land is not mentioned, nor is Israel mentioned as a political entity.[1]

When Paul wrote Romans the Jewish people were still in the land of Israel (under Roman occupation, admittedly), so a specific promise of a return to the land would have been out of place. It is difficult to imagine that the Apostle Paul could have conceived of the "covenants" of which he wrote in this section of Romans without relating this to Genesis 15 and 17, in which God's covenant with Abraham and his descendants clearly relates to the land.

In these three chapters it is clear Paul saw a continuation of the Jewish people after the birth of the Church and sought their inclusion into the believing Church. In fact he said it was the Gentiles who are included into the covenant God made with Israel, symbolised by the olive tree of Romans 11:11-24. For Romans 11:25-36 to be fulfilled it is necessary for Israel to remain a people until the return of the Messiah.

It is a remarkable testimony to the faithfulness of God's word that despite the dispersion of the Jewish people to the ends of the earth, persecution and assimilation, the Jews remain an identifiable people to this day. Even more remarkable is that after the worst period of persecution they

---

[1] J. Stott, "Foreword" in P. Johnstone and P Walker, eds. *The Promised Land* (Downers Grove, ILL: InterVarsity Press, 2000), 11.

have ever known, the Nazi holocaust, "am Israel chai" ("the people of Israel live") are once again in the land promised to Abraham. And despite all the traumas of their history many Jewish people in the land of Israel and in the dispersion are coming to believe that Jesus, or Yeshua, to give Him His Hebrew name, is the Messiah.

One advantage the Apostle Paul had over us when he told Jewish people about the Messiah was he did not have nearly two thousand years of history to deal with. These years have caused an enormous barrier to be erected which prevents many Jewish people from even considering that Jesus could be the Messiah. The barrier is actually two-fold: from the professing church and from the synagogue.

BARRIERS FROM WITHIN THE CHURCH

In Romans 10 Paul told Christians to pray for Israel that they might be saved. If we pray for our neighbour to be saved but he does not get saved, how do we respond to him? Do we go over to his house and throw stones through his window to show what a rotten person he is for not accepting the Lord? Of course not. We will try to show concern for him and to "provoke him to jealousy" that he might want what we have (Rom 11:14). Sadly, the professing church has done much more than throw stones through the windows of the Jewish people. As the church rejected Paul's teaching not to cut themselves off from the Jewish roots of the faith, so it became anti-Semitic, and in the process actually denied much of the teaching of the Lord Jesus and the Apostles. John Chrysostom, considered a saint and church father who lived in the fourth century, wrote:

The Jews are the most worthless of all men. They are lecherous, greedy and rapacious. They are perfidious murderers of Christ. The Jews are the odious assassins of Christ and for killing God there is no expiation possible, no indulgence or pardon. Christians may never cease vengeance and the Jews must live in servitude forever. God always hated the Jews. It is incumbent upon Christians to hate Jews.[2]

When Constantine established Christianity as the official religion of the Roman Empire in 312, he issued many anti-Jewish laws. Jews were forbidden to accept converts, while every enticement was used to make them forsake Judaism. At the Council of Nicea in AD 325 he said, "It is right to demand what our reason approves and that we should have nothing in common with the Jews."[3]

Augustine taught that the Church had replaced Israel: "For if we hold with a firm heart the grace of God which hath been given us, we are Israel, the seed of Abraham."[4] He made what must be one of the most wrong-headed interpretations of Scripture ever, concerning Psalm 59.11: "Kill them not, lest my people forget; make them totter by your power and bring them down." This he interpreted to mean the vagabond Jews was a testimony of God's dealing with them in judgment according to the Scripture.[5]

---

[2] *Homilae Adversus Iudaeos.* John Chrysostom (c 307-407) was a preacher with great powers of oratory from Antioch.

[3] In a letter to those not present at the Council (see Eusebius, Vita Const., Lib. iii., 18-20.), Fordham University's *Internet History Sourcebooks Project,* www.fordham.edu/halsall/source/const1-easter.html (accessed 18 February 2008).

[4] Augustine, *Expositions on the Book of Psalms* (vol 5), 114.3.

[5] Augustine, *The City of God,* 18.46.

In 1215 Pope Innocent III took up this theme when he condemned the Jews to eternal slavery by decreeing

> The Jews against whom the blood of Jesus Christ calls out, although they ought not to be killed, lest the Christian people forget the Divine Law, yet as wanderers ought they remain upon the earth until their countenance be filled with shame.[6]

Martin Luther, the founder of the German Reformation, hoped initially he would attract Jews to his Protestant faith, understanding they could not accept the superstitions and persecutions of Rome. But when they rejected his attempts to convert them, he turned on them and uttered words of hatred cited *verbatim* by the Nazis in their propaganda. He told the German princes how to deal with the Jews. This included setting their synagogues on fire, destroying their homes, forbidding rabbis to teach and depriving them of their prayer books. He said they should be forbidden to travel and to practice usury (the main occupation of Jews in the Middle Ages due to the restrictive laws of the time). In short he recommended enslaving them.[7]

Jewish people today are much more likely to know about this history than most Christians. For many, it is still played out in their experience of life. The singer Helen Shapiro gives her testimony of growing up in London in the 1950s and the shock of a child in primary school screaming at her, "You

---

[6] Innocent III, *Letter to the Count of Nevers,* 1208.
[7] Martin Luther, *Concerning the Jews and Their Lies* (1543 tract). For further details of Luther's view of the Jews see M. Vlach, "Martin Luther and Supersessionism", www.theologicalstudies.org/luther_supersessionism.html (last accessed 18 February 2009).

killed Jesus". Sometimes Christians say to me, "Why can't Jewish people see that Jesus is the Messiah?" When we look at the image of Jesus that has been given to Jewish people through the centuries it is more remarkable that Jewish people like Helen Shapiro can see that Jesus is the Messiah.

In John's Gospel Jesus makes it clear who is responsible for his death:

> For this reason the Father loves me, because I lay down my life that I may take it up again. No one takes it from me, but I lay it down of my own accord. I have authority to lay it down, and I have authority to take it up again. This charge I have received from my Father. (John 10:17-18)

The implication of this is clear. Jesus Himself takes responsibility for His own death. It happens at the time and manner of His choosing, in order that He might fulfil the Father's will by dying as the sacrifice for the sins of the world and rising again from the dead to give eternal life to those who receive Him. No human being, Jew or Gentile has the right or power to take Jesus' life from Him against His will.

This fulfils the prophecy of Isaiah 53, which states concerning the sufferings of the Messiah, "Yet it was the will of the Lord to crush him; he has put him to grief" (Isa 53:10). In this prophecy the responsibility for Messiah's sufferings is placed on God Himself. "It was the will of the Lord to crush him" means Jesus was put to death to fulfil the will of God.

According to the Book of Hebrews, those who believe come to "Jesus, the mediator of a new covenant, and to the sprinkled blood that speaks a better word than the blood of Abel" (Heb 12:24). The blood of Abel spoke of vengeance for Cain's sin of murder (Genesis 4), but the blood of Jesus speaks of mercy and forgiveness. Wrong church teaching, however, has turned this on its head and used the verse in Matthew's Gospel, "His blood be upon us and on our children" (Matt 27:25), to claim that the suffering of the Jewish people is the result of a self-inflicted curse, and even that Christians are therefore justified in persecuting the Jewish people in Jesus' name.

Nothing could be further from the truth. Jesus Himself prayed from the cross, "Father, forgive them, for they know not what they do", (Luke 23:34), thus expressing God's will that even those responsible for the death of Jesus, whether Jewish or Gentile, should find forgiveness through His name. Do we base our theology on the words of an enraged crowd or on the words of the Lord Jesus?

The answer to Jesus' prayer was to be found not long afterwards in the preaching of the Apostles. When Peter preached in the Temple after the Day of Pentecost, before him were people who had really been responsible for the death of Jesus in that they called for Him to be crucified. But even to them there was a message of hope and forgiveness. Explaining the meaning of the death and resurrection of Jesus Peter said:

> And now, brothers, I know that you acted in ignorance, as did also your rulers. But what God foretold by the mouth of all the prophets, that his Christ would suffer, he thus fulfilled. Repent therefore, and turn back, that your sins may be blotted out. (Acts 3:17-19)

The statement which really tells us who was responsible for the death of Jesus is to be found in Acts 4.27-28:

> For truly in this city there were gathered together against your holy servant Jesus, whom you anointed, both Herod and Pontius Pilate, along with the Gentiles and the peoples of Israel, to do whatever your hand and your plan had predestined to take place.

In this prayer all categories of people are implicated: Herod and Pontius Pilate with the Gentiles and the people of Israel. The Gentiles are actually mentioned before the people of Israel, therefore they have no right to claim any superiority or judgmental attitude towards the Jews. It is clear the physical act of crucifying Jesus was carried out on the orders of the Roman governor, by Roman soldiers in the Roman way. Strangely no one has ever suggested the Italians killed Jesus and should be placed under a curse because of this! All this happened "to do whatever your hand and your plan had predestined to take place", in other words to fulfil the predetermined plan of God. So again the ultimate responsibility for the death of Jesus rests with God Himself in order to fulfil His purposes.

A number of Christians react to anti-Semitism within Christianity by taking the view that Christians should not share the Gospel with Jewish people. Some then become involved in pro-Israel activities or in dialogue with Jewish people and deny Jews need salvation through Jesus the Messiah. A noted example of this view is John Hagee, who organises events to honour Israel and raises large sums of money from Evangelical Christians to give to Jewish charities in Israel. Hagee has said:

> The Jewish people have a relationship to God through the law of God as given through Moses. I believe that every Gentile person can only come to God through the

287

cross of Christ. I believe that every Jewish person who lives in the light of the Torah, which is the word of God, has a relationship with God and will come to redemption. The law of Moses is sufficient enough to bring a person into the knowledge of God until God gives him a greater revelation. And God has not.[8]

But the whole message of the New Testament is that God has given a greater revelation in Jesus. The book of Hebrews explains this "better covenant" which we enter into through faith in the Messiah. In fact, if Jesus is not the Messiah of the Jewish people then He is not the Messiah of anyone, because our very concept of Messiah comes from the Jews.

BARRIERS FROM WITHIN THE SYNAGOGUE

Modern Judaism fits in with Paul's words in Romans 10 where he speaks of Jewish people "seeking to establish their own righteousness" but not submitting to the "righteousness of God. For Christ / Messiah is the end of the law for righteousness to everyone who believes." Paul is saying Jesus the Messiah provides the solution to the sin problem and if we miss this then we are going to end up trying to establish our own system of religious good works in order to find salvation.

It can be shown that all religious systems including nominal Christianity do exactly this. All religions basically offer some system of good works in order to cancel out our sins and gain credit with God. Because none of them are based on God's revelation they all fail. In modern Judaism it

[8] 'San Antonio fundamentalist battles anti-Semitism', *Houston Chronicle*, April 30, 1988.

can be shown there is a religious system which is based on their own Messiah, their own way of atoning for sins and their own holy books.

Their Own Messiah

One of the most common objections to Jesus being the Messiah from Jewish people is that there has been no peace since Jesus came, and therefore He cannot be the Messiah. This is based on the view that the Messiah must fulfil Scriptures such as Isaiah 2:1-4 and 11-12 when He comes. Isaiah 2 is accepted as being a Messianic passage by the synagogue and the church. It promises a time when "nation shall not lift up sword against nation, neither shall they learn war anymore". Another objection is the Christian view of Jesus as the Son of God, and the implication that God is a plural unity of Father, Son and Holy Spirit.

According to Maimonides (1135-1204), the pre-eminent Jewish rabbi and teacher of the Middle Ages, the Messiah has to complete the following three tasks:

1. Re-gather the dispersed Jewish people to Israel
2. Rebuild the Temple in Jerusalem
3. Make world peace.[9]

By contrast it is pointed out since the coming of Jesus the following has happened:

1. The Jewish people were dispersed into the nations
2. The Temple in Jerusalem was destroyed
3. There have been wars and persecutions ever since.

---

[9] Maimonides Hilchos Melachim 11.1 and 4 from the Mishneh Torah.

Of course, Jesus never claimed He would bring world peace following His first coming and prophesied a long period of "wars and rumours of wars" (Matt 24:6), the destruction of the Temple (Luke 19:41-44) and the dispersion of the Jewish people into the nations (Luke 21:20-24). There will be a reversal of this process at the end of days when Jerusalem will no longer be "trampled underfoot by the Gentiles" (Luke 21:24), and its people will welcome Jesus as returning Messiah with the Messianic greeting "Blessed is he who comes in the name of the Lord" (Matt 23:39).

There is a hope for the time of peace and justice, of which the Prophets spoke, being fulfilled after the return of the Lord Jesus in the Millennium (Rev 20), or Messianic Age. Of course, the problem of explaining this to Jewish people today is much of the church takes the amillennial view that these prophecies are fulfilled in the church reigning today or in heaven. In fact much of the church misses the point about the future reign of the Messiah after His return, just as the Jewish people miss the fact that He has already come as Suffering Servant.

Isaiah actually gives two different portraits of the Messiah, one as a reigning king (Is 2) and the other as a suffering servant (Is 53). Isaiah 53:3, 5-6 describes the servant of the Lord as one who is

> despised and rejected by men; a man of sorrows, and acquainted with grief... But he was pierced for our transgressions; he was crushed for our iniquities; upon him was the chastisement that brought us peace, and with his wounds we are healed. All we like sheep have gone astray; we have turned—every one—to his own way; rand the Lord has laid on him the iniquity of us all.

Modern Judaism tries to interpret this passage as applying to the sufferings of Israel as taught by the French rabbi Rashi (1040-1105). However, according to Arnold Fruchtenbaum

> Every rabbi prior to Rashi, without exception, viewed Isaiah 53 as describing Messiah. When Rashi first proposed that this passage spoke of the nation of Israel, he sparked a fierce debate with his contemporaries. Maimonides stated very clearly that Rashi is completely wrong and going against the traditional Jewish viewpoint."[10]

There are various reasons why Isaiah 53 cannot refer to the sufferings of Israel on behalf of the Gentiles. The Suffering Servant of Isaiah 53 bears the sins of others. If the servant is Israel then Isaiah must be a Gentile because the people he identifies with ("all we like sheep") have their iniquity laid on him (Israel?). Of course, this is impossible and Isaiah is identifying the sins of himself and his people Israel being laid on this servant of the Lord. Isaiah has spent much of his prophecy speaking of the sins of Israel, as we see in the first chapter of his book: "Israel does not know, my people do not understand. Ah, sinful nation, a people laden with iniquity" (Is 1:3-4). A sinful people cannot bear the sins of others. Only one who is without sin Himself, as Paul states in 2 Corinthians 5:21, "For our sake he made him to be sin who knew no sin, so that in him we might become the righteousness of God."

Isaiah 53 was perfectly fulfilled by the sacrificial death of the Lord Jesus as recorded in the New Testament. The New

---

[10] Arnold Fruchtenbaum, *Messianic Christology* (San Antonio, TX: Ariel, 1998), 54.

Testament clearly teaches that the same Jesus will come again, this time as King of Kings and Lord of Lords and that He will judge the world in righteousness (Matt 24, Mark 13, Luke 21, Acts 1, Rev 6-19). In the time between His first and second coming the Gospel will go out to all nations to bring in the harvest of souls who are saved through repentance and faith in the Lord Jesus as Saviour / Messiah.

While the Messianic prophecies do not specifically state there will be two comings of the same Messiah, it is clear that there are two different portraits of the Messiah, one as a Suffering Servant and one as a Reigning King. There are rabbinic writings which acknowledge this and try to explain it by saying there are two Messiahs, one known as Messiah son of Joseph, who suffers and is then exalted as Joseph was in Genesis, and the other known as Messiah son of David who reigns as a king like David.[11] The better explanation is there is one Messiah who comes on two different occasions and whose name is Jesus / Yeshua.

On the issue of the divinity of the Messiah there are a number of prophecies which do indicate the coming one will be more than just a great man who brings peace. In Isaiah 9:6 we read of one to be born as a child, but who will also be Mighty God, Everlasting Father. In Micah 5:2 the one to be born in Bethlehem will have His origins in the "days of eternity". Only God has his origins in eternity. In Zechariah 14:4 the one whose feet stand on the Mount of Olives at the end of days is identified as the LORD (Yahweh). In Judaism, this prophecy is believed to be about the Messiah and it ties in with the New Testament promise of the return of Jesus (Acts 1:11-12).

---

[11] For details on this see David Baron, *Visions and Prophecies of Zechariah* (Whitefish, MT: Kessinger, 2007), 441.

THE GOSPEL AND THE JEWISH PEOPLE

There are also passages which speak of God as a plural unity in the Torah. In the very first verse of the Bible we read, "In the beginning God created the heavens and the earth" (Gen 1:1). The word for "God" (Elohim) is a masculine plural noun. The word for "created" (bara) is a singular verb. The very first sentence in the Bible, with a plural noun and a singular verb, opens up the possibility of God being a plural unity. In Genesis 1:26 God said, "Let us make man in our image, after our likeness." Why not "Let me make man in my image"? It cannot be that God is speaking to the angels, because man is not made in the image of angels. The rabbinic explanation, that it is the plural of majesty, does not add up either since there is no example in the Bible of kings addressing themselves in the plural. The likely explanation for this and other occasions where God speaks in the plural of Himself (Gen 11:7, Isa 6.8) is that God is a plural unity.

Atonement

Modern Judaism does not deal with the sin problem in the way the Torah requires. In order to cover sin and escape from its penalty (death) there must be repentance and sacrifice of another who dies in our place. Under the covenant with Moses this was the animal which sacrificed its blood (and therefore died) in accordance with the commandments given in the Torah. This was the only way in which the barrier between God and humanity, caused by sin, could be removed. God is holy and we are not, and the only way we can relate to the Holy One is on His terms, not ours. The Lord makes it clear He requires the shedding of blood in order to be able to come into relationship with his people. In Leviticus 17.11 we read:

> For the life of the flesh is in the blood, and I have given it for you on the altar to make atonement for your souls, for it is the blood that makes atonement by the life.

However, modern Judaism teaches that the blood of atonement is no longer required today. When the Temple was destroyed in 70 CE by the Romans, the Sanhedrin reconvened in Yavneh under the leadership of Rabbi Yochanan ben Zakkai, who developed a theology based on some verses of the Bible which seem to point to sacrifices being unnecessary as a means of mediating between God and humanity. For example:

> "What to me is the multitude of your sacrifices?" says the Lord; "I have had enough of burnt offerings of rams and the fat of well-fed beasts; I do not delight in the blood of bulls, or of lambs, or of goats... Bring no more vain offerings; incense is an abomination to me. New moon and Sabbath and the calling of convocations—I cannot endure iniquity and solemn assembly." (Isa 1:11, 13).

Based on these Scriptures Judaism developed a theology which relegated the sacrificial system to ancient history. The fact that the Temple no longer stood and therefore there was no access to the place appointed by God to offer the sacrifices seemed to confirm this view. Therefore the Rabbis decreed that God was able to forgive sins through repentance, prayers, fasting and good deeds which replaced the blood of the animal sacrifices.

So does God say that sacrifices are not needed to cover sins? In Isaiah 1 God tells His people they are offering sacrifices without sincerity and continuing in sin at the same time. God is not actually saying, "You don't need to offer any sacrifices". What He is saying is "Your sacrifices are meaningless because you are just going through the outward motions of pleasing me while your hearts and your actions are far from me". He is calling on them to repent *and* to offer the sacrifices from a true heart, not to repent *instead* of offering the sacrifices.

Under the old covenant the worshipper found forgiveness through repentance and faith in the sin offering prescribed by the Torah. He recognised he deserved to die, but God in His mercy accepted this sacrifice in his place. The blood of the animal itself only had value in that it pointed forward to the blood of the Messiah who was yet to come. Under the New Covenant the same principle applies. We find forgiveness through repentance and faith in the blood of the Messiah shed for our sins:

> (Christ) has appeared once for all at the end of the ages to put away sin by the sacrifice of himself. And just as it is appointed for man to die once, and after that comes judgment, so Christ, having been offered once to bear the sins of many, will appear a second time, not to deal with sin but to save those who are eagerly waiting for him. (Heb 9:26-28).

Under the New Covenant the same principle operates as under the Old Covenant: that those who come to God must repent of their sins and put their trust in the sacrifice He has appointed. Under the Old Covenant it was the blood of the sacrificed animal. Under the New Covenant it is the much better sacrifice of the blood of Jesus the Messiah. Through accepting this sacrifice we find our way back to a covenant relationship with God.

Holy books

In a way both Judaism and Christianity acknowledge that the Old Testament / Tenach on its own is not enough. Christians believe we need the New Testament to reveal the real meaning of Old Testament events. Judaism rejects the New Testament and therefore does not like to refer to the Hebrew Bible as the "Old" Testament. However Judaism has its own additional book, or rather a great library of books, known as the Talmud.

It is believed that when God gave the written word to Israel He also gave the Oral Torah, which was not written down but passed on by word of mouth from generation to generation, eventually to be codified in the Rabbinic writings known as the Mishna and the Gemara compiled in the Palestinian Talmud around 400 CE and the Babylonian Talmud around 500 CE. Rabbi Simmons writes:

> The Oral Torah is not an interpretation of the Written Torah. In fact, the Oral Torah preceded the Written Torah. When the Jewish people stood at Mount Sinai 3,300 years ago, God communicated the 613 commandments, along with a detailed, practical explanation of how to fulfil them. At that point in time, the teachings were entirely oral. It wasn't until 40 years later, just prior to Moses' death and the Jewish people entering the Land of Israel, that Moses wrote the scroll of the written Torah (known as the Five Books of Moses) and gave it to the Jewish people.[12]

---

[12] 'What is Oral Torah?' Aish ha Torah's Discovery Seminar, Aish website:

Admittedly we do not have any detailed record of how the Torah came to be written down, but at the same time we have no mention in the Bible of the existence of an oral Torah separate from the written Torah. Here is something very strange. If God had given Moses both the written and the oral Torah surely something would have been mentioned in the written Torah pointing to the existence of this other teaching, which was necessary to understand the written Torah. But what do we find? Not a word about it.

In fact we find evidence to the contrary. It is hard to see how Rabbi Simmons can justify the statement that the oral Torah preceded the written Torah when Exodus 24 says "Moses *wrote down all the words of the Lord...* then he took the *Book of the Covenant* and *read* it in the hearing of the people" (Ex 24:4-7). According to the text this happened immediately after Moses came down from the Mountain.

Moreover the Book of Joshua tells us Joshua (to whom Moses is supposed to have communicated the unwritten oral Torah) possessed a written word, which he read to the people of Israel as they entered the Land. This written word contained *all* that Moses had passed down:

> And afterward he (Joshua) read all the words of the law, the blessing and the curse, according to all that is written in the Book of the Law. There was not a word of all that Moses commanded that Joshua did not read before all the assembly of Israel, and the women, and the little ones, and the sojourners who lived among them. (Josh 8:34-35)

---

www.aish.com/shavuotsinai/shavuotsinaidefault/what_is_the_oral_torah$.
asp (last accessed 19 February 2009).

It is hard to reconcile these verses with the idea of an unwritten oral Torah, which precedes the written Torah and is equally inspired given by God at Mount Sinai.

In practice the Talmud is generally treated as more important than the Bible in the life of Jewish people. I once attended a lecture at a Jewish outreach centre in London during which the rabbi spoke about the Oral Torah. He told the following story found in the talmudic tractate *Bava Mezia* 59b. This follows a discussion according to halakha (halakha means the body of Jewish law supplementing the scriptural law and forming the legal part of the Talmud) in which the rabbis debated whether an oven that had become impure could be purified. While almost all the sages felt it could not be, Rabbi Eliezer, a lone voice but a great scholar, disagreed:

> On that day, Rabbi Eliezer put forward all the arguments in the world, but the Sages did not accept them. Finally, he said to them, 'If the halakha is according to me, let that carob tree prove it.' He pointed to a nearby carob tree, which then moved from its place a hundred cubits, and some say, four hundred cubits. They said to him 'One cannot bring a proof from the moving of a carob tree.'
>
> Said Rabbi Eliezer, 'If the halakha is according to me, may that stream of water prove it.' The stream of water then turned and flowed in the opposite direction. They said to him, 'One cannot bring a proof from the behavior of a stream of water.'
>
> Said Rabbi Eliezer, 'If the halakha is according to me, may the walls of the House of Study prove it.' The walls of the House of Study began to bend inward. Rabbi Joshua then rose up and rebuked the walls of the House of Study, 'If the students of the Wise argue with

one another in halakha," he said, 'what right have you to interfere?' In honor of Rabbi Joshua, the walls ceased to bend inward; but in honor of Rabbi Eliezer, they did not straighten up, and they remain bent to this day.

Then said Rabbi Eliezer to the Sages, 'If the halakha is according to me, may a proof come from Heaven.' Then a heavenly voice went forth and said, 'What have you to do with Rabbi Eliezer? The halakha is according to him in every place.' Then Rabbi Joshua rose up on his feet, and said, 'It is not in the heavens' (Deuteronomy 30:12).

What did he mean by quoting this? Said Rabbi Jeremiah, 'He meant that since the Torah has been given already on Mount Sinai, we do not pay attention to a heavenly voice, for You have written in Your Torah, 'Decide according to the majority' (Exod 23:2).

Rabbi Nathan met the prophet Elijah. He asked him, 'What was the Holy One, Blessed be He, doing in that hour?' Said Elijah, 'He was laughing and saying, 'My children have defeated me, my children have defeated me.'

The British-Jewish scholar and writer Hyam Maccoby has commented: 'This extraordinary story strikes the keynote of the Talmud. God is a good father who wants His children to grow up and achieve independence. He has given them His Torah, but now wants them to develop it....'[13]

<hr/>

[13] Source: Joseph Telushkin, *Jewish Literacy: The Most Important Things to Know About the Jewish Religion, Its People and Its History* (NY: William Morrow, 1991). Available on the Jewish Virtual Library: www.jewishvirtuallibrary.org/jsource/Judaism/Halakha_&_aggadata_&_midrash.html (last accessed 4 March 2009).

Hyam Maccoby actually misses the real point of this story. It means the Sages of Israel are treated as being a higher authority than God Himself and that the words of the Oral Torah are greater in importance than the words of God in the Bible. This was the issue Jesus faced with the religious leaders of His day, likewise Christianity today when writings of men and traditions become of greater importance than the word of God.

The Torah shows us that we all fall short of the glory of God and need to be made right with God by repentance and faith in the sacrifice God has appointed. Under the old covenant this was through the blood of the animals offered on Yom Kippur. Under the new covenant it is through the blood of the Messiah. In this way Messiah Jesus becomes our bridge to God, fulfilling His word, "I am the way, and the truth, and the life. No one comes to the Father except through me" (John 14:6).

Yeshua, Jesus, is the Messiah of whom Moses and the Prophets spoke, who has mediated the new covenant through which we can find the true bridge to God. Through His death and resurrection He has paid the price required for sin and made it possible for all humanity, Jewish and Gentile, to come to know God's forgiveness and eternal life. Those who truly accept Him as Messiah, Saviour and Lord experience the new birth which Jesus spoke about to Nicodemus which empowers us by the Holy Spirit to walk in newness of life and gives us the desire to keep His commandments. Although we remain liable to sin and still fall short of the glory of God, the blood Jesus shed is sufficient to cover our sins and to give us peace with God so that we know that when we appear before God on the Day of Judgment He will receive us into eternal life in His kingdom which shall never pass away.

CHAPTER 13

Faith and Politics in Today's Holy Land[1]

Calvin L. Smith

The past couple of decades or so have witnessed growing Evangelical interest in the Arab-Israeli conflict. I believe there are several reasons for this. First, a changing Arab-Israeli narrative in recent decades has caught the world's—and Evangelicals'—attention. Between the end of the Second World War and the 1967 Six Day War Zionism and the fledgling state of Israel enjoyed some, if somewhat begrudging, support in the West. The horrors of the Holocaust clearly contributed to this. Also, early Zionism was essentially collectivist (the communal kibbutz system being a prime example), thus garnering respect from some on the political left. Moreover, Israel's survival against the odds while surrounded by enemies seeking her annihilation won her much admiration, a plucky nation surrounded by enemies defending herself successfully against all the odds.

Yet Israel's nation-building success, a modern and innovative economy (compared with that of neighbouring Arab states) and military prowess have contributed to the

---

[1] This is a revised version of a paper originally delivered at Tyndale Fellowship conference, Cambridge, 9 July 2008.

CALVIN L. SMITH

Zionist narrative undergoing considerable change in recent decades, from a small pioneer movement to that of regional superpower. Also, from 1987 Palestinian *intifada* have contributed to raising the profile of the on-going Israeli-Palestinian conflict, inverting the David versus Goliath narrative. Meanwhile, the rise of Islamism, the events of 9-11, Western responses such as its adventurism in Iraq, together with hard-left anti-Americanism (a nation of which Israel is regarded as a client) have all contributed to how the Middle East conflict is viewed. The past couple of decades, then, have witnessed a hardening anti-Israel narrative, which is increasingly reflected in media reports and public perceptions of Israel.

This growing anti-Israel narrative has also been embraced by many Christians. A shift away from post-Holocaust theology—emerging as a result of considerable soul-searching by Europe's historic denominations in the wake of the Nazi horror—has contributed to this narrative. A growing number of denominations and Christian organisation have backed the Boycott, Divestment and Sanctions (BDS) movement, aimed not only at Israeli economic interests but arguably the nation's legitimacy itself. All this comes at a time when Evangelicals are moving away from private faith to engage more robustly with the political sphere.[2] In recent years, too, the Evangelical movement has witnessed the rise of a vocal Evangelical Left, which tends to be highly critical of Israel and Christian Zionism. Meanwhile, anti-Israel rhetoric by some Palestinian Christian leaders has also contributed to raising the profile of the Arab-Israeli

---

[2] For a brief discussion, see my "The De-privatisation of Faith and Evangelicals in the Public Square" in *Evangelical Review of Society and Politics* 1.1 (February 2007), 1-20.

conflict in Evangelical circles. Consequently there has emerged a counterpart to Christian Zionism, so-called "Christian Palestinianism",[3] which sides with the Palestinian people and is deeply critical of Israel. At times this criticism crosses over into the demonisation of the Jewish state. Thus, the debate between Christian Zionists and Christian anti-Zionists is becoming increasingly intense, polarised and bitter.

To date, Christian responses to Israel have tended to revolve around the study of certain biblical texts[4] or biblical theology themes such as the people of God or social justice. Especially popular is a focus on a theology of the land (whether from a Christian Zionist or pro-Palestinian perspective). This is not my starting point in my theological assessment of the relationship between the Church and Israel, together with the Middle East conflict. Neither am I, in principle, against giving up some land if it were to bring genuine peace to Israel and her inhabitants. However, I simply do not believe it can ever bring peace as long as Islamist Hamas, whose long-term strategy is the destruction of the Jewish state, remains in power in Gaza. Ariel Sharon's disengagement from Gaza demonstrated precisely this point. Hamas' charter calls for Israel's end, which is why the terrorist group will only ever contemplate a temporary truce (*hudna*) and not a permanent ceasefire. For Hamas, establishing pre-1967 borders is simply part of a piecemeal

---

[3] The term appears in Paul Wilkinson, *For Zion's Sake: Christian Zionism and the Role of John Nelson Darby* (Milton Keynes: Paternoster, 2007) and presumably coined by him.

[4] A useful book identifying and commenting on prooftexts cited by either side is *Ronald Diprose, Israel and the Church: The Origins and Effects of Replacement Theology* (Waynesboro, GA: Authentic Media, 2004).

strategy aimed at turning the clock back to *before* 1948 and even beyond.

Concerning giving up land for peace some Christian Zionists, of course, are strongly against such action for theological reasons. They do not believe Israel ever has the right to negotiate away its God-given inheritance. Such a position is fine, but it becomes problematic when some who hold it perceive somehow that God's plans are in jeopardy if, for example, someone like Ariel Sharon leaves Gaza. God's plans are final and irreversible, and no one, whether Ariel Sharon or anyone else, can reverse or influence the divine plan. What God has planned will be accomplished no matter what. More problematic is a minority of fringe pro-Israel Christians who consider their support for Israel as essential for God to fulfil biblical prophecy, as if the fulfilment of prophecy is somehow dependent on humans.[5] For my part, I prefer to focus on the Jewish people and challenge the supersessionist view that Church supersedes Israel. In the current anti-Israel atmosphere the land is far too emotive a starting point (though ultimately not one which can be ignored theologically at some stage). Yet by demonstrating from Scripture that God still retains a plan and purpose for the Jewish people, that God has not finished with Israel, is a battle half-won. Once Christians see the exegetical and theological problems supersessionist theology yields they begin to look at Israel, where approximately a half of the world's Jewish people live, in a new light.

---

[5] A point discussed by Stephen Sizer in *Christian Zionism: Road-map to Armageddon?* (Leicester: IVP, 2004). It is unfortunate that Sizer takes an unnecessarily polemical and sensational stance, as well as his tendency to parody most pro-Israel believers as extreme Christian Zionists, as any useful point such as this he makes is lost on a wider audience rejecting both his pejorative language and lack of objectivity.

Aside from these approaches to the relationship between the Church and Israel, less attention is given by Western believers to the situation of believers – both Jewish and Arab – in the Holy Land and what such an approach may bring to a Christian appraisal of the Middle East conflict. Certainly, in the current bitter debate between Christian Zionists and Christian anti-Zionists the latter accuse the Jewish state of adopting policies that oppress Arab Christians. Yet the situation of Christians in the Holy Land is not one which commands a great deal of attention by Western Christians.

As a regular visitor and study trip leader to Israel I am in a good position to do fieldwork, and so I decided to research the extent to which the evidence on the ground bears out this view among Christian anti-Zionists that Israel oppresses Arab Christians. As part of the research I also decided to explore the nature of relations between Jewish believers in the wider Jewish state. Such a snapshot can, I believe, serve as a useful contribution to how we view and debate the conflict in the Holy Land. This chapter, then, is based on on-going fieldwork, interviews and research in both Israel and the Palestinian Territories. While not yet complete, the emerging narrative contradicts blanket claims by pro-Palestinian Christians that Israel systematically oppresses its Arab Christian population. However, they do experience difficulties living among a predominantly Muslim population. My research also rejects some Christian Zionists' claims that Christians in the Holy Land enjoy full protection by the Israeli authorities. Jewish believers in Jesus are experiencing considerable difficulties in the Jewish state by virtue of their faith. We shall now look at both of these in turn.

ARAB CHRISTIAN RELATIONS WITH ISRAEL

Blanket claims that all Palestinian Christians are critical of Israel and reject her theologically are simply not true. The liberation theology views of organisations such as *Sabeel*, an ecumenical body promoting Palestinian liberation theology (e.g. coming perilously close to condoning suicide bombings on the basis of Samson's last act in the temple of Dagon)[6] are not embraced by all Arab Christians in the Holy Land. Neither do all Arab Christians blame Israel for their genuinely difficult situation.

First, it is essential to differentiate between Arab Christian leaders of the historic denominations and the grassroots laity. The former often express anti-Israel rhetoric, which some Arab Christians explained to me was a survival strategy by church leaders who recognise the peace process' focus on a two-state solution means one day they will come under the control of the Palestinian Authority. As such, these church leaders feel the need to establish their Palestinian nationalist credentials now if they and their congregations are to survive in the future. Arab Christianity already faces considerable challenges as a religious minority within the Territories. Moreover, research indicates how an historically secular Palestinian population has swung strongly towards militant Islamism in the past fifteen years or so,[7] which is

---

[6] Naim Ateek, "Suicide Bombers: What is Theologically and Morally Wrong With Suicide Bombings? A Palestinian Christian Perspective" in *Cornerstone* 25 (Summer 2002). This was originally posted on the *Sabeel* website but appears to have been removed since.

[7] See Loren. D. Lybarger, *Identity and Religion in Palestine: The Struggle Between Islamism and Secularism in the Occupied Territories* (Princeton University Press, 2007).

causing Christians in the Palestinian Territories considerable difficulties (discussed below).

Even in Israeli Arab areas Christians have experienced difficulties from their Muslim neighbours. One study details how Muslim Israeli Arabs have captured political control of Nazareth for the past two decades, where Christians were formerly in the majority, passing local laws which have had a detrimental effect on Arab Christianity resulting in many Christians leaving the town.[8] The emergence of Palestinian Islamism makes the future of Arab Christianity (whether historic denominations or non-denominational) in a future Palestinian state even more precarious, which helps to explain why some historic church leaders criticise Israel so vociferously. I do not suggest this is their only motive. Some Palestinian Christians clearly hold to a particularly triumphalist version of punitive supersessionism which also explains some of their anti-Israel rhetoric. But the survival issue also helps place some anti-Israel rhetoric within its endogenous political context.

This strongly critical view of Israel by church leaders is echoed by some grassroots Arab Christians, but certainly *not* all—or even the majority. Many grassroots believers are not convinced Israel is the cause of all Arab Christianity's problems. For example, a Catholic Jerusalemite currently researching Arab Christianity for a Ph.D. with a British university explained to me how many Arab lay Christians were disillusioned with their church leaders' failure to improve the situation of a Christian minority which feels increasingly under siege from economic difficulties, Islamic encroachment and a diminishing Christian population

---

[8] Raphael Israeli, *Green Crescent Over Nazareth: The Displacement of Christians by Muslims in the Holy Land* (London: Frank Cass, 2002).

through emigration.[9] These are real problems, he explained, which demand responses and action by Arab Christian church leaders. But instead all the mainstream church leaders do is blame everything on the Israeli occupation, a convenient scapegoat which excuses their own leadership failures. It is significant that this individual is a Palestinian nationalist who has little love for Israel. Yet his research and analysis lead him to conclude that Arab Christianity's problems cannot all be laid at Israel's feet. Ineffective church leadership within some of the historic denominations, which is at odds with its grassroots, is at least partly to blame.

Various lay Christians echoed similar views, and during my many interviews and conversations a distinct difference of opinion emerged between Arab Christian leaders and grassroots within historic denominations concerning their perception of Israel. Some lay Christians clearly had no love for Israel (though most claimed to get on quite well with their Jewish neighbours), but few expressed the same anti-Israeli rhetoric of their high-profile leaders, which appears to be aimed at a Western audience.

Several Christians from historic denominations were even quite generous towards the Israeli state and said they actually *preferred* Israeli rule to the prospect of coming under the Palestinian Authority. Joseph, an Orthodox Church Jerusalemite businessman, explained to me how he genuinely appreciated a great deal about the Jewish state.[10] Moreover, as an Arab Christian he said he far preferred being with Jews than Arab Muslims, with whom he and other Arab Christians he knew had faced various problems. He explained how a

---

[9] Interview, East Jerusalem, 4 February 2008. Given the difficulty of speaking out in in the present climate he asked not to publish his identity.
[10] Conversation, Jerusalem's Old City, 5 February 2008.

Muslim business rival kept making problems for him, as well as continuously suggesting he should emigrate, as so many other Arab Christians were doing. This issue of Islam came up frequently during the various interviews, with many Arab Christians expressing concern about their faith's existence as a diminishing minority under the Palestinian Authority, particularly with a shift towards Islamism among parts of the Palestinian population.

Aside from the differences of opinion between Arab Christian leaders and laity, it is also important to differentiate between mainstream historic denominations (for example, Lutheran, Anglican, Catholic, Eastern) and Evangelicals. The latter consists of both supersessionists and those who believe the Jews remain in some sense God's chosen people. Some even appreciate and talk openly about the Jewish root of their faith. In Haifa, there is an Arab pastor who leads a Messianic congregation.[11] Others speak out against replacement theology. For example, in Jerusalem I was introduced to a Pentecostal Arab former pastor who stated categorically the land belonged to the Jews and the Muslims had no right to it whatsoever.[12] I also met an Arab pastor who took a particularly strong Dispensationalist line, explaining how in the last days the land would be inhabited by Jews only, while God's covenant with the Arabs guaranteed them inheritances of territory alongside a Greater Israel.[13] Leaving aside his theology and links with American groups, such views fly in the face of claims that Arab Christians are all supersessionists. I do not want to give the impression all

[11] For details see Kai Kjær-Hansen and Bodil F. Skjøtt, *Facts and Myths About the Messianic Congregations in Israel* (Jerusalem: United Christian Council in Israel and the Caspari Center, 1999),163-7.
[12] Interview, Jerusalem's Old City, 2 February 2008.
[13] Interview, 5 February 2008.

Arab Christians monolithically view Israel positively. My point is quite the opposite: Arab Christian perceptions of Israel are *far* from homogenous. Many dislike Israel, yet others consider Israeli rule far more preferable to a future Palestinian authority. Some, like Samir, an Evangelical from Jerusalem, believe in a future divine plan for the Jews but maintain the Israeli occupation, together with economic problems, are partly to blame for the exodus of Christians.[14] The point I am simply making is that Arab Christianity's perceptions of Israel, both politically and theologically, are not, as some Christian anti-Zionists would have us believe, united in their hatred of the Israeli state, or that all Arab Christians in the Holy Land are supersessionists. This is a straw man argument.

As well as differentiating between leaders and laity, historic and Evangelical Christianity, and also the different theological and political views within Evangelicalism vis-à-vis Israel, it is also vital to take into account differing geographical experiences of Arab Christianity. Jerusalem is very different from the West Bank. In the Jewish capital Arab Christian are a double minority, squeezed between two far larger faiths (Judaism and Islam). Yet all three faiths do manage to get on, though tensions arise from time to time. (Samir explained how Jerusalem tends to be better for Christians, though the Danish cartoon protests shortly before we chatted had caused Christian-Muslim relations to deteriorate considerably in the city.)[15] In the West Bank, where Islam is dominant, Christians experience more problems. For example, Joseph explained how Muslims regarded Christian girls who did not wear a headscarf as

---

[14] Conversation, Jerusalem's Old City, 5 February 2008.
[15] Ibid.

promiscuous and an easy target.[16] (A report in the *Jerusalem Post* echoed how Jerusalemite Christian girls were also treated inappropriately by Muslim young men.[17]) I came across various other stories of difficulties West Bank Christians faced. Moreover, there is a difference between the West Bank and Gaza, where Christianity represents a tiny minority, and where there have been several high-profile cases of Christian oppression, including the murder of a prominent Christian leader, since Hamas took over.

What of Israeli perceptions and treatment of Arab Christians? Despite many Arab Christians' preference for Israeli rule, several said they were regarded with suspicion by the Israeli authorities in much the same way as Muslim Arabs. Joseph, who expressed some particularly strong pro-Israel comments, was nonetheless frustrated that the authorities often do not differentiate between Arab Christians such as himself, who likes Israel, and some of the very Arab Muslims he feels are causing problems for him and his fellow Christians.[18] Others echoed similar views. Arguably, Israel has reason to be suspicious of some Israeli Arabs, who have been implicated in terrorist plots, while several of their MKs (members of the Knesset, the Israeli parliament) have fraternised with Israel's enemies. Yet not all Israeli Arabs are against the state. For example, a sizeable number want to take up a new form of Arab national service (which Arab Israeli leaders have rejected).[19] Hence, many Arab Israelis (including

---

[16] Conversation with Joseph, op. cit.

[17] David Smith, "Christians Anonymous in *In Jerusalem* (a *Jerusalem Post* weekend supplement), 1 February 2008, 10-13.

[18] Conversation with Joseph, op. cit.

[19] Leslie Susser, "National Service Seeks Arab Volunteers" in *The Jerusalem Report* (28 April 2008), 12-16.

Arab Christians) are frustrated that they are by and large regarded with such suspicion by the Israelis.

Moreover, Israeli security policies have had an economic bearing on parts of the Arab Christian population, for example, in Bethlehem (though tourism is well up on previous years). Arab Christians are leaving Bethlehem in large numbers and the local economy as a result of the conflict have at least partially contributed to this emigration.

Yet it should be noted that Israeli security policy is not the only factor at work which indirectly affects Arab Christian wellbeing. One Palestinian businessman explained how, besides the security fence and long IDF checkpoints, poor Palestinian Authority administration and a monopoly of tourism by a handful of Arab families, or clans, were all contributing to Bethlehem's economic woes.[20] It is also important to move beyond the simplistic statement that Bethlehem's Christian population has been falling steadily since the state of Israel was founded in 1948. Indeed, in 1948 some 85% of Bethlehem's population was Christian, while by the end of the first decade of the twentieth century it was between 12-15%.[21] Some claim it has fallen considerably from these levels in the past five or so years. Thus, it is easy to extrapolate from these statistics that the founding of Israel is somehow responsible for the demise of Arab Christianity in Bethlehem. But there is much more to this story. Consider

---

[20] Jorg Luyken, "Room at the Inn?" in *International Jerusalem Post* 2460 (2007), 24-5.

[21] Lela Gilbert, "Bethlehem Beyond the Christmas Calm" in *International Jerusalem Post* 2461 (2007), 18-19; Khaled Abu Toameh, "The Beleaguered Christians in Bethlehem", *Gatestone Institute* website: http://www.gatestoneinstitute.org/501/the-beleaguered-christians-in-bethlehem (last accessed 11 May 2013).

how the Christian population in the city in 1967 was 42.6%.[22] This means it halved between 1948 and 1967, when Bethlehem was *not* under Israeli control. Moreover, the exodus of Christians has *increased* since the First Intifada, and since the Palestinian Authority took over Bethlehem the Christian population has shrunk considerably. The blame cannot be laid completely at Israel's feet.

Clearly, the economic situation is a major part of the problem, but anti-Christian Muslim feelings also contribute considerably to Christianity's demise in Bethlehem and the West Bank. Mention has already been made of the growing Islamism among the Palestinian population. During a visit to Bethlehem for several days, the then-Archbishop of Canterbury Rowan Williams observed that as well as life made intolerable by the security fence, there were "some signs of disturbing anti-Christian feelings among parts of the Muslim population". One Baptist minister claimed his church in Bethlehem had been attacked with Molotov cocktails 14 times.[23] Catholic Palestinian landowner in Bethlehem Jiryas Handal had land expropriated by Israel to build a neighbourhood on land annexed in 1967. But he also had land taken by his Muslim neighbours. The Palestinian authorities promised to intervene repeatedly, but nothing ever happened and the land was never returned.[24] There are various reports of Christians having their land seized by Muslims, together with instances of extortion by Muslim gangs.[25] Indeed, even a cursory search on the Internet for news about the maltreatment of Christians in Palestinian

[22] Barak Barfi, "Land Grab in Bethlehem" in *The Jerusalem Report* (7 January 2008), 24-6.
[23] Lela Gilbert, op. cit.
[24] Barak Barfi, op. cit.
[25] Khaled Abu Toameh, *Gatestone Institute,* op. cit.

CALVIN L. SMITH

Territories will yield numerous reports of the daily harassment they experience and their second-class (*dhimmi*) status. Reports by reputable news agents, as well as comment by some Arab political observers means pro-Palestinian or Christian attempts to explain away such reports as pro-Israel propaganda can only go so far. The evidence of the difficulties Palestinian Christians face has been well-documented and goes some way to explaining why Christians are leaving Bethlehem and the West Bank.

So clearly there are various factors at work explaining why Arab Christians are emigrating from the Holy Land. Yet many Christian anti-Zionists prefer to focus on Israel and ignore or fail completely to publicise the difficulties Arab Christians face from their Muslim neighbours. These issues must be dealt with if the haemorrhage of Christians from the land is to be stopped.

MESSIANIC BELIEVERS AND ISRAEL

If the perceptions and experiences of Arab Christians vis-à-vis Israel have been generalised and presented as homogenous, the nature and extent of relations between Messianic believers and society have been all but ignored by the bulk of Evangelical Christians in the West. At the turn of the decade the number of Jewish Christians was very small, somewhere between 10,000 and 15,000 (there are probably another 15,000 to 20,000 Christians who entered Israel under the right of return as relatives of Russian Jews).[26] Being such a

---

[26] There are various statistics for the Messianic movement in Israel, but the most detailed work has been carried out by the Caspari Center, Jerusalem. A useful book on the nature and extent of Messianic congregations is the important survey by Kai Kjær-Hansen and Bodil F. Skjøtt, *Facts and Myths* (op. cit.). Unfortunately, this work is now quite old.

314

small number, together with the view prevalent among Haredi (or Ultra-Orthodox) Jews that to become a believer in Jesus means one is no longer a Jew, has caused considerable problems for Israel's Messianic believers. Like their Arab Christian counterparts in predominantly Muslim areas, many feel under siege from the dominant religious faith.

Messianic Jews in Israel supposedly enjoy full religious freedom and legal protection of their rights. Moreover, the Israeli state and constitution is secular, as are many of its politicians, so in theory Jewish Christians are treated no differently from any other faith. But Israel is currently witnessing not only a growing Ultra-Orthodox population, but also one that is growing in political power. With every visit to Israel one is struck by an increasingly polarised society divided along religious-secular lines. Moreover, Ultra-Orthodox Jews are increasingly involved in Israeli politics through their own political parties, working towards the passing of laws which benefit them but which also have a bearing on secular and less religious Jews (for example, rules on Shabbat, smoking during Passover, and so on).

Not all Ultra-Orthodox Jews are Zionist, but many are, refusing to sanction calls to give away parts of Jerusalem to a Palestinian authority. Meanwhile, settler activity as a whole is driven by Jewish Ultra-Orthodox theology. (In an allusion to the rock group Guns and Roses, a T-shirt is available for sale in Jerusalem showing a picture of an Ultra-Orthodox face, complete with *peyot* (hair locks) above an image of two tablets of stone (the Decalogue) next to a machine gun. Underneath is the caption: Guns and Moses.)

The Ultra-Orthodox have formed their own political parties, such as Shas, a Sephardic party, or United Torah Judaism, which is Ashkenazi. Because of the nature of Israeli politics, which relies on coalition governments, such parties often punch far above their weight and their power is disproportionate to their size.[27] Importantly, coalition support from Shas and other Orthodox parties comes at a price, mainly in the form of getting their religious policies on the statute books. This growing religious political power in Israel has occurred at a piecemeal pace, but the Ultra-Orthodox impact on a secular Israel has been steady. The movement has a powerful voice in determining who can make *aliya* (immigration to Israel), has enjoyed important positions in the state bureaucracy, and has helped pass laws which make life increasingly difficult for Israel's Messianic Christian community, who are regarded by many Orthodox Jews as traitors.

At this stage, we shall consider briefly the nature of Haredi-Messianic relations. Ultra-Orthodox Jews regard Christianity and Judaism as completely incompatible: you cannot be Jewish and a Christian. (In fact, within Jewish Christianity the same debate is taking place, with some leaders, such as Baruch Maoz arguing for a complete break with Judaism, while others, notably Mark Kinzer, embracing a much more Judaic expression of faith in Jesus, including espousing a "bilateral ecclesiology" to allow for Jewish believers in Jesus to practice a Torah-observant form of communal living and worship, as well as a focus on preaching Messiah through example.)[28]

---

[27] A notable exception is this year's general election, where religious parties were frozen out of a coalition deal, the first time in over a decade.

[28] Both these positions can be summed up in the titles of books written by both Jewish Christian leaders: Baruch Maoz, *Judaism Is Not Jewish* (Christian Focus, 2003), and Mark. S. Kinzer, *Post-Missionary Messianic Judaism: Redefining Christian Engagement with the Jewish People* (Grand Rapids, Michigan: Brazos Press, 2005).

Missionary activity is despised by Orthodox Jews, who associate it with centuries of persecution and forced conversion in a Europe plagued with a history of Christian anti-Semitism. Messianic believers are deeply aware of such sensitivities, and many struggle themselves with determining the nature of their identity and relationship with the wider Church (as discussed in the previous two chapters). For some, even to call oneself a Christian suggests no longer being Jewish, as well as causing problems within the community and making one's Christian witness that much more difficult. Meanwhile, links with exogenous (external) Gentile Christian organisations fuels Ultra-Orthodox claims that Messianic groups are engaging in missionary activity to convert Jews to Christianity. All this is a real problem for Messianic Jews, but especially so in Israel, where the powerful Ultra-Orthodox community despises them. Arguably, much of this is also because the Haredim feel threatened by Jewish believers in Jesus. There are many secret believers in Yeshua among the Ultra-Orthodox (so-called Nicodemus Christians), and Haredi anti-missionary activity is intense, aggressive, and sometimes can be violent.

Foremost among the anti-missionary organisations is the organisation Yad L'achim. Baruch Maoz, a well-known Jewish believer and former leader in Israel, says Yad L'achim receives substantial financial support from the Israeli government. They also cull information on Messianic Jews and organisations from government files.[29] Examples of anti-missionary activity aimed at Jewish Christians include graffiti, tyres being slashed, telephone threats, and arson. During visits to Jerusalem I have stayed several times at an old church near the Jaffa Gate of the Old City. One of the

---

[29] As cited in Kai Kjaer-Hansen and Bodil F. Skjott, op. cit.

church trustees described how one day he caught three Ultra-Orthodox youths trying to set fire to the building. This is just one of several problems they have encountered in the past. I have also seen older Haredis walk by and curse and spit at the church. A favoured technique of Yad L'achim is to put up picture posters of local Messianic believers and organisations, including their addresses, in order to denounce them and warn the wider Jewish population off having anything to do with Messianic Jews. Several years ago hundreds of New Testaments which had been given to Ethiopian Jews by Messianic believers were publicly burned by *yeshiva* students in Or Yehuda. The Deputy Mayor, a Shas politician, was eventually forced to apologise to Christians worldwide.[30]

Sometimes, Ultra-Orthodox anti-Christian activity can be violent. Cases include besieging Christians in Arad, the burning of a church in Jerusalem, and a siege by up to a thousand Ultra-Orthodox upon a church in Beersheva. The pastor, Howard Bass, explained to me how a rumour had circulated that his church was about to bring in three busloads of Jewish children to baptise them into the Christian faith (in fact, only three Israelis were to be baptised that day, all of them aged eighteen or over).[31] Proselytising minors is against the law in Israel, while such conversions have historical parallels in Europe's abysmal treatment of its Jews. And so a large crowd of strict religious Jews descended upon the church, causing considerable damage and roughing up members of the congregation. It later transpired it had been Ultra-Orthodox anti-missionary leaders who had circulated the rumour and organised the protest.

---

[30] "In Brief" in *International Jerusalem Post* 2481 (23-29 May 2008), 6.
[31] Interview, Beersheva, 11 February 2008.

A few years ago during the Purim festival, a bomb was sent to a Christian family, which severely injured the pastor's son when it exploded. I later interviewed the family, saw pictures of the damage to the house and injuries sustained by the son, which were horrific. When interviewed by the *Jerusalem Post*, Howard Bass said anti-missionary violence has been going on for years in Israel, yet nobody would take a stand and help Messianic believers.[32] Indeed, threats against Messianic believers are frequent. They are regarded by some religious Jews as a dangerous cult, and organisations such as Jews for Jesus face intense opposition in their efforts to preach the Gospel to their fellow Jews.

Meanwhile, Evangelical organisations based in Israel sometimes face great difficulty getting visas renewed for their workers, this despite their pro-Israel stance. Messianic Jews also face problems making *aliya* (immigrating to Israel), because rabbis play a central role in determining whether or not someone is Jewish, based on their faith. Also, by capturing important positions in the state bureaucracy, Ultra-Orthodox Jews make life increasingly difficult for Messianic believers.

Aside from Israeli government financing of organisations such as Yad L'achim, how else does the Israeli state have a bearing on Jewish believers in Jesus? The authorities, particularly the police, often do not do much to help Messianic believers who experience persecution. But Baruch Maoz explained how, despite such persecution, when such matters came before the Israeli courts believers were nearly always vindicated.[33] Thus, Messianic groups have now taken to bringing Ultra-Orthodox anti-Christian harassment to the

---

[32] "In Brief" in *International Jerusalem Post* 2474 (2008), 8.
[33] Interview with Baruch Maoz, near Tel Aviv, 11 February 2008.

courts, even though this can take years to work its way though the legal system. For its part, the Israeli government's frequent reliance on Ultra-Orthodox political parties in coalition means that, indirectly at least, the Israeli state is having a detrimental impact on the plight of Jewish believers in Jesus. These Jewish believers are the descendants of the very first New Testament Church, which was Jewish, the first church in the land. Yet they face very much the same kind of religious persecution at the hand of religious Jews as described in the book of Acts.

CONCLUDING REMARKS

The main threat facing Christians in the Holy Land today is more religious than political. Or perhaps more accurately these difficulties are primarily religio-political, involving two rival faiths: Islam and Ultra-Orthodox Judaism, both of which (in the Holy Land) are increasingly militant and political, including towards believers in Jesus. Many Arab Christians have responded by emigrating from the West Bank. Messianic believers also face considerable opposition, though reports suggest not in the same manner or intensity as their Arab counterparts. Messianic believers consider themselves authentically Jewish (even if many religious Jews do not), and therefore do not appear to emigrate for religious reasons.

For their part, the governing authorities—whether Israel or the Palestinian Authority—appear to do little to support their respective Christian communities. This might be because they represent such tiny and insignificant minorities. Ironically, though, both Israel and the Palestinian Authority seem keen to project positive pro-Christian credentials to an exogenous audience. Thus, the State of Israel openly courts Christian Zionists, while for his part the late Yasser Arafat (and more recently Mahmoud Abbas) portrayed the Palestinian Authority as a defender of Christianity against Israeli aggression, choreographing media images of attendance at Christian places of worship and holy sites, such as the Church of the Nativity in Bethlehem. Islamist Hamas also seeks to portray itself as a defender of its tiny Christian community, though the reality is completely at odds with such clumsy propaganda, with the violence towards and harassment experienced by Gaza's Christians since Hamas came to power having been well-documented.

In Palestinian-controlled areas of the West Bank Christian Arabs encounter plenty of harassment (and worse) on the basis of their Christian faith. Some seek to prove they are good nationalists by criticising Israel, while downplaying the real political and religious difficulties they encounter. One Palestinian Christian cleric compared the behaviour "of Christian *dhimmis* [in the West Bank] to that of battered wives or children, who continue to defend and even identify with their tormentor even as the abuse persists".[34]

This situation, for which there seems to be plenty of evidence, demonstrates how it is disingenuous to blame all Arab Christian problems upon the Israelis. For some Christian anti-Zionists to ignore the Islamist threat, as well as day-to-day general harassment experienced by Arab Christians at the hands of some Muslim neighbours, is not only unhelpful, it is profoundly dishonest. This is a situation all Christians in the West, regardless of their view of the Middle East conflict, should be praying earnestly about, lifting our fellow Arab Christians before God and seeking His

---

[34] David Raab, "The Beleaguered Christians of the Palestinian Controlled Areas" in *Jerusalem Letter/Viewpoints* 490 (2003), Jerusalem Center for Public Affairs, available online at http://jcpa.org/jl/vp490.htm (last accessed 11 May 2013).

care and protection for them. To echo instead, despite evidence to the contrary, that any and all claims of Islamic persecution of Arab Christians in the West Bank is merely a lie peddled by Israel and her supporters for its own propaganda purposes raises serious questions about motive. The danger facing those Christian anti-Zionists not prepared to acknowledge the very real religious harassment many Arab Christians face leaves them wide open to claims that many pro-Palestinian activists are driven less by support for the Palestinian people, and more by seeing them as pawns in a wider ideological battle aimed at demonising Israel. I do not say all Christian anti-Zionists act or think this way, but some—based on their well-documented actions, views and alliances—clearly do.

To pro-Palestinian Christians I would also ask why it is that many Arab Christians, the actual people on the ground, do not demonise Israel as they do? The many interviews I conducted suggested that very many Arab Christians actually feel safer under Israeli control, even despite instances of unfair treatment some undoubtedly experienced because they were Arabs. Notwithstanding, many (not all) of my interviewees refused to make political capital out of the situation, unlike some Palestinian Christian leaders, choosing instead to turn the other cheek. That they choose to uphold this particularly challenging aspect of Scripture, a Christian virtue which sets us apart from other faiths, is both humbling and significant. It also leads one to ask why some Arab Christians facing genuine difficulties do not, unlike some Christian anti-Zionist activists, insist on over-simplifying the conflict and exploiting the plight of these Arab Christians to make their own anti-Israeli political statement. I suggest that such people are actually exacerbating (in several cases possibly even wittingly) the negative view of Arab Christians many Israelis hold. Some Israelis I spoke with assumed, on the basis of the anti-Israel rhetoric they had heard from some anti-Israel (and often Western) Christians, that *all* Arab Christians were indeed enemies of Israel.

By the same token, many Christian Zionists should give some thought to why, in their support for Israel, they are not more vocal in speaking out against the religious hounding of the tiny Messianic community in that land, or challenging the Israeli authorities to do more to protect them. It is important too, as good friends of Israel, to challenge security policies which unnecessarily cause suffering for Arab Christians. That is not to say Israel does not have a right to defend itself in difficult circumstances. I cannot understand the hypocrisy of a world that exacts a higher standard from Israel than other countries and seems to think her security alone does not matter. I have spent considerable time in Israel and seen first-hand the very real security threats and difficulties the country faces on a day-to-day basis. But neither should this mean we cannot criticise those occasions when Israel is unnecessarily heavy-handed. If Christian friends of Israel, the support of which the Jewish state deeply values, were to challenge gently but more consistently some of the problems Arab and Messianic Christians face, Israel would likely be more willing to take note.

Neither does engaging with Israel on these issues somehow mean Christian Zionists are betraying their love for the Jewish people or support for Israel, or failing to recognise the very real and dangerous threats she faces from external enemies seeking her annihilation. Yet some pro-Israel Christians feel – irrationally – that if they are critical of Israel *in any way* they are somehow denying the notion of the Jews as God's chosen people and are edging over into theological supersessionism. Consequently some take a completely unrealistic "Israel right or wrong" position. This is untenable. After all, if biblical Israel sinned, how can we say the secular nation of Israel today is without sin (as with any other people or nation)? Quite simply, Israel is not inerrant. An "Israel right or wrong" position can also distort our perceptions of our fellow Christians in the Holy Land. For example, one Christian shopkeeper in Jerusalem explained to me how an American Christian couple came to his shop and asked if he was Jewish. When he explained that he was both an Arab and a Christian they left, explaining their desire to buy from a Jewish shop in order to bless God's people. Such insensitivity by some Western Christians only serves to alienate Arab Christians.

If Christian Zionists are to avoid an "Israel right or wrong" mentality, by the same token, Christian anti-Zionists must reject an "Israel is *always* wrong" viewpoint. The evidence on the ground suggests this is simply not true. I would much prefer to be a Christian in Israel, despite the problems they face there, than in many neighbouring Muslim countries. It is one thing to believe God has called you to champion the Palestinian cause, or to take the Gospel to the Muslim people. We need many more people called to such vital ministry. But when such a calling degenerates into the demonisation of another people something is seriously wrong. It also makes the ministry of those of us called to share the Gospel with and minister to the Jewish people so much more difficult.

A Christian approach to the whole Israeli-Palestinian conflict, together with the situation Christians in the region find themselves, requires considerable honesty, nuance, reflection and objectivity. As Christians respond to this issue, we must strive to understand the highly complex nature of the conflict so as to avoid making simplistic or sensational pronouncements that merely echo the propaganda battle being played out in the secular sphere. Substantial nuance is required to understand the situation of Christians in the Holy Land. By ignoring these complexities we merely contribute to the present war of words.

IN MEMORY OF
HOWARD TAYLOR

CHAPTER 14

Israel and the Purposes of God

Howard Taylor

THE UNIQUENESS OF THE PEOPLE OF ISRAEL

One very significant apologetic tool for the truth of the Bible is the history of Israel. The human subject for most of the Bible (both Old and New Testaments) is the Jewish people and their history. There is no doubt that they are unique among the nations. This does not mean the individual Jew is different from other human beings, but rather as a people their story has demonstrated God's faithfulness, as recorded and prophesied in the Bible. Thus all who trust the God of the Bible can take strength from the Jewish people and their painful yet glorious history. Their story has relevance to the whole human race and this is so even if the Jewish people themselves do not recognise it.

The following quotes illustrate the uniqueness of the Jewish people as perceived by different people in recent history:

> Some people like the Jews, and some do not. But no
> thoughtful man can deny the fact that they are, beyond

any question, the most formidable and the most remarkable race which has appeared in the world.[1] *Winston Churchill*

The study of the history of Europe during the past centuries teaches us one uniform lesson: That the nations which received and in any way dealt fairly and mercifully with the Jew have prospered; and that the nations that have tortured and oppressed him have written out their own curse.[2]   *Olive Schreiner*

By the standards of others, once they had lost their country, the Jewish people should have fallen into decay long ago. But instead, uniquely [emphasis mine], they continued to maintain themselves as a nation, and by doing so became in the eyes of others an uncanny and frightening people.[3]   *David Vital*

The Jews constitute a tiny percentage of the human race. Properly the Jew ought, hardly to be heard of; but he is heard of, has always been heard of. He is as prominent on the planet as any other people, and his commercial importance is extravagantly out of proportion to the smallness of his bulk. His

---

[1] *Illustrated Sunday Herald*, 8 February 1920.

[2] Olive Schreiner, South African novelist, pacifist and political activist, quoted by Chief Rabbi J. H. Hertz, *A Book of Jewish Thought* (Oxford: Oxford University Press, 1966), 177, 180. Schreiner is best known for her novel *The Story of an African Farm*, which has been acclaimed for the manner it tackled the issues of its day, ranging from agnosticism to the treatment of women.

3 David Vital, *The Origins of Zionism*. (Oxford: Oxford University Press, 1980). David Vital is Emeritus Nahum Goldmann Professor of Diplomacy at the University of Tel Aviv.

contributions to the world's list of great names in literature, science, art, music, finance, medicine and abstruse learning are also way out of proportion to the weakness of his numbers. He has made a marvellous fight in this world, in all the ages; and has done it with has hands tied behind him. He could be vain of himself, and be excused for it. The Egyptian, the Babylon and the Persian rose, filled the planet with sound and splendour, then faded to dream-stuff and passed away; the Greek and the Roman followed, and made a vast noise, and they are gone; other peoples have sprung up and held their torch high for a time, but it burned out, and they sit in twilight now, or have vanished. The Jew saw them all, beat them all, and is now what he always was, exhibiting no decadence, no infirmities of age, no weakening of his parts, no slowing of his energies, no dulling of his alert and aggressive mind. All things are mortal but the Jew; all other forces pass, but he remains. What is the secret of his immortality?[4] *Mark Twain*

The once-Marxist Russian Nikolai Alexandrovich Berdyaev came to a similar conclusion:

I remember how the materialist interpretation of history, when I attempted in my youth to verify it by applying it to the destinies of peoples, broke down in the case of the Jews, where destiny seemed absolutely inexplicable from the materialistic standpoint... Its

4 From an essay entitled "Concerning the Jews" in *Harper's Magazine*, March 1898. Available at Fordham University's *Internet History Sourcebook Project,* http://www.fordham.edu/halsall/mod/1898twain-jews.html (last accessed 16 February 2009).

survival is a mysterious and wonderful phenomenon demonstrating that the life of this people is governed by a special predetermination, transcending the processes of adaptation expounded by the materialistic interpretation of history. The survival of the Jews, their resistance to destruction, their endurance under absolutely peculiar conditions and the fateful role played by them in history: all these point to the particular and mysterious foundations of their destiny.[5]

The historian Barbara Tuchman also wrote:

The history of the Jews is... intensely peculiar in the fact of having given the western world its concept of origins and monotheism, its ethical traditions, and the founder of its prevailing religion, yet suffering dispersion, statelessness and ceaseless persecution, and finally in our times nearly successful genocide, dramatically followed by fulfilment of the never-relinquished dream of return to the homeland. Viewing this strange and singular history, one cannot escape the impression that it must contain some special significance for the history of mankind, that in some way, whether one believes in divine purpose or inscrutable circumstance, the Jews have been singled out to carry the tale of human fate.[6]

---

5 *The Meaning of History* (London: Geoffrey Bles, 1936), 86-87. Nikolai Berdyaev was a political philosopher who later embraced religion.
6 Quoted by Sir Rabbi Jonathan Sacks in *Covenant and Conversation: Thoughts on the Weekly Parsha From the Chief Rabbi*, available from the Chief Rabbi's website, www.chiefrabbi.org/thoughts/balak5765.htm (last accessed 17 February 2009). Barbara Wertheim Tuchman was an

THREE CHRISTIAN VIEWS

King Louis XIV of France asked Blaise Pascal to give him proof of the supernatural. Pascal answered, "Why, the Jews, your Majesty, the Jews."[7] Elsewhere Pascal writes:

> It is certain that in certain parts of the world we can see a peculiar people, separated from the other peoples of the world, and this is called the Jewish people ... separated from all the other peoples of the earth, who are the most ancient of all and whose history is earlier by several centuries than the oldest histories we have. .... My encounter with this people amazes me and seems worthy of attention ... Lovingly and faithfully they hand on this book in which Moses declares that they have been ungrateful towards God throughout their lives, that he knows they will be still more so after his death, but that he calls heaven and earth to witness against them that he told them so often enough.[8]

Pascal's amazement includes the observation that the Jews preserve and transmit a book that is unflattering to them. This surely merits our attention. He also states:

American historian and author best known for *The Guns of August*, a history of the prelude to the First World War.

[7] This quotation is cited by Rabbi Blech, Associate Professor of the Talmud at Yeshiva University, in "The Miracle of Jewish History", *History News Network* website (George Mason University's Center for History and News Media), http://hnn.us/articles/38887.html (last accessed 17 February 2009).

[8] Blaise Pascal, *Pensees*, 454, 452. Version cited is *Pensees* (London: Penguin, 1966). Translated by A.J. Krailssheimer.

This people are not eminent solely by their antiquity, but are also singular by their duration, which has always continued from their origin till now. For, whereas the nations of Greece and of Italy, of Lacedaemon, of Athens and of Rome, and others who came long after, have long since perished, these ever remain, and in spite of the endeavours of many powerful kings who have a hundred times tried to destroy them, as their historians testify, and as it is easy to conjecture from the natural order of things during so long a space of years, they have nevertheless been preserved (and this preservation has been foretold); and extending from the earliest times to the latest, their history comprehends in its duration all our histories which it preceded by a long time.[9]

Karl Barth, who did not like proofs from nature for the Christian faith, said of the history of the Jews:

In fact, if the question of a proof of God is raised, one need merely point to this simple historical fact. For in the person of the Jew there stands a witness before our eyes, the witness of God's covenant with Abraham, Isaac and Jacob and in that way with us all. Even one who does not understand Holy Scripture can see this reminder. And don't you see, the remarkable theological importance, the extraordinary spiritual and sacred significance of the National Socialism (Nazism) that now lies behind us is that right from its roots it was anti-Semitic, that in this movement it was realised with a simple demonic clarity, that the enemy is the Jew.

---

[9] Pascal, 451.

Yes, the enemy in this matter had to be a Jew. In this Jewish nation there really lives to this day the extraordinariness of the revelation of God.[10]

The Anglican theologian and distinguished churchman, Alan Richardson, wrote:

In view of the remarkable history of the Jewish people it ought not to seem strange to us that they should have some unique destiny to fulfil in the providence of God. The history of other nations provides not even a single remote parallel to the phenomenon of Jewish existence down the ages and to this day. What other nation of antiquity has preserved its identity and character as the Jews have done, though exiled from their homeland and dispersed throughout the world? Throughout centuries of persecution the Jewish race has survived the catastrophes which have so often destroyed the national identity of other peoples. Religious or secularised a Jew remains a Jew - a voluntary or involuntary witness to the truth that is symbolised in the story of God's Covenant with Abraham. This striking fact of the persistence of the Jewish race has long been recognised as important evidence of the truth of the Biblical interpretation of history [11]

PEOPLE AND LAND

Redemption is primarily for people but also it is for the natural world. Genesis 1 is the account of how God created

---

10 Karl Barth, *Dogmatics in Outline,* 75-76.
11 *Christian Apologetics* (London: SCM, 1947). This is an excerpt from a larger passage found in pages141-143.

people and nature. Genesis 3 is about how humans sinned and brought decay to all of nature. Therefore land is not just a temporary sign (like the Temple sacrifices), rather it is part of the content of redemption.

To represent all people, God needed a Chosen People, and to represent all lands He needed a Promised Land. The relation of the Jewish people with the land which God entrusted to them represents in "peculiar intensity"[12] all of us and the lands which are entrusted to us.

Over and over again the Old Testament Prophets tell us that the history of the Jews will be unlike the history of any other people, and how towards the end of time, after great suffering, the Jews will return to the Promised Land where they will become the centre of hostility. This hostility will affect the whole world. Eventually God will reconcile them to their Messiah, cleanse them from their sin, judge the nations who have hated them, and make them a blessing to all peoples (for example, Isa 43, 49, Jer 30-33, Ezek 36-39, Zech 12, 13). We shall see that the New Testament confirms this Old Testament promise. Events this century seem to be fulfilling these prophecies.

There are often arguments about whether or not such verses refer to the return from Babylonian exile or even the initial entry into Canaan. To be convinced let us consider the principles that Moses gives Israel even before they enter the Promised Land for the first time.

(a) God's judgement against Israel's sin means that her people will be scattered from the land.

---

[12] Professor T. F. Torrance's oft used phrase to describe the Jewish people.

And the Lord will scatter you among all peoples, from one end of the earth to the other, and there you shall serve other gods of wood and stone, which neither you nor your fathers have known. And among these nations you shall find no respite, and there shall be no resting place for the sole of your foot, but the Lord will give you there a trembling heart and failing eyes and a languishing soul. Your life shall hang in doubt before you. Night and day you shall be in dread and have no assurance of your life. In the morning you shall say, 'If only it were evening!' and at evening you shall say, 'If only it were morning!' because of the dread that your heart shall feel, and the sights that your eyes shall see. (Deut 28:64-67)

Anyone who knows anything about Jewish history – especially during the last 1000 years – will recognise these words as striking indeed. They were spoken by Moses 3,300 years ago and have been remarkably fulfilled throughout Jewish history until this present day. Even liberal Bible scholars, who deny that Moses himself spoke these words, recognise that they are at least 2,500 years old.

(b) God's forgiveness to Israel will mean that God will restore its people to the land.

Then the Lord your God will restore your fortunes and have mercy on you, and he will gather you again from all the peoples where the Lord your God has scattered you. If your outcasts are in the uttermost parts of heaven, from there the Lord your God will gather you, and from there he will take you. And the Lord your God will bring you into the land that your fathers

337

> possessed, that you may possess it. And he will make you more prosperous and numerous than your fathers. (Deut 30:3-5)

These are the principles laid down in the book of the Law and therefore do not refer only to this or that event in the history of Israel. They describe God's dealing with Israel *in all its history*. They are expounded and applied over and over again in the Hebrew Prophets (Isaiah, Jeremiah, Ezekiel, Hosea, Zechariah). Indeed they are a major theme of most of the Prophets.

Although Israel's return to the land is usually linked to their return to the Lord it must not be interpreted to mean that God's purposes are conditional on good behaviour. (If they were there would be no hope for any part of the world or for any of us personally – it is by grace we are saved.) Jeremiah 31 is one of those many marvellous passages that speak of Israel's restoration and then towards the end of the chapter we read these words:

> Thus says the Lord: "If the heavens above can be measured, and the foundations of the earth below can be explored, then I will cast off all the offspring of Israel for all that they have done, declares the Lord." (v. 37)

It is true, as we have seen, that the full blessings of the covenant were dependent upon Israel's behaviour. But the fulfilment of His purposes through them and their land is not dependent upon them at all. These purposes extend to the end of time and belong to God's sovereign purposes that cannot be thwarted by man's folly (Rom 3:3-4)

But now to a very important question: does the New Testament have anything to say about the principles of scattering and re-gathering which Moses spoke of, or do these principles apply only to Old Testament times? In Luke 21:20-24 we read:

> *But when you see Jerusalem surrounded by armies, then know that kits desolation has come near. Then let those who are in Judea flee to the mountains, and let those who are inside the city depart...* for these are days of vengeance, to fulfill all that is written... *They will fall by the edge of the sword and be led captive among all nations, and Jerusalem will be trampled underfoot by the Gentiles, until the times of the Gentiles are fulfilled.* (Emphasis added)

This passage tells us that the *coming* scattering of Israel is the true fulfilment of the Old Testament prophecies. We therefore conclude these Old Testament prophecies cannot have referred only to the Babylonian exile hundreds of years before Christ! Thus, the Old Testament prophecies about the restoration after exile must also refer to events after Christ as well as events before His time on earth. This is confirmed by the last words in the above quote which show us that the coming Jewish exile from Jerusalem *is not forever.*

There is also another very interesting word from our Lord found in Matthew 24:34-35:

> Truly, I say to you, this generation will not pass away until all these things take place. Heaven and earth will pass away, but my words will not pass away.

What does "generation" mean in this passage? To answer this let us consider which Old Testament passage this seems to be based on. We have already referred to part of it above. Jeremiah 31 is one of the many great passages speaking of the restoration of Israel to its land in the last days. In verse 36 and 37 the Lord says:

> "If this fixed order [the rational principles of nature which make science possible] departs from before me", declares the Lord, "then shall the *offspring* of Israel cease from being a nation before me forever." Thus says the Lord: "If the heavens above can be measured, and the foundations of the earth below can be explored, then I will cast off all the *offspring* of Israel for all that they have done, declares the Lord." (Emphasis added)

The Greek version of the Old Testament is called the Septuagint, and it was widely used by the Jews at the time of Jesus. The Septuagint word for offspring, or "descendants" in Jeremiah 31 is the very same word that Jesus uses in Matthew 24, and which, in our New Testaments is translated "generation" from the Greek. In the Greek it is the word *genea* and literally means "family", "race" or "generation". It seems to me that Jesus is doing what He does over and over again in His teaching, namely, quoting or paraphrasing the Old Testament Scriptures. In this particular case, in saying, "this generation will not pass away" He is confirming the promise given through Jeremiah, that in spite of all the Jews have done wrong, God will preserve them to the end of the world. Jeremiah makes this prophecy in the context of God's pledge to bring the Jews back to the Promised Land near the end of the age and Jesus sets His seal on it.

OBJECTIONS TO THE SIGNIFICANCE OF ISRAEL IN GOD'S PURPOSES

There are political as well as theological objections to the continuing significance of Israel. In this writer's view they are the overwhelming reason why the unique significance of Israel is overlooked these days. They can be summarised as follows.

Political Objections

If one sincerely believes that, in 1947-48 the Jews turned up from Europe and, with overwhelming odds, expelled much of the long standing local population and then expanded this conquest in 1967, it will be very difficult to believe that the hand of God was in such clearly unjust events.

Further if one sincerely believes that, if only Israel would withdraw to the pre-1967 boundaries, the huge Islamic world would give up its former aim of destroying Israel, then one will certainly place the blame for the continuing tragic events upon Israel. If, however, one believes an Israeli withdrawal would greatly increase its vulnerability to suicide bombs and invading armies, then one will understand why a withdrawal at this moment in time would be near suicidal. (The country would be a mere nine miles wide at its middle-populated area). If one believes that over half the Israeli population were from the Middle East and not from Europe and were fleeing Arab persecution, then one will be more sympathetic to these new immigrants. This sympathy will be strengthened if one believes the Arab nations started the 1967 war with the purpose of destroying Israel.

Theological Objections

If one believes God's relationship with his creation is purely spiritual (i.e. He does not interact with the physical space-time of this world) then one will find it difficult to believe He is active in history so as to give the Jews a unique history among the nations – a history which has now resulted in their re-gathering. If one does hold this view (a form of Deism), one must still come to terms with what is widely observed (even by the non-religious), namely that Jewish history is remarkable in its uniqueness. If, on the other hand, one believes God can and does act in the space-time of this world, then they will not have a theological problem with the uniqueness of Jewish history and perhaps its restoration to the land.

If one believes the Old Testament is concerned with a particular people and land and not with all the world, and that the New Testament gives this a universal application, then one will find it difficult to see how God could have any continuing special purpose for Israel and its land. If, however, one believes both Old and New Testaments hold the particular and universal together (this is the argument of Paul in Rom 2-3 and 9-11), then one will find it easier to see the continuing significance of land.

If one holds the view based on such texts as 1 Peter 2:9, that the mission of ancient Israel has been *transferred* to the Church (i.e. replacement theology or supersessionism), then one will call the Church the new Israel and one will not hold that modern Israel has a unique significance in the purposes of God. This is precisely the kind of conclusion that the Apostle Paul refuses to draw at the end of Romans 2 and the beginning of Romans 3, when discussing the relationship between the new circumcision and the old. If on the other hand we hold that the privileges of ancient Israel are not transferred but used merely to *describe* the Church, then we will not have any difficulty in recognising the continuing significance of the history of the Jewish people.

If one believes the salvation of Christ is only for the spiritual part of human beings, then one will find it difficult to believe the land is significant. If one believes, however, that the redemption of Christ embraces all creation then one will be able to see that land is significant. Since Paul (Rom 9-11) reaffirms God's ancient covenant with Jewish Israel and that at the *heart* of this ancient covenant is "land", one will see why Paul does not need to refer explicitly to their restoration to the land, especially as, at that time, they were not even in exile from the land.

If one believes Christ fulfils Israel's unique destiny and that fulfilment includes in its meaning a "putting an end to", then one will find it difficult to see the continuing relevance of Israel in the story of redemption. If, however, one believes that Christ fulfils Israel's destiny from Abraham *to the end of time,* then one will see Israel's continuing history as "in Christ" – even if Israel itself does not recognise it.

If one believes the temple (a temporary sign of the covenant) is equivalent to the "land", then one will believe (on the basis of the letter to the Hebrews[13]) that "land" has lost its significance. If, however, one distinguishes between "sign" (e.g. temple and its sacrifices) and "content" (God, people, land) then one will see the continuing significance of land.

THE MYSTERY OF JEWISH IDENTITY

The question "What is a Jew?" still puzzles the authorities in the State of Israel, as they agonise today over whom their "law of return" applies. One of the points the Apostle Paul makes in Romans 9:7ff is that ethnicity – mere physical descent from the patriarchs – was never a guarantee of belonging to the people of Israel. He uses the examples of Ishmael and Esau who were not seen as part of the chosen people, even though they were descended from Abraham to

---

[13] For example, Hebrews 8:13.

whom God's call and promise were given. The Hebrew Scriptures also record numerous examples of people who were not physically descended from Jacob being counted as Israelites, for example Ruth, Uriah the Hittite, Hushai the Archite, and many others. This is still true today: Israel is one of the most racially mixed nations in the world. As the whole Bible makes clear, families include adopted children who are to be regarded of the same worth and given the same privileges as their natural children.

If we cannot define a Jew in racial terms, neither can we do so by looking to religion. Many Jews today are secular. Even historically we would not be able to identify Jews just by their religious beliefs and practices. The Hebrew Scriptures are quite clear that there were many Jews who rejected and effectively rebelled against the God of their fathers.

So, although it is difficult to push Jewishness into a pigeonhole of race or religion, it cannot be denied that the Jewish identity has existed distinctively for thousands of years and continues to endure today. Jewishness is a startling fact of world history. In the letter to the believers in Rome, in which Paul discusses the history of the identity of God's people, he explains "it does not depend on human will or effort, but on God's mercy"[14]. In other words, we cannot define Jewishness. It is something sustained by the grace of God. The extraordinary persistence of the distinct Jewish people provides the lesson that, good or bad, we live only by God's grace.

---

[14] Rom 9:16.

DEATH OF CHRIST

Who was responsible for the death of Christ? Often, but not always, the Orthodox, the Roman Catholics and the Lutherans have described the death of Jesus as the death of a martyr.

The New Testament, while not excusing the human perpetrators of the deed, presents it, primarily, as a sacrifice of atonement, purposed by God. In his letter to the Romans, Paul struggles with the following conundrum: God elected Israel, yet they rejected the Messiah. However, God purposed that they reject the Messiah, so that the Gentile world would be forgiven through the death of Christ. In other words, they were *disobedient for our sake*[15]. Therefore what is the relationship between the Church and Jewish Israel? Paul's answer is that God's purposes for Israel still continue and the Church must behave well towards Israel or else it will be held responsible for their unbelief.

---

[15] For example Rom 11:28.

SCRIPTURE INDEX

351

352

SUBJECT INDEX

Abraham
27, 30, 31-32, 45, 56, 63, 107, 126, 130, 143-44, 149, 151-53, 156, 165, 170, 180, 203, 204, 213, 215, 216, 218, 219-223, 224, 226, 227-30, 245, 248, 281, 282, 283, 334-35, 343

alien (within biblical Israel)
14, 165, 181-88, 225

allegorical interpretation (see also hermeneutics)
14, 24-25, 28, 30, 32, 33, 34, 47-48, 55, 58-59, 171, 191-94, 206, 207-08

anti-Semitism
4, 7, 26, 51-53, 66, 67-89, 140, 141-42, 143, 244, 259, 262, 266-67, 269, 273, 274, 277-78, 287, 288, 317

Apostles, as Jewish
1, 147-48, 191, 208, 222, 269

Arab-Israeli conflict
301-03

Arab Israelis
16, 268, 305, 307, 311-12

Aristotle (see Greek philosophy)

Augustine (of Hippo)
33-35, 54, 55-60, 61, 62, 64, 83, 86, 121, 192, 244, 283

Balfour, Balfour Declaration
13, 94-100, 109, 110

Bar Kokhba
38, 39, 226, 243

Barth, Karl
154, 249, 334-35

Blackstone, William
94-100, 114-16

Bethlehem
53, 265, 292, 311-13, 314, 321,

Borough Park Symposium
238-40, 248, 254

Calvinism (see Reformation, Reformed theology)

Catholicism (in Germany)
68, 71-73, 78-79, 80-81, 82-83, 85, 86, 87

chosenness
6, 27, 97-98, 130, 143, 165, 177, 185-86, 259, 309, 323, 336, 343

Christian Zionism
5, 6, 8-9, 10, 13, 91-116, 185-86, 188, 302-03, 305, 310, 323-24

Christian anti-Zionism
4-5, 7, 11, 164-65, 183, 185-86, 188, 190, 262, 268, 273, 302-03, 305, 310, 314, 321-23, 324-25; and the Messianic movement, 15, 262

Chrysostom
50-53, 58, 62, 64, 146-47, 282-83

circumcision
132, 148, 215, 220-22, 342

Clement of Alexandria
47, 121, 193,

Darby, John Nelson
100, 105-09, 110, 113-16,

David, Davidic kingdom
59, 76, 150, 179-80, 218-19, 223, 228, 265, 292, 302

Dead Sea Scrolls
150, 197-99

Dispensationalism (see also John Nelson Darby)
10, 14, 106, 196, 212, 309
Dome of the Rock
180, 206
Early Church (as Jewish)
2, 13, 37-40, 122, 158, 191, 197, 198-99, 242-43
Edersheim, Alfred
102, 209
eschatology
41-59, 104-09, 169, 175-80, 204-07, 211-12, 232, 289-91, 339
ethnicity, also ethnic Israel
14, 56, 64, 120-37, 139, 148, 160, 166-67, 171-73, 184-87, 191, 212, 215, 220-22, 224, 230, 232, 237-39, 241-42, 248, 249-50, 255, 256, 258-260, 272, 343-44
Eusebius
38-40, 62, 283
Evangelicals in Germany
75-76, 85
Flannery, Edward
71, 90, 91-92
Fourth Lateran Council
71, 244
Galatian error
150, 264, 271
Gaza
16, 184, 303, 304, 311, 321
Glaser, Mitch
Preface, 11, 250
gnosticism
44-46, 193-94, 208
Greek philosophy
13, 19-35, 192-93,
Hamas
303-04, 311, 321

Haredi, Haredim (see also Judaism)
15, 167-68, 185, 315; and Messianic believers, 316-20; and politics in Israel, 315-17
hermeneutics
6, 14, 28, 29-30, 48, 119-37, 145, 163-64, 168-70, 191-210, 213-14, 219-20, 268, 304
Holocaust
3-4, 65-89, 141, 256-57, 274, 275, 281-82, 284, 302
Ignatius of Antioch
25-26
Irenaeus
44-47, 121, 244
Islam, Muslims
5, 7-8, 190, 305, 307-09, 310-14
Islamism (see also Hamas)
7-8, 302, 303, 306-307, 313
Israel
before Independence, 13, 94-95, 102-03, 267; biblical theology theme of, 1-2, 14, 163-89; congregation of, 165-66, 182-88; election/ covenants/ continued divine plan and purpose for, 64, 66, 139, 140, 155, 156, 160, 169-70, 171, 186, 215-16, 218, 220, 227-, 253, 263, 295, 329-45; future salvation of, 120, 133-37, 174-79; God's servant, 2, 165; God of, 1, 9, 63-64, 160, 168, 170, 188, 257; land of, 120, 164-65, 169-70, 188, 211-33, 303-04, 335-40; modern society, politics, 7-8, 231-32, 274, 305; remnant, 57, 129-30, 132, 173-76
Jacob
27, 44-45, 108, 130, 280, 334, 344

Jerome
53-55, 62, 68, 76
Jerusalem
1, 37, 41, 102-03, 218, 222,
225, 231, 241, 289, 310;
destruction of, 38, 60, 148,
167, 205-06, 226, 243-44, 294,
311
Jesus
as Jewish, 1, 37, 152, 165, 166-
67, 172, 208, 269 ; as Messiah,
1, 30, 32, 150, 160, 165, 166-
67, 170, 172, 173, 200-01, 249,
252, 258, 272, 284-85, 288, 345
Jewish evangelism
12-13, 14, 146, 231, 259, 268,
276-77, 279-300, 317-18
Judaism (see also Rabbinic
Judaism, Mosaic law, Haredim)
25-26, 44, 66, 125, 140, 143,
156, 192, 246, 247, 250, 270,
288-99
Justin Martyr
26-27, 41-44, 121, 122, 244
Kinzer, Mark
248-49, 250, 316
Luther, Martin
3, 70, 77, 284
Maimonides
289, 291
Maoz, Baruch   248-50, 252, 254,
316, 317, 319
Messianic movement
14-15, 202, 237-60, 261-78,
320; and Gentiles, 254-55;
and Israel, 15, 231, 314-20;
and Jewish identity, 251, 247-
48, 249, and relations with
the Church, 13, 14-15, 247-50,
258-60; and Torah, 239, 247

Mosaic Law (see also Torah and
Messianic movement)
1, 23, 151, 181-83, 220, 221-23,
239, 247, 250-53, 300
Old Testament
as Jewish, 69-71, 169, 186-7,
198-99; and prophecy, 30-31,
37, 158-59, 183-84, 216-17, 339
olive tree analogy
2-3, 133-34, 57, 133, 174-76,
184, 266, 281
Origen
27-30, 33, 34, 47-50, 54, 121,
193, 244
Orthodox and Ultra-Orthodox
Jews (see Haredim, Judaism)
Palestinian Authority
306, 308, 309, 313,
Palestinians
16, 93, 181-83, 188, 268, 302,
312; Arab and Palestinian
Christians, 305, 306-315, 320-
21
Passover
62, 183, 204, 308, 264-65, 315
Paul (apostle)
23, 33, 51, 53, 64, 127-28, 131,
133-34, 141-42, 150-51, 152,
167, 172-73, 188-89, 199, 203,
208, 220, 223, 224, 226, 230,
240, 242, 266, 277, 279-81,
282, 288, 343, 345
Pentecost, Day of
178-79, 286
Pharisees
141, 201, 242, 243
Philo (see Greek philosophy)
Plato (see Greek philosophy)
Pogroms
3, 34, 95

post-Holocaust theology
4, 66, 302

Puritans
94, 100, 195-96

Protestantism (in Germany)
68, 70, 77, 85, 284

Rabbinic Judaism (see also Judaism)
1, 26, 125, 197-207,

Reformation, Reformed theology
10, 14, 62-63, 193, 194, 211-16

replacement theology (see also supersessionism)
27, 28-29, 35, 143, 157, 168, 213, 214-20, 226-28, 272

Roman empire
38, 42, 95, 226, 281, 282, 287

Rome, NT church of
2-3, 174-75

Samaritan woman
1, 220-21

Sharon, Ariel
303-04

Six Day War
246, 301, 303, 313, 341

Soulen, R. Kendall
46-47, 63-64, 168-69, 188-89, 257

Spanish Inquisition
3, 84

supersessionism (see also replacement theology)
and the Jewish people, 272-75; effect upon Jewish believers, 238-39, 247-60, 261-78; punitive, 65-89, 168, 189-90, 257, 307; structural, 170-71, 188-89; Church as the new Israel, 2, 27, 34, 43-44, 56-57, 68-69, 120, 121, 130, 139, 156, 157-58, 171-72, 175,185-86, 211-12, 214-16, 237, 342

Taylor, Howard
14-15, 327-45,

Temple
19, 38, 45, 170, 205-06, 207, 225, 243, 286, 289, 290, 294, 336, 343

Torah (see also Mosaic law and Messianic movement)
8, 142-43, 151

United States
7, 9, 94, 95-100, 111-13, 302,

West Bank
16, 184, 310-11, 313, 314, 320-21, 322

Vlach, Michael
9

Yad L'achim
317-20